The Da Vinci Hoax

CARL E. OLSON and SANDRA MIESEL

The Da Vinci Hoax

Exposing the Errors in
The Da Vinci Code

IGNATIUS PRESS   SAN FRANCISCO

Cover art:
The Last Supper
Leonardo da Vinci
S. Maria delle Grazie, Milan
© Scala/Art Resource, New York

and

Mona Lisa
Leonardo da Vinci
photo: R. G. Ojeda
Louvre, Paris
© Réunion des Musées Nationaux/Art Resource, New York

Cover design by
Carl E. Olson
Roxanne Mei Lum

© 2004 Ignatius Press, San Francisco
All rights reserved
ISBN: 1-58617-034-1
Library of Congress Control Number 2004103531
Printed in the United States of America ∞

To Francis Cardinal George, O.M.I.,
in gratitude for courageously proclaiming the Gospel
and standing up for the Truth

CONTENTS

ACKNOWLEDGMENTS

The authors and publisher would like to thank Random House, Inc., New York, for permission to use excerpts from *The Da Vinci Code*, by Dan Brown, published by Doubleday, a division of Random House, Inc. and © 2003 by Dan Brown. All rights reserved and used by permission.

The authors would both like to thank their families for their support, encouragement, and patience during the research and writing of this book. They also want to thank the many friends and colleagues who have assisted in many ways, big and small, in making this book a reality.

FOREWORD

The title of this book by Carl Olson and Sandra Miesel says it all. The novel *The Da Vinci Code* is engaging and intriguing. It is a thriller presented as a historical novel. It is fiction, yet it seeks to convince the reader that it is based on fact. It pushes an attack on the Catholic Church and claims to do so in the name of historical authenticity and sound scholarship. The claim is preposterous, but for many it is persuasive.

The authors of *The Da Vinci Hoax* deserve our gratitude for exposing in considerable detail and with sure touch the fabrications of Dan Brown's book. Theirs is the definitive debunking. In the end, the fallacy of Brown's book is a common one. It approaches the Christian faith as though its contents were to be found in words and documents rather than in the witness and collective memory of the community Christ himself left behind, the Church.

There have been such writings before, and, no doubt, there will be again. Why single out this novel? I read it because so many people who read it kept asking me questions about it. It has had a remarkably large and credulous readership, reminding me of the dictum that those who have lost or do not know the faith are likely to believe anything. It matters what we read, what films and television shows we watch. If we feed our minds on error, we risk losing touch with the truth about who we are and how we ought to live.

We find salvation through self-surrender in faith to Christ, not from personal ideas or inspirations. Once the anchor of the Church's authentic witness and teaching is abandoned, gnostic or other false theories inevitably appear. Antagonism to the Church and her teaching ultimately entails some kind of rejection of Jesus Christ as he has revealed himself in history. His truth is always a challenge to every egocentric vision of reality and to an unbounded will for human autonomy. Besides, does anyone really think that all those martyrs went to their deaths to protect the secret that Jesus and Mary Magdalene were married?

— † Francis Cardinal George, O.M.I.
Archbishop of Chicago
March 30, 2004

INTRODUCTION

The Da Vinci Code is an anomaly in recent publishing history, in that mere "thrillers" seldom rank at the very top of the best-seller lists, much less are they solemnly discussed by supposedly serious people. When such occurs, there is more going on than meets the eye, but at the same time, where Dan Brown's *The Da Vinci Code* is concerned, there is also a great deal less than meets the eye, as Carl E. Olson and Sandra Miesel show so effectively in this book.

Most of the publishing industry is now driven by the balance sheet in ways that, at least according to legend, were not true a generation ago, when major commercial publishers were eager to publish books by serious authors, even if sales did not justify their publication. Whether those same publishers rejected potential best sellers because they did not agree with them is less clear.

In the atmosphere of contemporary publishing, *The Da Vinci Code* justifies itself solely on the basis of sales. But if Doubleday's motives are partly cynical ("the book will sell; who cares whether it's a lot of nonsense"), in another sense it is a very serious book, as the publishers no doubt also realize, since it is nothing less than an attack on the very foundations of historical Christianity, an attack that would be little noticed if it were presented in the form of a historical or theological treatise. (Not very many years ago Doubleday, in its Image Books, brought out a series of Catholic works of the highest quality, something that today would be unthinkable.)

People who do not read serious books are reading *The Da Vinci Code*, and for many it is the closest to a "real" book they will ever come. There is an odd assumption, detectable even among some professed Christians, that Dan Brown's book would not have been published, would not have become a best seller, if it were not true. In speaking about the book to Catholic audiences I have found that there are people who, if they cannot deny that it is a work of fiction, are nonetheless unwilling to concede that it is not reliable as history. Such people latch onto peripheral items ("isn't it true that Opus Dei owns a big building in New York?") and use those things to "prove" the accuracy of the entire fantastic plot.

For many people today, including some professed Christians, the Good News is bad news. At one time Christians found deeply troubling the claim that the Bible was unreliable history, and if they accepted the claim they did so with a heavy heart. But today some church members would be troubled if presented with incontrovertible evidence that the Scriptures are historically accurate, because such a revelation would require them to rethink their entire relationship to their faith. Paradoxically, many people who might be thought of as unusually active church members, the kind who frequent Bible-study groups, workshops, and adult-education classes, often seem to do so precisely because they have, as St. Paul warned, "itching ears". They yearn to hear novelty. They rejoice to have sacred truths "deconstructed". Thus there are parish groups that have made *The Da Vinci Code* the subject of their study, treating it with more credulity than they ordinarily give to the Bible itself.

For two hundred years the primary Western assault on Christianity was the rationalism of the Enlightenment, the claim that traditional religion was simply a set of fairy stories believed by the gullible in the face of growing evidence to the contrary. Because of this critique, until fairly recently it seemed necessary to choose between religious faith and a rather sterile rationalism. But the "counterculture" of the 1960s inevitably discovered "spirituality", which is now touted even in the business world. Prosperous people in the advanced Western countries cannot deny themselves anything, and at some point it occurs to them that religious believers are "enjoying" something that the secularists have denied themselves.

The historical forms of Christianity stand in the way of this new spirituality, however. Creeds require individuals to rise above themselves, to submit to a truth much greater than themselves, to become real disciples. By contrast, contemporary New Age religion is simply the worship of the self, or at best the worship of deities that the self has created. (How many New Agers really believe in goddesses?)

The moral implications of this are also obvious. The "sexual revolution" is the single most formidable dividing line between the culture and serious Christians. But if religion is a human invention, there cannot be an objective moral law, and all things are permitted. In an often unrecognized way, the passion that drives debates about *The Da Vinci Code* has more to do with abortion and homosexuality than it does with the origins of Christianity. New Age religiosity invites people to make up their own deities, and *The Da Vinci Code* invites them to invent their own history, to replace the Gospel of Jesus Christ with scriptures that cater to contemporary preoccupations like feminism.

Christianity makes fundamental historical claims about itself—that, if Jesus did not live, die, and rise again as the Gospels announce, our faith is in vain. This is a daring claim that makes Christianity vulnerable to attack precisely through its history, and Brown invites the reader to see Christianity as nothing less than a gigantic fraud perpetrated over two thousand years, a conspiracy of power that long held a monopoly on the things of the soul and is now being exposed. Shallow though the book is, it is a major weapon in the campaign to discredit the Christian faith once and for all.

The purported scholarly roots of this attack lie in the gnostic gospels, which, although written later than the New Testament, are often treated as more reliable than the New Testament. Elaine Pagels, who has done the most to promote the gnostic gospels, is quite candid about her own agenda—"spirituality" freed from the constraints of creeds.

If Brown offered his arguments in the form of a historical treatise, they would be dismissed as sheer fantastic speculation. Both he and his publisher are dishonest in that they invite the public to accept the book as history and then, if challenged, retreat to saying "but it's just a story". It is another example of a pernicious genre now practiced by, for example, the film-maker Oliver Stone and the novelist Gore Vidal—exploiting the public's ignorance of history by serving up mixtures of fact and fiction and failing to delineate between the two, scoring points through fiction that could not be made with fact. It is more than ironic that so much obloquy is now being heaped on Mel Gibson's *The Passion of the Christ*, which is based almost entirely on the New Testament, while many of the people who excoriate the film see nothing wrong with *The Da Vinci Code*.

Carl E. Olson and Sandra Miesel have done a superb and meticulous job of dissecting the fraud that is *The Da Vinci Code*. Not only Christians, but all fair-minded people owe them a debt of gratitude.

—James Hitchcock

The Da Vinci Code Phenomenon

An Introduction

> Be as careful of the books you read as of the company you
> keep, for your habits and character will be as much influ-
> enced by the former as the latter.
>
> —Paxton Hood

"Have you read *The Da Vinci Code*?"

If you are reading this, it is likely you have been asked that
question. It is also likely that you *have* read *The Da Vinci
Code*, the best-selling novel by Dan Brown and the publishing phenomenon of 2003. If you have read that novel, you
probably have some questions about it: Is it as factual and
well researched as the author claims? Is it telling the real story
about the history of Christianity? What should readers think
about its statements about Jesus, the Catholic Church, and
Mary Magdalene? How about the gnostic gospels—should
they be included in the Bible? What do they tell us about
Jesus? And what about the novel's numerous claims about
Leonardo da Vinci, the Templar Knights, the Priory of Sion,
and a grand conspiracy involving the Vatican? The questions
go on and on.

This book has been written to answer the seemingly endless questions raised by *The Da Vinci Code*. Why? Because
they are important, influential questions and much depends
on the answers. The issues and questions raised by *The Da Vinci*

Code are not simply matters of trivia or ancient history but rather have to do with what people believe, how they live their lives, and how they understand the world. More than "just fiction" or an entertaining book, the chart-topping novel was purposefully written to challenge what people believe about God, Jesus, the Bible, Mary Magdalene, religion, history, and the nature of truth itself. The author readily admits this is so. In a June 9, 2003, interview on *The Today Show*, host Matt Lauer said to Brown, "You ask the reader to—to challenge certain long-held beliefs or truths about religion." Brown answered, "Yes." He then went on to say that while some readers have found the book to be "a little bit shocking", the majority of readers "love it".

Many readers and critics obviously do love the novel, as a trip to amazon.com or Brown's web site indicates. There is no denying the success—and controversy—Brown has generated with *The Da Vinci Code*.

The authors of this present book were introduced to Brown's novel in the summer of 2003 by friends and family members who had read it and were annoyed, even angered, by its contents. For Sandra, it was a daughter who had read the book and was irritated by what she thought were anti-Catholic statements. Sandra, a medieval historian, science-fiction writer, and widely published journalist, read the novel and then wrote a review of it, titled "Dismantling *The Da Vinci Code*", which appeared in the September 2003 issue of *Crisis* magazine and caught the attention of the Christian and secular media.

Carl, the editor of *Envoy* magazine, was told about the novel by a good friend who was outraged by what he believed were lies and half-truths. Having read the book the same month that Sandra's article appeared and having read dozens of reader's reviews on the Internet, Carl decided to write a book in response to the novel. Familiar with Sandra's work and her review of *The Da Vinci Code*, Carl contacted her and asked if she would co-author such a book. She agreed, and the rest is history, as they say.

Where We Are Coming From

Both of us are Christians who take our faith seriously and believe that we have an obligation to defend and promote the truth about matters large and small. We believe the evidence shows that many of Brown's statements about the Catholic Church are false; as Catholics we also find those statements offensive and upsetting. But we are not interested in censorship or making unsubstantiated charges against Brown. Rather, we want to examine *The Da Vinci Code* carefully and with fairness, relying upon available scholarship—Christian and non-Christian—and sound thinking.

We realize that some fans of Brown's work may immediately reject this book, possibly without even reading it, simply because we are Christian. Criticizing a popular book such as *The Da Vinci Code* is bound to upset some people. For example, after writing her review of *The Da Vinci Code*, Sandra received a number of negative responses, including this one from a professor of humanities: "All I can do is to *laugh* about your article on the Da Vinci code [sic]. . . . Your comments on the book are uneducated Christian propaganda." Others have informed us that we have been duped by the Catholic Church, that Brown's novel is "the truth", and that any response given is simply sour grapes. The position of these writers seems to be that only *we* are biased—*they* are as objective and fair as the day is long. Such attitudes are themselves biased and unfair. After all, if Brown is going to become rich and famous by making controversial comments at the expense of others, should a response to his claims not be taken seriously, or at least acknowledged?

As Christians, we believe that all truth ultimately comes from God, the Father of lights (Jas 1:17), his Son Jesus Christ, who is "the way, and the truth, and the life" (Jn 14:6), and the Holy Spirit, who guides us into all truth (Jn 16:13). We also believe that faith is not blind or contrary to fact but is in accord with reason—including scholarship, logic, and common sense. We have nothing to fear by examining the claims put forth by *The Da Vinci Code*. On the contrary, we have much to be confident in, as well as much to share with those who wish to know the facts behind the fiction.

And so, with that in mind, the remainder of this introduction will be spent providing some background to *The Da Vinci Code*, looking at its tremendous success, examining Brown's motives in writing the novel, and offering some reasons why we believe the novel is so popular. We will also examine some reader reactions and point out what we see as major problems.

The *Da Vinci Code* Phenomenon

In April 2003, Doubleday published *The Da Vinci Code*, Brown's fourth novel.[1] A combination of murder mystery, thriller, conspiracy tale, romance novel, religious exposé, and historical revisionism, the novel had instant success. Glowing reviews from leading newspapers and magazines, combined with the buzz from Brown's previous novel *Angels and Demons*,[2] helped *The Da Vinci Code* debut as number one on the *New York Times* best-seller list. As of early May 2004, *The Da Vinci Code* had been on the *New York Times* best-seller list for sixty weeks and had been number one or two for most of that time. There are nearly seven million copies of

---

[1] See www.danbrown.com for information on all of Dan Brown's novels.
[2] Dan Brown, *Angels and Demons* (New York: Pocket Books, 2000).

The Da Vinci Code in print, and it is being translated into over forty languages.

Described by the *New York Times* as a "riddle-filled, code-breaking, exhilaratingly brainy thriller", *The Da Vinci Code* garnered effusive, even ebullient, praise from numerous reviewers. The *Library Journal* raved, "This masterpiece should be mandatory reading"; the *Chicago Tribune* marveled that the book contained "several doctorates' worth of fascinating history and learned speculation"; *Salon* magazine described the novel as "an ingenious mixture of paranoid thriller, art history lesson, chase story, religious symbology lecture and anti-clerical screed". Numerous critics noted how "smart", "intelligent", and well-researched the novel appeared to be ("his research is impeccable" stated the *New York Daily News*),[3] a point that surely pleased the author, who insisted in interviews and on his web site[4] that his thriller is thoroughly researched and factual in all respects. In addition, the novel features an opening page titled "FACT", which states: "All descriptions of artwork, architecture, documents, and secret rituals in this novel are accurate."

Readers have enthusiastically embraced the book and many of them point to the historical, artistic, religious, and theological details it contains as central reasons for their fascination with it. A reader's review on amazon.com states that *The Da Vinci Code* is "one of the best books I have ever read—makes you see the world a little differently after reading it!" Another gushes, "You will be amazed at the revelations that come forth in this book." Another elaborates:

> *The Da Vinci Code* has to be one of the most remarkable books I've read. It is a wonderful—and very effective—mix of history, mystery, action, puzzles and suspense. The pace is

---

[3] All comments from reviews found on Brown's web site.
[4] See, for example, www.danbrown.com/novels/davinci_code/faqs.html.

so powerful, the book just wouldn't let go! The story line is almost too brilliant to conceive, the sheer genius and fascinating craftsmanship that Dan Brown uses in his book are breathtaking. The idea behind the story may seem controversial, but once you think about it, it really does become quite real and even natural.

Another reader provides a more muted and relativistic assessment:

> The historical events and people explored in the book are real. But no one knows the Truth . . . nor will we ever, probably. I think that some things are meant to be a mystery. With all the world's diverse religions and each individual's belief in what is Divine—the Truth would have to destroy the beliefs, hopes and lives of many of the world's population. So, perhaps, in the divine scheme of things, there are many more Truths than one. Don't take the book too seriously.[5]

Despite the skepticism of some readers, *The Da Vinci Code* proved so popular, so quickly, that within a matter of weeks after being published, Columbia Pictures bought the film rights to the book (and to Brown's *Angels and Demons* as well). Noted director Ron Howard is reportedly on board and Columbia plans to bring the book to cinematic life sometime in 2005.[6]

Brown's Agenda and the Purpose of *The Da Vinci Code*

In an article about the intentions of *The Da Vinci Code*, historian Dr. James Hitchcock makes the following remark:

[5] Readers' comments from www.amazon.com.
[6] From www.comingsoon.net.

The Da Vinci Code can be viewed as merely an ephemeral artifact of popular culture, but its immense sales ensure that it will have influence on people who never read serious books. Brown has found a formula for becoming rich: sex, sensationalism, feminism, anti-Catholicism, and the occult. But it is also obvious that he sincerely hates Christianity and sees himself as engaged in an anti-crusade. The culture is ripe for such a debased book, so that even professing Christians are being seduced by it.[7]

This sober assessment is in stark contrast to the adulatory reviews of the book written in the secular press. In her glowing *New York Times* review of the novel, Janet Maslin writes: "As in his *Angels and Demons*, this author is drawn to the place where empirical evidence and religious faith collide. And he creates a bracing exploration of this realm, one that is by no means sacrilegious, though it sharply challenges Vatican policy." [8] More than a challenge to "Vatican policy", *The Da Vinci Code* challenges beliefs that are central to Christianity: the celibacy and divinity of Jesus, the place of the apostles, and the purpose of the Church. The novel insists that Jesus was married to Mary Magdalene and had children, that Mary Magdalene—not Peter—was the head apostle, that the Catholic Church has kept these "facts" hidden through force and terror, and that Jesus was, not truly divine, but merely a good man "deified" by Emperor Constantine in A.D. 325. As Hitchcock indicates, Brown (who has described himself as a nontraditional Christian) appears to have a sincere, even deep, dislike for historical, traditional Christian beliefs.

He also has a strong belief in a variety of feminist notions about God. His novel is obsessed with radical feminist notions

[7] James Hitchcock, "Fantasy Faith", *Touchstone* (December 2003), 16.

[8] Janet Maslin, "Spinning a Thriller from the Louvre", *New York Times*, March 17, 2003. Accessed at www.nytimes.com.

of the "sacred feminine" and ancient goddess worship, all served up in a syrupy, breathless fashion reminiscent of romance novels.[9] The major theme of Brown's novel is the call to a recovery of the "sacred feminine" and a revitalized worship of a goddess or goddesses. In responding on his web site to the question about his novel being "empowering to women", Brown states that, "Two thousand years ago, we lived in a world of Gods and Goddesses. Today, we live in a world solely of Gods. Women in most cultures have been stripped of their spiritual power. The novel touches on questions of how and why this shift occurred ... and on what lessons we might learn from it regarding our future."[10] In an interview with CNN, Brown emphasized this point more than once, stating, "In the early days ... we lived in a world of gods and goddesses.... Every Mars had an Athena. The god of war had the goddess of beauty; in the Egyptian tradition, Osiris and Isis.... And now we live in a world solely of gods. The female counterpart has been erased." He continues: "It's interesting to note that the word 'god' conjures power and awe, while the word 'goddess' sounds imaginary." Then, revealing his understanding of how his novel might affect "traditional" Christians, he remarks, "There are some people in the church for whom this book is a little bit shocking. But the reaction from the vast majority of clergy and Christian scholars has been positive." He adds: "Nuns,

---

[9] Stephanie Mittman, a romance novelist, lists seven key elements in a successful romance novel: (1) a wonderful, lovable, sympathetic heroine; (2) a similar hero; (3) a major event that brings the two together; (4) an insurmountable obstacle for them to overcome; (5) a difficult moment; (6) a twist that complicates the resolution; and (7) the happy ending. Accessed at http://groups.msn.com/RomanceWritingTips/romanceformula.msnw. This is not to suggest that *The Da Vinci Code* is simply a romance novel, but it does suggest that, despite its esoteric subject matter, it follows a standard formula that appeals to a specific demographic.

[10] Accessed at www.danbrown.com.

in particular, are exceptionally excited about the strong feminist message of the book."[11]

It should be noted that when Brown, in interviews or in his novel, refers to "the church" or Christianity, he means the Catholic Church. *The Da Vinci Code* betrays little awareness that there are non-Catholic Christians such as the Eastern Orthodox and Protestant denominations; there is only brief, negative mention of the Church of England (346).[12] Otherwise, all references are to the Catholic Church, often referred to as "the Vatican", a term for which Brown seems to have a special affinity. However, he is not a Catholic, nor does he appear to be a former Catholic. When asked on his web site if he is a Christian, Brown offers an oxymoronic mixture of "yes" and "no" in his reply:

I am, although perhaps not in the most traditional sense of the word. If you ask three people what it means to be Christian, you will get three different answers. Some feel being baptized is sufficient. Others feel you must accept the Bible as immutable historical fact. Still others require a belief that all those who do not accept Christ as their personal savior are doomed to hell. Faith is a continuum, and we each fall on that line where we may. By attempting to rigidly classify ethereal concepts like faith, we end up debating semantics to the point where we entirely miss the obvious—that is, that

[11] CNN, July 17, 2003. An examination of columns and articles written about the novel in the past year by Christian clergy reveals a mostly negative and often highly critical perspective. Some praise the novel as an entertaining read that is inaccurate and full of nasty comments about the Catholic Church. Fr. Andrew Greeley, a best-selling novelist and sociologist, praises *The Da Vinci Code* as a "skillfully written read" that is also anti-Catholic and full of inaccuracies. Greeley states, "Brown knows little about Leonardo, little about the Catholic church, and little about history" ("DaVinci Code Is More Fantasy than Fact", *National Catholic Reporter*, October 3, 2003. Accessed at www.ncronline.org).

[12] All page numbers within the text of this book without additional citation refer to *The Da Vinci Code* (New York: Doubleday, 2003).

we are all trying to decipher life's big mysteries, and we're each following our own paths of enlightenment. I consider myself a student of many religions. The more I learn, the more questions I have. For me, the spiritual quest will be a life-long work in progress.[13]

In other words, he is certain of nothing *except* that traditional Christian beliefs are false. This is echoed in comments made by *The Da Vinci Code*'s main character, Harvard "symbologist" Robert Langdon. "*Every* faith in the world is based on fabrication", he states, adding that faith is the acceptance of what we imagine is true but that cannot be proven. Religion explains God through the use of "metaphor, allegory, and exaggeration", but those metaphors should not be understood in a literal fashion: "Those who truly understand their faiths understand the stories are metaphorical" (341–42).[14]

Ironically, *The Da Vinci Code* hinges upon Langdon having a profound—and apparently non-metaphorical—faith experience at the novel's conclusion, an experience bound

---

[13] Accessed at www.danbrown.com.

[14] The point appears to be that since man uses metaphors in speaking about God, those metaphors cannot be trusted to convey truths about God. Compare that to this statement in the *Catechism of the Catholic Church*: "Since our knowledge of God is limited, our language about him is equally so. We can name God only by taking creatures as our starting point, and in accordance with our limited human ways of knowing and thinking. God transcends all creatures. We must therefore continually purify our language of everything in it that is limited, image-bound or imperfect, if we are not to confuse our image of God—'the inexpressible, the incomprehensible, the invisible, the ungraspable' [*Liturgy of St. John Chrysostom*, Anaphora]—with our human representations. Our human words always fall short of the mystery of God. Admittedly, in speaking about God like this, our language is using human modes of expression; nevertheless it really does attain to God himself, though unable to express him in his infinite simplicity. Likewise, we must recall that 'between Creator and creature no similitude can be expressed without implying an even greater dissimilitude' [Lateran Council IV: DS 806]; and that 'concerning God, we cannot grasp what he is, but only what he is not, and how other beings stand in relation to him' [St. Thomas Aquinas, SCG 1, 30]" (nos. 40, 42–43).

up in the "sacred feminine" and Mary Magdalene. Also revealing is how Brown continually questions any sort of authority, especially that of the Catholic Church, but has such
confidence in his personal research into a large number of
complex areas of study—even areas where his lack of knowledge is obvious. This is disconcerting in light of his relativistic attitude toward religion and his suspicious view of history.
He openly questions whether we can even know the truth
about the past:

> Since the beginning of recorded time, history has been writ-
> ten by the "winners" (those societies and belief systems that
> conquered and survived). Despite an obvious bias in this
> accounting method, we still measure the "historical accu-
> racy" of a given concept by examining how well it concurs
> with our existing historical record. Many historians now
> believe (as do I) that in gauging the historical accuracy of a
> given concept, we should first ask ourselves a far deeper ques-
> tion: How historically accurate is history itself? [15]

This may strike some as thoughtful commentary, but it is
simple sophistry, based on a mixture of popularized postmodernism and deconstructionism. [16] As someone once noted

---

[15] Accessed at www.danbrown.com.

[16] Postmodernism, generally speaking, is based on the premise that meaning comes from one's social group and culture and that transcendent knowledge and meaning do not exist. Inherently antirational, postmodernism seeks
to dissolve and undermine history and the belief in "facts" and "objectivity".
This leads to deconstructionism, which asserts that language cannot articulate
truth in an objective manner. "For the deconstructionists, all truth claims are
suspect and are treated as a coverup for power plays. Reason, objective truth,
science, and all 'Western claims to serenely self-aware rationality' are challenged.... Scholars attack received ideas with withering skepticism, while
constructing new models as alternatives. Those who celebrate the achievements of Western civilization are accused of a narrow-minded 'Euro-centrism';
this view is challenged by 'Afro-centrism,' which exalts Africa as the pinnacle of civilization. Male-dominant thought is replaced by feminist models.

about history, something either happened, or it didn't. The comment, "How historically accurate is history itself?" is nonsensical since it rests on the premise that "accuracy" is in the eyes of the beholder and therefore cannot ever be objectively gauged. This is based on the illogical premise that nothing is really true except the statement, "Nothing is true." Ironically, Brown claims that his book is based on facts and sound historical research. And he does admit, in an interview with the *Washington Post*, that he is not "entirely convinced [history] is unknowable.... We're entering an age ... when we've started to question everything. In the past, knowledge was something that was handed down by authority figures; now we seek and discover for ourselves." [17] As we will see, discovering the truth for yourself, for Brown, oftentimes means relying on the authority of dubious, conspiracy-minded works that few, if any, scholars take seriously.

Brown apparently hopes *The Da Vinci Code* will be more than just a best seller; he wants it radically to change perceptions of history, religion, and Western civilization. Asked if the novel might be considered controversial, Brown again asserts his desire to promote the "sacred feminine" and to challenge commonly accepted understandings of Western culture and Christianity: "As I mentioned earlier, the secret I reveal is one that has been whispered for centuries. It is not my own. Admittedly, this may be the first time the secret has

---

'Patriarchal religions' such as Judaism and Christianity are challenged and replaced with matriarchal religions; the influence of the Bible is countered by the influence of 'goddess-worship'" (Gene Edward Veith, Jr., *Postmodern Times: A Christian Guide to Contemporary Thought and Culture* [Wheaton, Ill.: Crossway Books, 1994], 56, 57).

[17] Roxanne Roberts, "The Mysteries of Mary Magdalene: 'The Da Vinci Code' Resurrects a Debate of Biblical Proportions", *Washington Post*, July 20, 2003. Accessed at www.washingtonpost.com.

been unveiled within the format of a popular thriller, but the information is anything but new. My sincere hope is that *The Da Vinci Code*, in addition to entertaining people, will serve as an open door to begin their own explorations." [18] As noted, these intentions have not been lost on readers, and many of them revel in the subversive agenda that Brown undertakes in his thriller. One mesmerized reader summarizes this fascination quite well: "With his impeccable research, Mr. Brown introduces us to aspects and interpretations of Western history and Christianity that I, for one, had never known existed . . . or even thought about. I found myself, unwillingly, leaving the novel, and time and time again, going online to research Brown's research—only to find a new world of historic possibilities opening up for me".[19] For his part, Brown claims he is neutral about the effect his novel will have. He will be satisfied, he indicates, if he opens up avenues for discussion: "I have no vested interest in whether people believe one history of Magdalene or another. . . . However, I think it's wonderful that people are . . . discussing their spirituality on new levels." [20]

The *Code* Is Causing Confusion

The immense success of *The Da Vinci Code* and its strong language about early Christianity and the Catholic Church has resulted in substantial confusion over many of the "facts" within its pages. Not only is the novel influencing the views of non-Christian readers, it is raising difficult questions in the minds of many Christians, some of whom are being asked about Brown's interpretation of Church history and theology. One such reader recently wrote to us, saying: "I own a

---

[18] Accessed at www.danbrown.com.
[19] Accessed at www.amazon.com.
[20] Roberts, "Mysteries of Mary Magdalene".

Catholic bookstore. We are getting bombarded daily by people who are buying into the garbage in this book. You cannot believe how many people have been exposed to this book. . . . We even had an elderly aunt talking about Opus Dei tonight and yelling at us that the book is true or it couldn't be printed." Another reader openly admitted the doubts that *The Da Vinci Code* has raised in his mind:

> Honestly, [reading the book] shook my whole faith. I realize that the book is fiction, but much of what he wrote about seemed like it was based on historical facts aside from the characters. Since I am not a Christian scholar I don't even know where to begin to refute these claims. As the Catholic church holds much of the evidence that would refute the drivel in *The Da Vinci Code*, I was wondering if you could point me in the right direction to a scholarly non-Christian book that might help me make better sense of the whole historical chain of events. If Christianity is nothing more than a big accommodation, it becomes relegated to a lifestyle choice and not a religion, which I do not want to believe.[21]

We have heard many similar stories in recent months and expect to hear more; this is the main reason our book has been written. Just as the *Left Behind* books have been used to promote a premillennial dispensationalist understanding of Scripture and the end times, *The Da Vinci Code* has proven to be an effective tool for attacking Christian doctrine and undermining the faith of those uncertain of how to respond to the many accusations leveled against the Church.

Sadly, it is not surprising that a work of fiction has produced confusion among some Christians about Church history and doctrine at a time when catechesis and basic knowledge of the faith are so poor. It is even less surprising

---

[21] Personal e-mails to the authors, Fall 2003.

that non-Christian readers would be taken in by Brown's revisionist history of the Church. After all, it is a demonstrated fact that most Americans are illiterate about major events in the history of their own country. For example, one recent study of historical literacy among young Americans found that most "college seniors could not identify Valley Forge, words from the Gettysburg Address, or even the basic principles of the U.S. Constitution."[22] So why should we expect people to be able to discern fact from fiction when it comes to early Church history and the complex debates over the divinity and person of Jesus Christ that took place in the first four centuries of the Church? An example of this is a recent online article about a group that met to discuss *The Da Vinci Code* at a Catholic parish.[23] The author of the article, David Rotert, writes:

> I queried several in the audience why they were there, and what their reaction was to the book and the evening's discussion. One woman told of her teenage son who was reluctant to go through the sacrament of Confirmation, yet after reading the book found a more believable, understandable, even human Jesus. That actually inspired him to continue the path. Another person said that such material added to the mystery, and in doing so served to strengthen her faith. For one it called into question the credibility of the teaching of the Church, yet [that person] felt that faith needs to be challenged to be pursued. Others voiced the idea that this book reinforced a disenchantment with the Church.

[22] Anne D. Neal and Jerry L. Martin, "Restoring America's Legacy: A Report by the American Council of Trustees and Alumni" (September 2002), 1. Accessed at http://www.goacta.org/publications/Reports/america%27s_legacy.pdf. The report notes, "Not a single one of the top 50 national and liberal arts colleges as defined by *U.S. News and World Report* in 2002, requires a course in American history" (2).

[23] David Rotert, "St. Joan's Discusses *The Da Vinci Code*" (September 25, 2003). Accessed at www.stjoan.com/er3/davinci/small.htm.

This group, and others similar to it, obviously emphasize opinion and feelings over careful and objective study. This ambivalent approach to the claims of the novel are summarized well in Rotert's remark: "Fortunately the evenings [sic] participants did not come expecting Yes/No answers." The same remark could be made about religious education in many parishes and churches today, again highlighting the need for a more rigorous approach to popular works such as *The Da Vinci Code*.[24]

Fiction, especially best-selling, popular fiction such as *The Da Vinci Code*, has become a major means of "educating" the masses about many varied topics, but especially about issues that are controversial and can be easily sensationalized. The belief that Jesus was married to Mary Magdalene, had children, and was not divine has existed for several decades in American pop culture, was popular among various esoteric and feminist groups in the nineteenth century, and its roots go back to even earlier times. Yet many, if not most, readers of Brown's novel seem unaware of this—even though the novel provides the titles of several books written in the last two or three decades proposing such beliefs.[25]

---

[24] A Jewish author, David Klinghoffer, writes, "If I were a Christian, though, I think I would find it a little disturbing that some fellow Christians do in fact view this novel as a threat to their faith. Some Catholic magazines have published detailed refutations of *The Da Vinci Code*; that they believe this is necessary indicates that many Catholics, and many in the general reading public, are taking this book far more seriously than they ought to. This also suggests that the problems in Catholic religious education are every bit as severe as Catholic conservatives have been alleging for some time now. If the professional educators were doing their job, any believing Catholic past elementary-school age would know that Brown's book is—a total falsehood" ("Religious Fiction", *National Review*, December 8, 2003. Accessed at www.nationalreview.com).

[25] See *The Da Vinci Code*, 253. Those titles include *The Templar Revelation: Secret Guardians of the True Identity of Christ*, by Lynn Picknett and Clive Prince (1997; New York: Simon and Schuster, 1998); *Goddess in the Gospels: Reclaiming the Sacred Feminine* (Rochester, Vt.: Bear, 1998) and *The Woman with the Alabaster Jar: Mary Magdalen and the Holy Grail* (Rochester, Vt.: Bear, 1993), by

What's the Matter with the *Code*?

Here is a list of what we believe are the major problems with *The Da Vinci Code*:

1. It claims to be historically accurate and based on fact, but often it is not

Many novelists who write historical fiction take some liberties with facts. This is usually not malicious, but rather it oftentimes is meant to help drive the plot or help develop characters. In other words, the background is changed a bit in the interest of the story. However, Brown's novel (which is not historical fiction, strictly speaking) is unique because its historical claims *are* the central focus—they are the real characters and plot. A serious reading of *The Da Vinci Code* reveals that the characters are simply devices meant to help promote Brown's central concerns, which are ideological. Without its radical rewriting of historical fact, Brown's novel does not exist in any shape or form. *The Da Vinci Code* also includes the before-mentioned "FACT" page, and Brown insists in interviews that his book is thorough and accurate in its representations of events, historical personages, and beliefs. But this simply is not the case, as this book will show in detail. Considering the sort of claims Brown makes, historical accuracy is a major issue with his novel.

2. It repeatedly misunderstands or misrepresents people, places, and events

The Da Vinci Code misrepresents, purposefully or otherwise, many historical events, persons, and institutions. These are

Margaret Starbird; and *Holy Blood, Holy Grail* (1982; New York: Dell, 1983), by Michael Baigent, Richard Leigh, and Henry Lincoln. As we will see, Brown relies heavily on *The Templar Revelation* and *Holy Blood, Holy Grail* for much of his supposed research.

discussed in detail in the pages that follow, but some examples will help make the point.

Brown confuses the Vatican and the Catholic Church and writes as though they were synonymous, with references to "the Vatican" often used in place of the Catholic Church. He has his fictional character the historian Leigh Teabing state that Constantine created a "new Vatican power base" (233), an amazing feat considering the fact that in Constantine's day the Vatican did not exist; the land it would one day occupy was then still a swampy marsh. The Vatican did not become the official residence of the pope until the fourteenth century.

Similar confusion exists about the status of Opus Dei, a Catholic group maligned at several points in the novel. A key character is Silas, a "hulking albino" monk (12). Never mind that Opus Dei is not a religious order and that it consists of mostly lay people, with fewer than 2 percent of its members being priests.[26] Brown has a Vatican secretarius tell the bishop heading Opus Dei, "You will be a church unto yourself" (415). Opus Dei is not a church, nor can it be. Other descriptions are also flawed, as Peter Bancroft of the Opus Dei Information Office in the United States explains:

> The various permutations of "personal prelature" the author uses to describe Opus Dei are redolent of something like the papal equivalent of a personal army, i.e., an extra-legal operation not subject to the rest of the Church's established authorities. But personal prelature is a jurisdictional status provided for by Canons 294–97 of the *Code of Canon Law*. "Personal" does not mean that Opus Dei belongs personally to the Pope or Vatican officials, but refers to the fact that the prelature's

---

[26] See www.opusdei.org. Brown seems to have a special dislike for Opus Dei; his novel even includes the address of a web site (30) devoted to "awareness" of the prelature.

jurisdiction applies to persons rather than a particular territory. Lay faithful of a personal prelature are subject to the bishop of their local diocese in just the same way as other lay faithful; the prelature's jurisdiction over them pertains only to guidance given to their spiritual life and apostolate.[27]

Other people or groups that are depicted in dubious or strange ways include Mary Magdalene, Emperor Constantine, Leonardo da Vinci, the Knights Templar, and the Priory of Sion.

Perhaps this should not be a surprise. In his previous novel *Angels and Demons*, a main character states that Copernicus (1473–1543) was "murdered" by the Catholic Church[28] (actually, Copernicus, a devout Catholic, was bed-ridden for several days and then died of a cerebral hemorrhage at the age of seventy) and that Galileo was a member of the Illuminati and was "severely punished" for believing that man was not the center of the universe (Galileo was put under house arrest for three years and was assisted by his daughter, a nun). *Angels and Demons*, which is set largely in and around the Vatican, features a "FACT" page and also an Author's Note stating: "References to all works of art, tombs, tunnels, and architecture in Rome are entirely factual. . . ."

3. It promotes a radical feminist, neo-gnostic agenda

The fact that the "sacred feminine" and rediscovering the goddess are a major theme of the novel may mean little to some readers, but it is a serious matter to many fans of *The Da Vinci Code*. The past few decades have witnessed a rapidly

---

[27] Personal letter to Carl Olson, January 22, 2004. In the novel, a bishop, Bishop Manuel Aringarosa, is described as saying Opus Dei is "a Catholic Church" (29)—a comment that no bishop would ever make since it is both false and confused. Opus Dei is a personal prelature of the Catholic Church, not a church in and of itself.

[28] Brown, *Angels and Demons*, 31.

growing interest in these topics, and that interest has influenced political and cultural opinion about sexuality and morality. As Philip G. Davis explains in *Goddess Unmasked: The Rise of Neopagan Feminist Spirituality*, "Goddess spirituality makes dramatic claims about anthropology, archaeology, ancient and modern history, social organization, psychology, art, and human biology, as well as religion."[29] *The Da Vinci Code* draws much of its inspiration from goddess spirituality. As Davis shows, the goddess movement involves a mixture of neo-paganism, neo-gnosticism, wicca, occultism, and radical feminism, all of which are mentioned, at least in passing, within Brown's novel. In a passage about his studies of goddess spirituality that could just as easily apply to *The Da Vinci Code*, Davis laments that "it is perplexing that claims so easily disproved are nevertheless in wide and increasing circulation. An important lesson of this book is the ease with which patent falsehoods may clothe themselves in the garb of scholarship and masquerade as truth."[30]

4. It incorrectly and unfairly misrepresents Christianity and traditional Christian beliefs about God, Jesus, and the Bible

Where to begin? A sampling includes: Jesus and Mary Magdalene were married. Prior to A.D. 325 no one believed Jesus was divine. Emperor Constantine declared Jesus to be God. Constantine rejected dozens of other "gospels" and rewrote the four that are in the Christian Bible. The Catholic Church burned over five million witches. The Catholic Church's leaders continue to keep the truth about Jesus from the masses through lies, deception, and violence.

[29] Philip G. Davis, *Goddess Unmasked: The Rise of Neopagan Feminist Spirituality* (Dallas: Spence, 1998), x.
[30] Ibid., ix.

These and other false claims fill *The Da Vinci Code*. And although few scholars would take any of them seriously, many readers do not have the background, time, or inclination to find out the truth. Even worse, many readers accept Brown's claims without consulting an encyclopedia or other resources, apparently believing that if it is in print, it must be true. Or perhaps they want it to be true. Or maybe truth is not a concern to them. Regardless, the misrepresentation of Christian beliefs in the novel is so aggressive and continual that we can only conclude that it is the result of willful ignorance or purposeful malice.

5. It propagates a relativistic, indifferent attitude toward truth and religion

One of the great dangers of a popular, entertaining work such as *The Da Vinci Code* is that it reinforces the relativistic attitudes that are already prevalent in Western culture and offers additional reasons for readers to embrace such attitudes. Hitchcock notes, "Millions of people read *The Da Vinci Code* not because they necessarily believe its absurd story but because it creates a myth that serves certain emotional needs and allows them to be 'religious' without submitting to any of the demands of faith." [31] This idea is evident in remarks made by the character Robert Langdon, who talks about "faith" as being built upon "fabrication" and beliefs that cannot be proven in any way (341). The appeal of such notions is obvious. It frees people from any sense of obligation or discipline, and it allows them to perceive reality in whichever way best suits their desires.

Unfortunately, many Christians who are fans of the novel do not seem to appreciate that it is an attack upon the core beliefs of the Christian faith. *The Da Vinci Code* "is not merely another liberal 'revision'", writes Hitchcock. "It is nothing

[31] Hitchcock, "Fantasy Faith", 16.

less than the claim that Christianity has been a deliberate fraud almost from its beginning, that the true story of Jesus was suppressed, and that only now are we finally learning what it was all about." [32] The lack of awareness of the novel's assaults on history, fact, and logic is evidence of a deep erosion of basic thinking and studying skills as well as an ambivalent attitude toward truth.

Deciphering the Success of the *Code*

Why has *The Da Vinci Code* been so successful? Why has it become such a force in popular culture? Why is it being taken so seriously by so many readers as well as by the mainstream media? There are no simple answers to these questions. Rather, there are a number of intertwining reasons, some of them obvious and others less apparent.

As Brown has stated, [33] most of the ideas in the novel are not original with him. The intellectual, ideological, and spiritual heritage of *The Da Vinci Code* can be traced back many decades, even centuries. However, what Brown has accomplished is the creation of a popular myth that distills and presents vital statements of belief in a way that is not demanding but entertaining and attractive. This myth works on more than one level, being a mystery novel, a romance, a thriller, a conspiracy theory, and a spiritual manifesto, all at once.

---

[32] Ibid., 15.

[33] Brown's contention that "this may be the first time the secret has been unveiled within the format of a popular thriller" is being challenged by Lewis Perdue, author of *The Da Vinci Legacy* (1983; New York: Tor Books, 2004) and *Daughter of God* (2000; New York: Forge, 2001). Perdue is suing Brown for alleged plagiarism, claiming that *The Da Vinci Code* took material from both of his novels and is largely based on the plot, characters, and premises of *Daughter of God*, a thriller that takes up neo-gnostic and feminist themes and combines them with excursions in the world of art. See www.daughter-of-god.com for more information.

On an immediate level, fans of the novel find it to be a quick and exciting read—a thriller with twists and turns, conspiracies, and mystery. However, it is less a thriller than a romance novel, filled with the usual conventions of the romance genre: extreme personality types, exotic locations, snobbish references to Harvard and Oxford, excessive amounts of conversation, and intentionally empty characters whose physical appearance needs to be supplied by the imagination of the reader. For example, Sophie's facial features are barely described—only her walk, clothing, eyes, and hair (50). The book reads much like a made-for-television movie, with short chapters, curt conversations, little character development, and sparsely constructed backdrops. There is an overwhelming emphasis on what the characters are feeling. At one point, in a span of five pages, readers are told that Sophie felt uncertain, surprised, troubled, confused, uneasy, skeptical, surprised (again), and unsure (158–62). Though this is not good writing, it makes for the sort of quick, emotionally driven, and superficial reading that dominates the mass market.

There are other, deeper, reasons for the novel's success. Although not immediately obvious, these reasons help explain why the book has become more than just a "good read" and nearly achieved a cult status. Although Brown is not a great writer, he has proven to be a clever, adept promoter of his beliefs—or at least of beliefs that he (correctly) thought would sell well.

Perhaps most important is the gnostic aspect of *The Da Vinci Code*. *Gnosis* is a Greek word for "knowledge"—connoting a special, hidden knowledge available only to an elite few. Seven million readers might not sound like an elite few, but readers' comments confirm how thrilled they are to "discover" the hidden "truth": "You will be amazed at the revelations that come forth in this book!"[34] Brown's novel promises hidden knowledge and an alternative view of history and reality open to those willing to believe, to risk going against "the winners" and the faceless authority figures. Having read the book, readers feel they have been initiated into a forbidden, dangerous world, where the truth behind the façade called "Christianity" is revealed in all of its shocking glory.

This promise of secret knowledge comes wrapped in a number of appealing layers. One is a distrust of authority, especially religious authority. The Catholic Church, the Vatican, bishops, Opus Dei, and the Catholic police officer Fache are presented as deceptive, extremist, misogynist, and mostly evil. These portrayals play on the long-standing discomfort and dislike that many Americans have experienced toward the Catholic Church.[35] "I think anti-Catholicism is a contributory factor [to the novel's success]," states Philip Jenkins, professor of history and religious studies at Pennsylvania State University, "but the main reason for the book's popularity is deeper, a fundamental suspicion of traditional claims to authority, where they conflict with contemporary ideas and standards, especially over sex and gender. It mainly

---

[34] Reviews provide evidence of the same. BookReporter.com states that Brown's "surprising revelations on Da Vinci's penchant for hiding codes in his paintings will lead the reader to search out renowned artistic icons such as *The Mona Lisa, The Madonna of the Rocks* and *The Last Supper. The Last Supper* holds the most astonishing coded secrets of all and, after reading *The Da Vinci Code*, you will never see this famous painting in quite the same way again." The *Louisville Voice-Tribune* writes, "Readers with advanced degrees in comparative religion, European history, symbology, art and cryptology, will have a grand old time with Dan Brown's *The Da Vinci Code*." The novel is "a mystery that challenges our intelligence" states ReviewsofBooks.com, and the *Atlanta Journal* encourages readers to "look closely at the epilogue, in which Langdon returns to where everything began, and determine if the most viable truth is the one gained from personal discovery."

[35] See Philip Jenkins, *The New Anti-Catholicism: The Last Acceptable Prejudice* (New York: Oxford University Press, 2003).

illustrates a broader suspicion about orthodoxy generally, and the idea that the truth is out there." [36]

Added to these suspicions is an appeal to individualism and the exaltation of the experiential. In negative terms, this means a renouncement of doctrine, dogma, and rules; positively, it is the celebration of self and "my truth". Emotion is the preferred guide to spirituality, as Langdon experiences at the supposed resting place of Mary Magdalene, where he is filled with "a sudden upwelling of reverence" (454). And so the cool, rational hero, an academic and scholar, admits his need for the divine—as he sees fit, alone and in direct contact with the spirit of the "sacred feminine".

The steadily growing interest in New Age beliefs, neognostic attitudes, and radical feminist notions has undoubtedly fed the frenzy surrounding *The Da Vinci Code*—and fed off of it as well. A January 2004 e-letter from *Publishers Weekly* reports that "the continuing popularity of Dan Brown's *The Da Vinci Code* and Elaine Pagels' *Beyond Belief* has prompted an unprecedented resurgence of interest in gnosticism" and goes on to detail the recent success of older books (*Holy Blood, Holy Grail* [1983] and Susan Haskins' *Mary Magdalene: Myth and Metaphor* [1993]) and newer titles (*The Resurrection of Mary Magdalene* [2002], by Jane Schaberg, and *The Gospels of Mary: The Secret Tradition of Mary Magdalene, the Companion of Jesus* [2004], by Marvin Meyer).[37]

Another factor in the success of *The Da Vinci Code* is that many readers implicitly share Brown's distrust of history. Many Americans are not only historically illiterate, they are chronologically condescending—the more ancient the history,

[36] Quoted by Gary Stern in "Unraveling the Myth: Catholic Church Decries 'The Da Vinci Code,' Academia Dismisses It", *Gannett News Service*. Newspress.com. December 27, 2003.

[37] *Publishers Weekly* January 2004 e-letter. Accessed at Amy Welborn's weblog: http://amywelborn.typepad.com/.

the less regard they have for it. Why? Mostly because they believe or at least act as though the world revolves around them. And those who have little use for history are more willing to rewrite and revise it to suit their ideological, spiritual, and emotional needs. A related problem is that many people simply do not care that they are historically illiterate. Historical facts are boring, but fictional stories are exciting. And so fictional narrative—whether in books, television, or movies—has become a primary source of historical "education" for the masses. People learn about Native Americans by watching *The Last of the Mohicans*, find out about merry old England by viewing *Robin Hood: Prince of Thieves*, and get in touch with World War II by sitting down to *Pearl Harbor*. It is not surprising *The Da Vinci Code* is being made into a major motion picture. Besides being an obvious money-maker, its breezy style, sensationalism, and postmodern approach is perfectly suited for a society oriented toward amoral, lightweight visual entertainment.[38]

Finally, a pervasive relativism has paved the road for works such as *The Da Vinci Code*. Not only does Brown's novel rest on distrust of traditional avenues of history, religion, and truth, it harbors the notion that truth ultimately cannot be known. In the words of a correspondent angered by our criticisms of *The Da Vinci Code*: "Religion says 'I know'. True spirituality says 'I have not found it and must continue to search.' "[39] Put bluntly, this means that we are free to do as we like, as long as we label it a "search". The truth *is* out there but is strangely unobtainable. Ironically, the comment is self-defeating: the correspondent *knows* what "true spirituality" is but insists that that spirituality consists of not being in possession of knowledge.

[38] See Gene Edward Veith, Jr., *Postmodern Times* (Wheaton, Ill.: Crossway Books, 1994), 93–142, for more on postmodernism in entertainment. Also see Veith's *Reading between the Lines: A Christian Guide to Literature* (Wheaton, Ill.: Crossway Books, 1990).

[39] E-mail to Carl Olson, January 2004.

He is certain that nothing is certain. Buttressing this internally confused outlook is the trendy conviction that "truth" can be reworked and remade in our image. Truth is malleable. Truth is what works for me. Truth is what makes me feel good. "Facts" are mythical constructs of an old, uptight Eurocentric way of looking at reality. "Reality" is what you make of it.

Whether out of cleverness or by accident, Brown has written a novel that takes a potent mixture of divergent elements and shapes them into a popular, postmodern myth. Playing to his readers' biases and weaknesses, he insists history cannot be known, but he still offers a history based on "fact" and "research". He claims that religion is a crutch, but he has written a book permeated with an esoteric, syncretistic religiosity. He implies that there is no truth, but he offers up secret *gnosis* about reality. He says that women need and deserve more attention, but only two of his main characters are women and one of those—Mary Magdalene—is dead. He sings the praises of androgyny, but he relies on the traditional formula of a handsome man meeting an attractive woman under stressful conditions and then falling in love. He wants readers to think for themselves, but he himself relies almost exclusively on a small collection of recent books laden with conspiracy theories unsubstantiated by reputable scholarship. In a word, the novel is a mess—and its very messiness is part of its appeal, for nearly everyone can find something in it to relate to, whether it be a character, an idea, or a situation. As Gene Edward Veith, Jr., explains "Many people find this loss of truth liberating. If we construct our own reality, then there are no limits to our freedom. In the words of a writer paraphrasing the punk rock band Johnny Rotten and the Sex Pistols, 'If nothing [is] true, everything [is] possible'"[40]— including *The Da Vinci Code* and its remarkable success.

[40] Veith, *Postmodern Times*, 59.

Chapter 1

Gnosticism

The Religion of the *Code*

> The method of salvation for Gnosticism ... does not involve struggle and suffering through time, the stance of faith as an act of trust in God's power to recover his fallen creation. The Gnostic instead demands an immediate glimpse of the inner workings of the cosmos, a decisive clue that deciphers the riddles of heaven and earth.
>
> —Carl A. Raschke, *The Interruption of Eternity: Modern Gnosticism and the Origins of the New Religious Consciousness*

Drawing deeply upon gnostic ideas about spirituality, Jesus Christ, Mary Magdalene, and the early Church, *The Da Vinci Code* weaves elements taken from that ancient belief system into a modern-day story of murder, intrigue, and conspiracy. In doing so, Brown has tapped into a form of religion and spirituality that has seen a tremendous increase of interest over the past three or four decades. Far more than an esoteric religion or antiquated set of spiritual guidelines, gnosticism is alive and well, a vibrant part of the world of alternative faiths. In essence, as even its adherents proudly note, it is the perennial heresy that continually follows

Christianity, seeking to subvert and invert essential beliefs of the orthodox Christian faith.[1]

For students of gnosticism today, the "gnostic gospels" and the ideas in them offer a more inclusive, ambiguous, accepting, and individualized version of Christianity, one free of unneeded doctrine and stifling dogma. Princeton professor and scholar Elaine Pagels, whose 1979 work *The Gnostic Gospels*[2] was a watershed in popularizing gnosticism and who is mentioned in *The Da Vinci Code* (245), writes in her recent best seller, *Beyond Belief*, that gnosticism is about being a seeker—someone who seeks for God—not a believer.[3] She laments those elements of orthodox Christianity that she "cannot love: the tendency to identify Christianity with a single, authorized set of beliefs—however these actually vary from church to church—coupled with the conviction that Christian belief alone offers access to God".[4] She states that orthodox Christianity is too rigid and keeps people from making their own choices about good and evil, truth and falsehood. "Orthodoxy tends to distrust our capacity to make such distinctions and insists on making them for us", she remarks. "Many of us, wishing to be spared hard work, gladly accept what tradition teaches."[5]

These comments touch on gnostic themes found within *The Da Vinci Code*: suspicion of tradition, distrust of authority, dislike for dogma and objective statements of faith, and

[1] By "orthodox Christianity" we refer to that general body of belief about which Catholics, Orthodox, and most Protestants would agree, including the belief in a personal, transcendent God, the Trinity, the divinity and humanity of Jesus Christ, the salvific work of the Cross, the Resurrection, the reality of sin and salvation, the Church, and the Second Coming.

[2] Elaine Pagels, *The Gnostic Gospels* (1979; New York: Vintage Books, 1989).

[3] Elaine Pagels, *Beyond Belief: The Secret Gospel of Thomas* (New York: Random House, 2003), 29.

[4] Ibid.

[5] Ibid., 184.

the pitting of the individual against the institution. There is also the promise of secret knowledge, which is one of the reasons for the novel's success. Readers believe that they are being let in on a secret that has been hidden for centuries—a bloody and damning cover-up by an ancient and powerful institution. This has always been the promise of gnosticism: freedom from authority, insight into reality, and enlightenment that goes beyond normality. Dr. Carl A. Raschke, in his insightful analysis of modern gnosticism, *The Interruption of Eternity: Modern Gnosticism and the Origins of the New Religious Consciousness*, explains that gnosticism is a "'religion of revolt' against conventional religion":

> Gnosticism consists in a rebellion not only against an oppressive and increasingly irrelevant structure of religious meaning, but also against an intolerable social and political system which the Gnostic, perhaps unconsciously, regards as the source of his spiritual discomfort. This relationship between Gnostic heterodoxy and social disenfranchisement may be confirmed not only by the fact that his religion finds its greatest appeal during periods of political corruption and the loss of coherent authority, as in the anarchy of Hellenistic times and the later phases of Rome's decline, but also by the tendency of Gnostic morality to be deviant and frequently antinomian.[6]

Simply put, gnostics—or neo-gnostics or "seekers"— historically have a reputation for rebelling, making a scene, and thumbing their noses at what they consider to be the status quo. There is little doubt that authority, whether political, religious, social, or otherwise, is not held in high regard in Western culture today. Questioning and attacking authority has become a rite of passage for many youth and an

---

[6] Carl A. Raschke, *The Interruption of Eternity: Modern Gnosticism and the Origins of the New Religious Consciousness* (Chicago: Nelson-Hall, 1980), 34.

addictive practice for many who are older. All of these elements can be found in *The Da Vinci Code* and, just as importantly, in its success and the controversy it has caused.[7] A closer look at the gnostic sources and ideas behind Brown's novel will perhaps help us gain a better understanding of this cultural phenomenon in our own day.

Dualism and the Promise of Knowledge

Gnosticism was the greatest challenge to the fledgling Christian faith of the second and third centuries. Yet, despite its influence, it is a difficult movement to define precisely because of its esoteric, decentralized, and eclectic nature.[8] In general, gnosticism is dualistic, focused on hidden spiritual knowledge (*gnosis*), antagonistic toward or uninterested in time and history, and distrustful—even hateful—toward the physical realm and the human body. Gnosticism seeks to escape the limits of time and space, to transcend the physical and historical realm, and it attempts to obtain salvation through secretive, individualistic means. "In its most essential form," explains James A. Herrick, "gnosticism is the systematic

---

[7] This is not to say that *The Da Vinci Code* embraces all gnostic beliefs, something that would be impossible since some forms of gnosticism contradict others. As for the novel questioning authority, especially that of the Catholic Church, many readers have told us stories of being confronted by friends, family members, or co-workers who believe the novel accurately depicts Catholic beliefs and events in the Church's past.

[8] Karen King of Harvard University, for example, writes: "Why is it so hard to define Gnosticism? The problem, I argue, is that a rhetorical term has been confused with a historical entity. There was and is no such thing as Gnosticism, if we mean by that some kind of ancient religious entity with a single origin and a distinct set of characteristics. Gnosticism is, rather, a term invented in the early modern period to aid in defining the boundaries of normative Christianity. Yet it has mistakenly come to be thought of as a distinctive Christian heresy or even as a religion in its own right" (Karen L. King, *What Is Gnosticism?* [Cambridge, Mass.: Belknap Press of Harvard University Press, 2003], 2).

spiritual effort to escape the confines of history and physical embodiment through secret knowledge (*gnosis*) and technique (magic). Gnostics seek to rise above the crowd of ordinary mortals who lack the will to break the chains of time and earthly existence."[9]

In his seminal study *The Gnostic Religion: The Message of the Alien God and the Beginnings of Christianity*, Hans Jonas explains that the "radical dualism" of gnosticism exists on many levels: "God and the world, spirit and matter, soul and body, light and darkness, good and evil, life and death".[10] Ancient gnostics believed that the true God is not only beyond the world and the material realm, he had nothing to do with the creation of matter: "The world is the work of lowly powers which though they may mediately be descended from Him do know the true God and obstruct the knowledge of Him in the cosmos over which they rule."[11] Stated another way, the material realm is evil, and man must escape it. This can be accomplished only through *gnosis*, or secret knowledge, of the true God.

This *gnosis* is rooted in the belief that man is not meant for this evil, material world. Dr. Bart D. Ehrman, author of *Lost Christianities: The Battles for Scripture and the Faith We Never Knew*, writes that according to this view, "we are trapped here, imprisoned. And when we learn who we are and how we can escape, we can then return to our heavenly home." He notes how this concept resonates with modern readers, "many of whom also feel alienated from this world, for whom

[9] James A. Herrick, *The Making of the New Spirituality: The Eclipse of the Western Religious Tradition* (Downers Grove, Ill.: InterVarsity Press, 2003), 179. See pp. 176–203 of Herrick's book for a helpful introduction to gnosticism and its current influence in Western culture.

[10] Hans Jonas, *The Gnostic Religion: The Message of the Alien God and the Beginnings of Christianity* (1958; Boston: Beacon Press, 1963), 31.

[11] Ibid., 42.

this world does not make sense, readers who realize, in some very deep and significant way, that they really don't belong here".[12] It is also the case that the individualistic, relativistic, and syncretistic character of gnosticism is appealing to modern men and women who are distrustful of the Church, believe Christianity to be anti-woman, and who have a generally negative view of any structure of authority.

Pagels explains that some of the early gnostics claimed "that humanity created God—and so, from its own inner potential, discovered for itself the revelation of truth".[13] In this form of gnosticism, which is popular in our own day, rather than being outside of—and separate from—humanity, God is a creation of mankind. Salvation is not about overcoming sin through and by God's assistance; rather, it is the overcoming of ignorance through self-knowledge.[14] Ignorance insures destruction, while self-knowledge provides liberation and escape from suffering. This means that Jesus was not the God-man who came to save mankind from sin, as orthodox Christians believe, but is a "teacher, revealer, and spiritual master" who is human only but who points the way to "the Christ". In gnostic teaching, Jesus is not greater than the student, but he will help the student to transcend him in knowledge and "Christ consciousness".

Another key concept embraced by many gnostic groups— and an idea that is popular among modern feminists—was that of an androgynous God, a deity who is a perfect balance of feminine and masculine. Some gnostic groups believed that the divine should be considered "masculofeminine— the 'great male-female power.' Others claimed that the terms were meant only as metaphors, since, in reality, the divine is

---

[12] Bart D. Ehrman, *Lost Christianities: The Battles for Scripture and the Faith We Never Knew* (New York: Oxford University Press, 2003), 114.

[13] Pagels, *Gnostic Gospels*, 122.

[14] See ibid., 123–24.

neither male nor female. A third group suggested that one can describe the primal Source in either masculine or feminine terms, depending on which aspect one intends to stress." Pagels adds: "Proponents of these diverse views agreed that the divine is to be understood in terms of a harmonious, dynamic relationship of opposites—a concept that may be akin to the Eastern view of *yin* and *yang*, but remains alien to orthodox Judaism and Christianity." [15]

The gnostic deity is both god and goddess, and the gnostics despised the Christians for "suppressing" the feminine nature of the Godhead. In *The Da Vinci Code*, Langdon lectures Sophie about this, telling her that the Priory of Sion believes that Emperor Constantine and his successors "successfully converted the world from matriarchal paganism to patriarchal Christianity" by employing "a campaign of propaganda that demonized the sacred feminine", destroying goddess worship and insuring that modern religion would be male-oriented (124). This suppression resulted, Brown's novel tells readers, in a warped and unbalanced humanity, overly masculine and lacking in feminine balance: "The days of the

---

[15] Ibid., 51. Androgynous can mean either possessing the traits of both genders (hermaphroditic) or lacking the traits of both genders (genderless). There is a sense in which it is true to say both of God. God possesses the perfections of both men and women, and God is neither male nor female. Manfred Hauke writes, "Images like 'Father' for the first Divine Person, and 'Son' for the second, must always be interpreted as analogies. They merely express an element of similarity, while that of dissimilarity always remains greater" (*God or Goddess? Feminist Theology: What Is It? Where Does It Lead?* [San Francisco: Ignatius Press, 1995], 149). Many feminists insist that the masculine images used for God need to be "balanced" with feminine images in an act of "democratization". For a detailed treatment of this topic, see Hauke, *God or Goddess?* 135–60. As for Pagels' remark about "harmonious, dynamic relationship of opposites", it can be said that in the relational opposition of the Persons of the first and second Persons of the Holy Trinity there exists something akin to such a relationship: the first Person is unbegotten and the begetter, and the second Person is begotten and the non-begetter.

goddess were over. The pendulum had swung. Mother Earth
had become a *man's* world, and the gods of destruction and
war were taking their toll." Readers are informed that the
"male ego" has run amuck, without being balanced or controlled at all by its feminine counterpart. This has led to the
"obliteration of the sacred feminine in modern life", resulting in imbalanced lives, "testosterone-fueled wars", woman-
hating societies, and "a growing disrespect for Mother Earth"
(125–26).

Many gnostics believed, not only that the true God[16] is
androgynous, but that humanity was also meant to be androgynous, or "masculo-feminine". Some gnostics interpreted
Genesis 1:27 as saying God created "male-female", not "male
and female". Certain gnostic texts describe the Divinity as a
"bisexual Power" and state that humanity is a "male-female
being". There are references to God as Father and Mother—a
"dyad" of both masculine and feminine.[17] This focus on an
androgynous ideal is often referred to in contemporary, neo-
gnostic works as "wholeness", a favorite term among many
feminists as well.[18] Margaret Starbird, whose books *The Woman
with the Alabaster Jar* and *The Goddess in the Gospels* are referred
to in *The Da Vinci Code*, repeatedly refers to "the partnership

---

[16] A core premise of gnosticism was that the god of this world—the God
of the Jews and Christians—is a lesser being (or group of them) who created
this world against the wishes of the true God, who is transcendent and "hidden from all creatures and is unknowable by natural concepts" (Jonas, *Gnostic
Religion*, 42). These lesser beings are often called archons, and they tyranni-
cally rule the world and keep the "inner man" of humans from being freed
of the material realm and returning to the true God. See Jonas, *Gnostic Religion*, 42–47.

[17] See Pagels, *Gnostic Gospels*, 56–57.

[18] "Fundamental to the 'androgyny'-oriented mainstream in feminist theology is the thesis that every person combines in himself both 'feminine' and
'masculine' aspects. Here, it is seen as crucial to achieve a state of balanced
'wholeness'" (Hauke, *God or Goddess?* 100; see pp. 100–117 for a full treatment of this concept).

paradigm",[19] which she describes as "the imaging of the Divine as both Bride and Bridegroom". This is necessary, she explains, so that the "collective psyche" of humanity will be healed, made whole, and restored. The essential purpose of this? "We must value our own feelings and emotions, our own intuitions, our own experience, our own selves. We must honor our own journeys."[20] Wholeness, it seems, is merely self-absorption and narcissism.

The idea of an androgynous, "whole" humanity makes an appearance in *The Da Vinci Code*. In talking to Sophie about the *Mona Lisa*, Langdon claims that the *Mona Lisa* is "neither male nor female", but an androgynous portrait that is "a fusing of both" (120). This is wishful thinking on the part of Langdon (and Brown), since reputable art historians agree the portrait has nothing to do with androgyny but is simply a masterful painting of an Italian lady (most likely Mona Lisa Gherardini, the wife of merchant Francesco del Giocondo).[21] However, the idea that the *Mona Lisa* depicts an androgynous person does fit with the gnostic beliefs that those who were enlightened by gnosis needed to be in

[19] Margaret Starbird, *Goddess in the Gospels: Reclaiming the Sacred Feminine* (Rochester, Vt.: Bear, 1998), 145, 153. Starbird, *The Woman with the Alabaster Jar: Mary Magdalen and the Holy Grail*, is also published by Bear (1993). Starbird has been described by Episcopal bishop John Shelby Spong as "a seeker after truth, not a defender of doctrine. She recognizes that orthodoxy is orthodox because it won and not necessarily because it is true" (from back cover of *The Woman with the Alabaster Jar*). Starbird admits that she turned her back on orthodox Catholic teachings (she was a religious educator) after reading *Holy Blood, Holy Grail* in the 1980s: "The more deeply involved I became with the material, the more obvious it became that there was real substance in the theories set forth in reading *Holy Blood, Holy Grail*. And gradually I found myself won over to the central tenets of the Grail heresy, the very theory I had originally set out to discredit" (*Woman with the Alabaster Jar*, xx–xxi). *Holy Blood, Holy Grail* (1982; New York: Dell, 1983) was written by Michael Baigent, Richard Leigh, and Henry Lincoln.

[20] Starbird, *Goddess in the Gospels*, 145.

[21] See chap. 9 below, "The *Code* Puts on Artistic Errors".

pairs—male and female—forming a perfect whole, or syzygy. Thus, Jesus would require a female counterpart who would make him complete; in gnostic writings that woman, of course, was Jesus' "consort", Mary Magdalene.

The interconnection between these ancient gnostic notions and feminist attacks on core Christian beliefs, especially upon the male priesthood, should be apparent. If the male and female genders are not unique in vital, but equal, ways—as the Catholic Church teaches—but are the results of an incomplete anthropology, then there is no reason to keep women from the priesthood or episcopal authority. If there is no essential difference or distinction between men and women, then the Church's refusal to ordain women is simply a matter of misogyny, not of theological, doctrinal truth. This connection is readily apparent in the activities of religious feminist groups, such as "Women-Church", that are intent on getting women ordained as Catholic priests (or priestesses). Such groups insist that the early Church was an egalitarian community and that the gnostic scriptures provide a truer picture of what Jesus intended the Christian community to be. Redemption "consists essentially in knowledge of one's self", which is a "basic principle of ancient Gnosticism".[22] Christianity becomes whatever the individual desires, based on subjectivity and ideology, not objectivity and theology.

Feminist Dreams of the Gnostic Early Church

One difficulty in defining gnosticism, whether ancient or modern, is its syncretistic nature. As Jonas states, "the gnostic systems compounded everything—oriental mythologies, astrological doctrines, Iranian theology, elements of Jewish

[22] Hauke, *God or Goddess?* 208. See 205–15 for an examination of feminist views of the Church.

tradition, whether Biblical, rabbinical, or occult, Christian salvation-eschatology, Platonic terms and concepts." [23] Today there are numerous esoteric groups and movements that utilize gnostic concepts and writings: wiccans, New Agers, occultists, radical feminists, neo-pagans, and a host of others. *The Da Vinci Code* makes reference to a number of esoteric and occult groups and movements, but it is especially enamored with a radical feminist interpretation of Church history.

The beliefs about the early Church, gnosticism, and Mary Magdalene set forth in Brown's novel date back to the nineteenth century and the advent of modern feminism. Philip Jenkins points out, in *Hidden Gospels: How the Search for Jesus Lost Its Way*, that "late nineteenth-century activists saw Jesus and his first followers as protofeminists, whose radical ideas were swamped by a patriarchal orthodoxy." In addition to feminists, this "idea that the Gnostics retained the core truths of a lost Christianity was commonplace among occult and esoteric writers, many of whom shared the contemporary excitement over women's suffrage and other progressive causes".[24] These writers looked to heretical, gnostic forms of early Christianity for material to bolster their belief that Jesus was really a radical feminist, that the Church was initially founded as an egalitarian and non-dogmatic body, and that women were among the first apostles—or were, as in the case of Mary Magdalene, the *primary* apostles.

One of the first gnostic texts used effectively by feminists was *Pistis Sophia*, sometimes called "The Books of the Savior", published in English in 1896. In this work, Mary Magdalene is depicted as the foremost apostle of Jesus, while

---

[23] Jonas, *Gnostic Religion*, 25.

[24] Philip Jenkins, *Hidden Gospels: How the Search for Jesus Lost Its Way* (New York: Oxford University Press, 2001), 125.

the male disciples are frustrated by the lack of attention they received from Jesus. But it was the discovery of numerous gnostic texts in 1945 at Nag Hammadi, Egypt, that provided even more ammunition for those looking to undermine Church authority and change the structures and theology of the Catholic Church. Pagels, whose work in this area is both scholarly and popular, writes, "The Nag Hammadi sources, discovered at a time of contemporary social crises concerning sexual roles, challenge us to reinterpret history—and to re-evaluate the present situation." [25]

As Pagels' comment indicates, the timing of the Nag Hammadi discovery was fortuitous for those wishing to reinterpret Jesus in their own image and to attack traditional, orthodox understandings of Christianity. Those gnostic writings have provided the means of creating radical new interpretations of who Jesus was and what he wanted to accomplish. They provide the means, Jenkins notes, "for interpreting theological statements in a purely symbolic and psychological sense, and for challenging dogmatic or legal rules on the basis of the believer's subjective moral sense. Generally, the hidden gospels offer wonderful news for liberals, feminists, and radicals within the churches, who challenge what they view as outdated institutions and prejudices." [26]

This perfectly describes the intent of *The Da Vinci Code*, which uses a fictional vehicle to promote the same agenda that a number of feminist and postmodern scholars have been working on since the 1960s. Those fans of Brown's novel who think the author has somehow stumbled upon new and never-before-seen information might be surprised to know how commonplace his views are within the realm of gnostic

[25] Pagels, *Gnostic Gospels*, 69.
[26] Jenkins, *Hidden Gospels*, 16.

and feminist studies. Jenkins' depiction of the literature produced within that world could just as well describe *The Da Vinci Code*: "Over the last century, the literature on hidden gospels, genuine and fraudulent, has been pervaded by conspiratorial speculations which suggest that some powerful body (usually the Roman Catholic Church) is cynically plotting either to conceal the true gospel, or to plant bogus documents to deceive the faithful."[27] As Jenkins notes, these conspiratorial ideas can be found in a number of recent books and films, including the movie *Stigmata*, which depicts the Vatican as attempting to cover up the existence of a "Jesus Gospel", apparently patterned after the *Gospel of Thomas*.

It would take an entire book to address thoroughly all of these intertwining topics and answer each of the questions they raise.[28] But here, in short order, are some of the essential points about these issues that play such a prominent role in *The Da Vinci Code*.

The feminist belief that the early Church was an egalitarian body led by both female and male bishops and priests is based on flimsy premises and lacks historical evidence. This has even been partially admitted by Pagels, who stated in the 1998 PBS program *From Jesus to Christ*, "I don't see a picture of a golden age of egalitarianism back there. I see a new, unformed, diverse, and threatened movement which allowed a lot more fluidity for women in certain roles for a while, in some places and not in others."[29] Feminist scholars speculating about the first few decades of the early Church usually treat the New Testament documents with suspicion,

[27] Ibid., 18.

[28] Jenkins' *Hidden Gospels* is an excellent place to start. Donna Steichen's *Ungodly Rage: The Hidden Face of Catholic Feminism* (San Francisco: Ignatius Press, 1991) is an indispensable study of feminism, especially among Catholics. A more involved and theologically complex resource is Hauke's *God or Goddess?*

[29] Accessed at www.pbs.org.

claiming that they are the work of those men who finally gained control over the Church through the suppression of women. Using a "hermeneutics of suspicion", these scholars must ignore early evidence that the Church was founded by Christ and her leadership on earth given to twelve men (Mt 10:1ff; 19:28; Lk 22:25–30; Jn 20:20–24) led by Peter (Mt 16:15–19), and they must instead insist upon using texts that were written anywhere from fifty to three hundred years after the New Testament documents.

In addition, there is the misleading notion that the gnostic writings are consistently pro-woman, while the New Testament writings—and therefore the authors of those books—are anti-woman. This idea also arises in *The Da Vinci Code*. After quoting from the *Gospel of Mary Magdalene*, in which Peter complains about Mary's closeness to Christ, Sir Leigh Teabing states: "I daresay Peter was something of a sexist" (248). He then remarks that "Jesus was the original feminist" and that he meant for "the future of His Church to be in the hands of Mary Magdalene" (248). But Pagels notes that the gnostics did not affirm women in a unanimous way, "nor were the orthodox unanimous in denigrating them". Many gnostic texts, in fact, clearly refer to the feminine with great contempt.[30]

But Brown never bothers to have his characters quote from the final verse of the *Gospel of Thomas*, the most famous of the gnostic texts. That verse states: "Simon Peter said to them: 'Let Mary leave us, for women are not worthy of life.' Jesus said, 'I myself shall lead her in order to make her male, so that she too may become a living spirit resembling you males. For every woman who will make herself male will enter the kingdom of heaven'" (v. 114). This passage and others do not fit well with the feminist view of the gnostics. Some

[30] Pagels, *Gnostic Gospels*, 66.

popularized feminist works (and *The Da Vinci Code*) ignore this passage. Pagels, to her credit, addresses it: "Strange as it sounds, this simply states what religious rhetoric assumes; that the men form the legitimate body of the community, while women are allowed to participate only when they assimilate themselves to men."[31] Strangely enough, this "if you can't beat them, join them" approach has been embraced by many feminists, who believe that the way to "equality" with men is to adopt masculine traits and qualities.

Feminists routinely claim that Christianity is antiwoman and that the history of the Church has been one of repressing and subordinating women. In *Beyond God the Father: Towards a Philosophy of Women's Liberation*, Mary Daly states, "Christian theology widely asserted that women were inferior, weak, depraved, and vicious. The logical consequences of this opinion were worked out in a brutal set of social arrangements that shortened and crushed the lives of women."[32] She refers readers to the work of Simone de Beauvoir (1908–1986), a leading French feminist and longtime companion to the existentialist (and atheist) philosopher Jean-Paul Sartre. Known for her statement, "One is not born, but rather becomes, a woman",[33] de Beauvoir believed that "the good for woman lies in making herself as

---

[31] Ibid., 49. Susan Haskins writes, "In the *Gospel of Thomas*, the disciple has to strip off his fleshly garment and 'pass by' his mundane existence in order to participate in the spiritual world. Jesus says that Mary Magdalen too may become male, that is to say, 'spiritual,' under his tutelage; and that she has evidently become so is reflected in her mysterious pronouncement in the *Gospel of Mary*: 'he has prepared us [and] made us into men'" (*Mary Magdalen: Myth and Metaphor* [New York: Riverhead Books, 1993], 40–41). The gnostics, then, equated being "spiritual" with maleness, hardly a pro-feminist perspective.

[32] Mary Daly, *Beyond God the Father: Towards a Philosophy of Women's Liberation* (Boston: Beacon Press, 1973), 95.

[33] *The Oxford Companion to Philosophy*, ed. Ted Honderich (Oxford: Oxford University Press, 1995), 179.

similar as possible to man." [34] As Manfred Hauke observes, this approach leads only to a deeper, more radical contempt for femininity, and those who embrace it actually align themselves with "the most infamous woman haters of our epoch". Hauke writes, "The most misogynous pronouncements known to us stem not from antiquity or the Middle Ages but from the 'enlightened' nineteenth and twentieth centuries, from Kant, Schopenhauer, Virchow and Nietzsche up to Esther Vilar." [35] Whatever the failings of individuals throughout history, Daly's broad claims of Christian cruelty toward women do not hold water; indeed, they are based in a radical feminism that hates both men and Christianity with an intense, nearly demonic hatred. "In its depth, because it contains a dynamic that drives beyond Christology," Daly writes, "the women's movement does point to, seek, and constitute the primordial, always present, and future Antichrist. It does this by breaking the Great Silence, raising up female pride, recovering female history, healing and bringing into the open female presence." [36]

Daly's teaching and writing has influenced a host of other feminists and feminist groups. In addition to the works of Daly, many of these groups use gnostic writings to buttress their arguments for female priests. One such feminist group is the "Catholic" organization FutureChurch, whose web site contains an article insisting that "the Montanist and Valentinian Churches, which had both male and female leaders,

---

[34] Manfred Hauke, *Women in the Priesthood? A Systematic Analysis in the Light of the Order of Creation and Redemption* (San Francisco: Ignatius Press, 1988), 470.

[35] Ibid. Hauke provides some "samplings". Schopenhauer: Woman is "in every respect the backward second sex". The "veneration of women" is the "highest blossoming of Christian-Germanic stupidity". Disraeli: "Every woman should marry—and no man." Nietzsche: "Woman is God's second mistake."

[36] Daly, *Beyond God the Father*, 96. For more on Daly, see Steichen, *Ungodly Rage*, 297–301.

were eventually suppressed. Scholars say that the Montanist and Valentinian communities were orthodox. They were suppressed not because their teachings were heretical, but because women as well as men engaged in leadership."[37] In fact, almost all scholars, including some feminist authors, acknowledge that the Montanists and Valentinians were outside the Church and considered heretical for numerous reasons, including attacks on the deity of Christ (Valentinians) and the authority of the Church (both groups), an obsession with prophetic utterances (Montanists), and dualist views (Valentinians). Even Pagels observes that "Valentinian gnosticism" was "the most influential and sophisticated form of gnostic teaching, and by far the most threatening to the church".[38] Unfortunately, such attempts to use ancient, heretical movements for modern, ideological ends are common. They are also quite successful, in part because many readers of works such as *The Da Vinci Code, The Templar Revelation*, or *The Goddess in the Gospels* know little if anything about ancient gnosticism or about whether the "gnostic gospels" can rightfully be placed on the same level as the four Gospels of the Christian Bible.

The Gnostic Gospels and the Dating Game

Correctly dating the New Testament writings and the gnostic writings is essential in order to place ideas found in *The Da Vinci Code* and the works of neo-gnostic enthusiasts in their proper historical context. If gnostic works such as the *Gospel of Mary Magdalene* (also called *The Gospel of Mary*) and the *Gospel of Thomas* were written at the same time as the canonical Gospels, the Pauline corpus, and the other New

---

[37] Author unknown, "Mary of Magdala—Apostle to the Apostles". Accessed at www.futurechurch.org/marym/index.htm.

[38] Pagels, *Gnostic Gospels*, 31.

Testament books (which are dated from A.D. 50 to 100, even by many scholars who are not considered "conservative" or "orthodox"), then the early Church resembles the picture painted by feminist scholars—one in which various groups existed equally, at least for a while, within a democratic, theologically fluid era. According to this premise, the hierarchical and male-dominated Church came much later, in the second and third centuries, and Jesus was not deified as the God-man until the time of Constantine. This is essentially the scenario depicted in *The Da Vinci Code* (230–62).

However, if the gnostic books were not written until several decades, or even centuries, after the New Testament books, a different picture emerges. In it, the gnostic writings are the result of the intense struggle of heretical sects against the established teachings of the Church and the apostles. In fact, precisely such struggles did erupt in the second century, were especially noticeable around A.D. 135 to 165, and continued for quite some time. The nature of this struggle can be seen in the writings of orthodox apologist Irenaeus, who wrote his great polemic refuting gnosticism (especially the Valentinians), *Against Heresies*, around A.D. 180.

Put another way, gnosticism began to infiltrate the Church in full force in the early to mid-second century, many decades removed from the life of Christ, the apostles, and the formation of the Church—a distance in time similar to that experienced by modern-day scholars looking back at the lives of Abraham Lincoln or even George Washington. Gnosticism was thus a movement arising outside of Christianity, even though some overlapping of language and concepts may have existed, due in part to a shared culture and the gnostic interest in the Old Testament. Some gnostic proponents claim that a full-fledged gnosticism is evident within the Church in the person of Simon Magus (Acts 8:9–13), but this view is speculative at best. Jonas writes that Simon was "not a dissident Christian, and if the Church Fathers cast him in the role of the arch-heretic, they implicitly admitted that Gnosticism was not an inner-Christian phenomenon".[39]

An important characteristic of gnostic writings is how much they vary in character from the canonical writings: they are non-historical, or even anti-historical, in style and content, and they contain little narrative or sense of chronology. The Nag Hammadi documents, as highly touted as they are, have offered few, if any, new or illuminating details about the life of Christ or events in the early Church. This is due in part to the documents having been written generations after the fact as well as to the anti-historical bias of gnosticism, which scorns the belief that the true God would care about the material, historical realm. In concluding his examination of the veracity of the *Gospel of Mary* and other gnostic texts, Jenkins notes that at the time those noncanonical texts were written, the hierarchy of the Church was already formed and established. The canonical gospels were known and accepted as the primary sources and authorities about Jesus and his life, and Christians were many years removed from meeting in house churches. "[The *Gospel of*] *Mary* and its like come from a time when the church had already fixed its gospel canon at four." [40] Although proponents such as Karen King insist that the *Gospel of Mary* was unfairly excluded from the Christian canon because it had an overly positive view of women and female leadership, the late date of its writing seriously undermines such arguments.

---

[39] Jonas, *Gnostic Religion*, 103.

[40] Jenkins, *Hidden Gospels*, 141. "Canon" comes from the Greek word meaning "measuring rod", or "rule". The Old Testament and New Testament canons were collections of divinely inspired writings that were eventually defined by Church authority over the course of lengthy periods of time. A helpful introduction can be found in J. N. D. Kelly's *Early Christian Doctrines*, 5th rev. ed. (San Francisco: Harper and Row, 1978), 52–79.

Jenkins' conclusions are supported by the majority of biblical scholars. For example, Dr. Bart Ehrman of the University of North Carolina, in his book *Lost Christianities:The Battles for Scriptures and the Faiths We Never Knew*, dates none of the gnostic gospels before the "early 2nd century". Many are dated in the third, fourth, and fifth centuries.[41] The introductions to the gnostic works contained in *The Nag Hammadi Library*,[42] edited by James M. Robinson, acknowledge the same dates, even though they argue that the gnostic writings should be considered just as authoritative as the four Gospels. The moderate *New Jerome Biblical Commentary* states that the *Nag Hammadi* writings are translations "of texts composed in Greek during the flourishing growth of gnostic sects from the mid-second century to the third century".[43] And Pagels is clearly straining when she writes that "*some*" of the Nag Hammadi manuscripts "can hardly be later than c. A.D. 120–150" since Irenaeus, writing around A.D. 180, observes that the gnostics "boast that they possess more gospels than there really are",[44] which is to say that *some* of the gnostic texts *may* have been written in the early to mid-second century.

All of this flies in the face of Teabing's assertion in *The Da Vinci Code* that "more than *eighty* gospels were considered for the New Testament, and yet only a few were chosen for inclusion—Matthew, Mark, Luke, and John among them" (231). By the mid-second century there were only five or six still being considered, and by the late second century the early Church recognized the Gospels of Matthew,

[41] Ehrman, *Lost Christianities*, xi–xv.

[42] James M. Robinson, general ed., *The Nag Hammadi Library*, 3rd rev. ed. (San Francisco: HarperSanFrancisco, 1988).

[43] Raymond E. Brown, Joseph A. Fitzmyer, and Roland E. Murphy, eds., *The New Jerome Biblical Commentary* (Englewood Cliffs, N.J.: Prentice Hall, 1990), 1065.

[44] Pagels, *Gnostic Gospels*, xvi. Emphasis added.

Mark, Luke, and John as the four inspired by the Holy Spirit and meant for the canon of the New Testament. As Jenkins shows, "the process of determining the canon was well under way long before Constantine became emperor, and before the church had the slightest prospect of political power. The crucial phase occurred in the mid-second century." [45]

In fact, there was already a growing consensus about the entire New Testament canon by the middle of the second century, even though it would not be defined on an official (though not universal) level until the late 300s and early 400s in a series of local synods. Justin Martyr, writing around A.D. 150 and explaining the liturgy of the Christians to his non-Christian readers, speaks of the apostles and says, "the memoirs composed by them, which are called Gospels, have thus delivered unto us what was enjoined upon them." [46] Tertullian, writing around the same time, defends the four Gospels, the Acts of the Apostles, thirteen Pauline epistles, the epistle to the Hebrews, and 1 John and the Apocalypse against the gnostic ideas of Marcion. [47] A couple of decades later Irenaeus specifically refers to the four Gospels and their authors and implies that they are granted a unique status within the Church:

> Matthew also issued a written Gospel among the Hebrews in their own dialect, while Peter and Paul were preaching at Rome, and laying the foundations of the Church. After their departure, Mark, the disciple and interpreter of Peter, did also hand down to us in writing what had been preached by Peter. Luke also, the companion of Paul, recorded in a book the Gospel preached by him. Afterwards, John, the disciple of the Lord, who also had leaned upon His breast, did himself publish a Gospel during his residence at Ephesus in Asia. [48]

[45] Jenkins, *Hidden Gospels*, 85.
[46] Justin Martyr, *The First Apology* 66.
[47] Tertullian, *Five Books against Marcion* 4.2, 4.5.
[48] Irenaeus, *Against Heresies* 3.1.1.

A bit farther on, Irenaeus writes, "It is not possible that the Gospels can be either more or fewer in number than they are",[49] and again he prominently mentions Matthew, Mark, Luke, and John, further proof that the number of Gospels recognized as authoritative within the Church was set at four at least 150 years prior to Constantine and the Council of Nicaea.

The Gnostic Jesus

A serious question ignored by *The Da Vinci Code* is this: Why should the writings of the gnostics be considered more dependable than the canonical writings, especially when they were written some fifty to three hundred years later than the New Testament writings? It is easy for writers such as Brown, who are sympathetic to the gnostics (or at least to some of their ideas), to criticize the canonical Gospels and call many of the stories and sayings contained in them into question. But without the canonical Gospels there would be *no* historical Jesus at all, *no* meaningful narrative of his life, and *no* real sense of what he did, how he acted, and how he related to others.

As we pointed out, the "gnostic gospels" are not gospels at all in the sense of the four canonical Gospels, which are filled with narrative, concrete details, historical figures, political activity, and details about social and religious life. Contrary to Teabing's assertion that "the early Church literally *stole* Jesus" and shrouded his "human message . . . in an impenetrable cloak of divinity", and used it to expand her own power (233), the Church was intent, from the very beginning, on holding on to the humanity and divinity of Christ and on telling the story of his life on earth without washing

[49] Ibid., 3.11.8.

away the sorrow, pain, joy, and blood that so often accompanied it. The Church fought to keep Christianity firmly rooted in history and fact "rather than the random mythologies reinvented at the whim of each rising Gnostic sage. The church was struggling to retain the idea of Jesus as a historical human being who lived and died in a specific place and time, not in a timeless never-never land." [50]

The Jesus of the gnostic writings is rarely recognizable as a Jewish carpenter, teacher, and prophet dwelling in first-century Palestine; instead, he is often described as a phantom-like creature who lectures at length about the "deficiency of aeons", "the mother", "the Arrogant One", and "the archons"—all terms that only the gnostic elite would comprehend—hence their secretive, gnostic character. One strain of gnosticism, known as docetism, held that Jesus only seemed, or appeared, to be a man. [51] Adherents believed this because of their dislike for the physical body and the material realm, a common trait among gnostics. The tendency toward a docetist understanding of Jesus—if not a fully formed docetist Christology—existed in the first century and was addressed in some of the later writings of Paul (Colossians and the pastoral epistles) and John (cf. 1 Jn 4:2; 5:6; 2 Jn 7). In the second century, docetism became a developed theology and made its appearance in various gnostic writings, including the *Acts of John*, written in the late second century:

> Sometimes when I would lay hold on him, I met with a material and solid body, and at other times, again, when I felt him, the substance was immaterial and as if it existed not at all. And if at any time he were bidden by some one of the Pharisees and went to the bidding, we went with him, and there was set before each one of us a loaf by them that had

[50] Jenkins, *Hidden Gospels*, 211.
[51] Docetism comes from the Greek word *doceo*, which means "I seem".

bidden us, and with us he also received one; and his own he
would bless and part it among us: and of that little every one
was filled, and our own loaves were saved whole, so that
they which bade him were amazed. And oftentimes when I
walked with him, I desired to see the print of his foot, whether
it appeared on the earth; for I saw him as it were lifting himself up from the earth: and I never saw it.[52]

If the material realm is evil, as almost all gnostic groups
believed, why would a being such as Christ have anything to
do with it? And why should we be concerned at all with
history and the common life of ordinary people? The gnostic Christ is not interested in earthly, historical events as much
as freeing the spirit from the entrapment of the body. In many
gnostic texts, Christ and Jesus are posited as two separate
beings—Christ being from above and Jesus, the bodily vessel
that Christ dwelled in for a time on earth, from below. "This
kind of Christology could be called 'separationist,' in that it
saw two clear and separate persons, the human being Jesus
and the divine aeon Christ who temporarily dwelled in him",
notes Ehrman. "According to some forms of these Gnostic
views, the Christ descended into Jesus at his baptism, empowering him for his ministry, and then left him prior to his
death. Thus it was that the divine Christ escaped suffering.
Jesus, in this view, suffered alone." [53]

Gnosticism was exclusive, elitist, and esoteric, open only
to a few. Christianity, on the other hand, is inclusive and

---

[52] *Acts of John* 93. Accessed at www.gnosis.org.

[53] Ehrman, *Lost Christianities*, 223–24. "In the second-century Gnosticism
described by the Father", writes Ronald Nash, "Christ was one of the higher
aeons, or intermediary beings, who descended to earth for the purpose of
redeeming man. Christ came into the world, not in order to suffer and die, but
in order to release the divine spark of light imprisoned in matter. The Gnostic
Jesus was not a savior; he was a revealer" (*The Gospel and the Greeks*, 2nd ed.
[Phillipsburg, N.J.: P and R Press, 2003], 209).

exoteric, open to all those who acknowledge the beliefs of the faith handed down by Jesus and enter into a life-giving relationship with him. Jesus Christ of the canonical Gospels is a breathing, flesh-and-blood person; he gets hungry, weeps, eats and drinks with common people, and dies. Jesus Christ of the gnostic writings is a phantom, a spirit who sometimes inhabits a body and sometimes does not, and who talks in ways that very few could understand. Once again, *The Da Vinci Code* has it backward.

The novel's statements about Jesus and his followers fail to make sense of some daunting questions. If the first followers of Jesus did not believe he was divine and if they thought that he had not risen again from the dead, why did so many of them willingly die as martyrs? Why would these follow-ers, who are so clearly confused and distraught when Jesus is taken away to be executed, re-emerge a few weeks later and begin boldly proclaiming their belief in their fallen leader? If Jesus had remained in the tomb where he was placed after his death, could the authorities not have shown his body and stopped once and for all the audacious teachings of the sud-denly confident Christians?

Put simply, if Jesus were merely mortal and not consid-ered anything more until the fourth century, then it is impos-sible to make any sense of Christianity and how it came into existence. Historian Paul Johnson writes that "in order to explain Christianity we have to postulate an extraordi-nary Christ who did extraordinary things. We have to think back from a collective phenomenon to its agent. Men and women began frantically and frenetically to preach Jesus' gospel because they believed he had come back to them from the dead and given them the authority and the power to do so." [54]

[54] Paul Johnson, *A History of Christianity* (New York: Atheneum, 1976), 27.

An implicit assumption behind the remarks of the fictional Teabing and Langdon in *The Da Vinci Code* is that Christians—whether of the first, fourth, or twenty-first centuries—are mindless drones who simply believe what they are told by their leaders. Thus, Constantine deified a man whom no one ever thought of as divine, and none of the Christians were bothered by it. And so the same people who often suffered and died for their beliefs were now willing to accept a radical, wholesale change in doctrine without so much as a peep? This is not only impossible to accept as logical, it is contrary to history and fact. Those who study the historical record do not have to believe that the early Christians were correct in believing that Jesus was divine, but they will have to acknowledge that *that* is exactly what those Christians did believe.

The New Gnosticism

The history of gnosticism is that of a series of silences and eruptions, fitting for a belief system that thrives on secrecy, subversion, ambiguity, and syncretism. Although the outer trappings of gnosticism have often changed throughout time, its radical dualism, distrust of authority, and dislike of the material realm have been relatively constant, even if a proper, concise definition of it is nearly impossible. The appeal of secret knowledge and the promise of elite techniques for harnessing the spiritual realm make gnosticism appealing to a diverse range of cultures and peoples, from second-century Valentinians to the medieval Cathars of France to the nineteenth-century followers of the American Joseph Smith and modern-day New Agers.

Both the mystery and appeal of neo-gnosticism were evident in the tragic 1997 mass suicide in California by thirty-nine members of the Heaven's Gate UFO cult. Initially, the bizarre group and deadly act seemed just as incomprehensible as the group's beliefs. But Heaven's Gate proved to be a variation—a horrific and extreme variation—on the gnostic themes of escaping their bodies ("shedding their containers"), moving to the next spiritual level, and following the call of secret knowledge. Although Heaven's Gate leader Marshall Applewhite had mixed in a number of elements drawn from the modern world (UFOs in particular), the "chosen ones'" goal of escaping this world and returning to their proper, original home was as ancient as the earliest gnostic writings.

More benign forms of gnosticism (at least on the physical level) can be found in a wide range of New Age groups and movements, self-help materials, and teachings of self-proclaimed gurus and spiritual guides. A well-known example was Joseph Campbell (1904–1987), author of many books and presenter of the popular television special *The Power of Myth*, hosted by Bill Moyers on PBS. Campbell claimed that the core ideas and mythologies of religions are essentially the same—only the temporal externals differ. These "elementary ideas" include the idea that humans are divine: "Deities are the symbolic personifications of the very energies that are yourself." [55] God, Campbell taught, is, not the personal, transcendent Being of the Judeo-Christian tradition, but an impersonal consciousness—the "Ultimate Reality". [56] For Campbell, "the basic Gnostic and Buddhist idea" is that God was in Christ and is also in all human beings in the same way, if only they will accept and realize it. The problem with humans, according to both modern and ancient gnostics, is ignorance and an attachment to the physical world.

---

[55] Herrick, *Making of the New Spirituality*, 241.

[56] Douglas Groothuis, *Searching for the Real Jesus in an Age of Controversy* (Eugene, Ore.: Harvest House, 1996), 77.

The gnostic believes he knows what others do not or cannot. The gnostic, Raschke writes, "is the person who 'knows' what he feels others are too ignorant to comprehend, what affords him singular opportunity for mastery and for sovereignty otherwise denied to him".[57] Raschke points to the Marquis de Sade and Nietzsche as examples of this. Arrogance and elitism are natural results of the gnostic perspective, for the gnostic "is the aristocratic shaman weaving with his erudite symbols and fantastic arcana a magic spell of words which lends him power over his ill-defined combatants. His 'sun' is the ganglion of radiant energy, his inflated self. That is why we find at the hub of all Gnostic speculation the irrepressible mythologem—the unrecognized messiah who is one's own will power."[58] This elitist attitude, ironically, comes through clearly in Dan Brown's best-selling, mass-produced novel. *The Da Vinci Code* depicts Christianity as a deliberate sham, Christians as mindless followers of lies and superstition, and Church leaders as deceptive, power-hungry murderers. "The greatest story ever told", Teabing sneers, "is, in fact, the greatest story ever *sold*" (267). On the other hand, feminists, neo-gnostics, wiccans, and non-fundamentalist Christians —which means only those who accept revisionist Christianity—are peace-loving, open-minded, and seeking. They know better: "Those who truly understand their faiths understand the stories are metaphorical" (342). And so gnosticism lives on, now firmly situated atop the best-seller charts and on supermarket book racks, an invitation to knowledge and freedom and a heresy intent on destroying Christianity.

---

[57] Raschke, *Interruption of Eternity*, 34.

[58] Ibid., 35. Raschke offers this biting word of warning: "He the gnostic finds happiness as he luxuriates in the glow of his own consciousness, which may however turn out to be a reflected light from the fire that is burning his own house down" (239).

Chapter 2

The Magdalene

Saint, Sinner, or Goddess?

> Maria Magdalene, quae fuerat in civitate peccatrix, amando veritatem, lavit lacrimis maculas criminis. (Mary Magdalene, who was a sinner in the city, by loving truth, washed away the stains of sin with her tears.)
>
> —Saint Gregory the Great, *Homily 25 in Evangelia.*

Mary Magdalene is the central character in *The Da Vinci Code.* However, the Mary Magdalene depicted by Brown and his characters is not always—or even occasionally—the Mary Magdalene depicted in the Gospels, revealed in history, and celebrated by the Church.

That is right—celebrated by the Catholic Church, as well as by the Eastern Orthodox and some Protestant denominations. This might come as a surprise to anyone who has formed his understanding of Mary Magdalene by reading Brown's novel. For many readers, *The Da Vinci Code* is their first encounter with Mary Magdalene; for others, it is the first time they have heard an alternative history of the mysterious disciple of Jesus—a history fraught with serious problems. In the course of about twenty-five pages (236–61), readers of Dan Brown's novel are exposed to a flood of claims about Mary Magdalene, her identity, her supposed relationship to Jesus, her role in the early Church, and what she supposedly has to do with the Holy Grail.

A quick overview of the novel's basic plot will help establish some context to the specific claims made about Mary Magdalene. Most of the novel takes place in a period of about one day, beginning with the murder of the curator of the Louvre. Robert Langdon, a Harvard symbologist,[1] is asked by the French police to help interpret a strange cipher left on the body of the deceased. Langdon is joined in his investigation by an attractive young cryptologist, Sophie Neveu. Soon they are suspects in the case and are fleeing from authorities. In the course of trying to escape and solve the murder, they ally themselves with wealthy historian and Holy Grail fanatic Leigh Teabing, an acquaintance of Langdon.

Chased by authorities and an albino "monk" who is a member of Opus Dei, this small band of iconoclasts and Grail enthusiasts travel from Paris to London. Woven throughout the narrative are a series of lectures by Langdon and Teabing on the identity of the Holy Grail, the importance of Leonardo da Vinci and *The Last Supper*, and the "truth" about Jesus and the Catholic Church. After some obligatory twists and turns, the novel concludes with Langdon having a sort of spiritual epiphany at the supposed burial place of Mary Magdalene. Suddenly filled with reverence, the skeptical academic falls to his knees and believes that he hears a female voice—the voice of Mary Magdalene: "the wisdom of the ages ... whispering up from the chasms of the earth" (454).

In the course of its 454 pages, the novel asserts the following:

---

[1] An expert in religious and esoteric symbolism.

1. Mary Magdalene, not an inanimate chalice, is the Holy Grail (236–39; 243–46; 249; 253). Jesus taught that Mary was the Holy Grail (242), and Leonardo da Vinci depicted her as such in *The Last Supper* (243). The quest for the Holy Grail is the search, not for the chalice used at the Last Supper, but for the resting place of Mary Magdalene (257).[2]

2. The Catholic Church launched a "smear campaign" against Mary Magdalene at a very early date, slandered her name (244, 249, 254, 261), and labeled her a prostitute out of spite (244) and "in order to erase evidence of her powerful family ties" (249). This secret campaign has included murder and violence (266). The Church's opposition to the "truth" about Mary Magdalene continues today, although in a less violent manner (407).

3. Jesus and Mary were married, and this "fact" has been examined in detail and explored endlessly by historians (245, 249). It is part of the "historical record" and is known through the gnostic gospels, including *The Gospel of Philip* (246) and *The Gospel of Mary Magdalene* (247). Jesus and Mary had children; after Jesus' death, Mary fled to France, persecuted by the Catholic Church (255, 257).

4. Mary Magdalene was the first and greatest apostle (247–48). She was of royal blood and of the house of Benjamin (248–49). By marrying, Jesus and Mary established themselves as heirs to Solomon's kingship (249).

Seeking the Real Mary Magdalene

In order to make sense of these claims we need to start at the beginning, with the biblical accounts of Mary Magdalene.

---

[2] The supposed place of Mary Magdalene in Leonardo da Vinci's *The Last Supper* will be discussed in chap. 9, "The *Code* Puts on Artistic Errors".

There are at least a dozen references to Mary from Magdala (a town on the western shore of the Sea of Galilee) in the four Gospels.[3] She is described as a woman who had suffered from demonic possession and from whom Jesus had expelled seven demons (Mk 16:9; Lk 8:2). She is prominently mentioned as one of the women who accompanied Jesus in his ministry (Lk 8:2), as a witness of the crucifixion (Mt 27:56; Mk 15:40; Jn 19:25), Jesus' burial (Mt 27:61; Mk 15:47), and of the empty tomb (Mt 28:1–10; Mk 16:1–8; Lk 24:10). After his Resurrection, Jesus appears to her alone at the tomb (Mk 16:9; Jn 20:1–18).

In the Western tradition, Mary Magdalene eventually became identified with the sinful woman of Luke 7:37–50. That passage immediately precedes the description of "Mary, called Magdalene, from whom seven demons had gone out" in Luke 8:2, and the two descriptions were harmonized together:

> Because the woman in Luke's anointing was a "sinner" or, in the *Jerusalem Bible*, one "who had a bad name in the town" and Mary Magdalen had "seven demons" cast out of her, it has been traditional to say that Mary Magdalen was a reformed prostitute, and this tradition has dominated Western thinking about, and artistic representation of her for centuries— witness, for example, the name Magdalens given to homes for reformed prostitutes.[4]

A third woman was also identified, in the Western Church, with Mary Magdalene: Mary of Bethany, the sister of Martha and Lazarus, described in Luke 10:38–42 and John 11. However, in the Eastern Church the three women were identified

---

[3] See Mt 27:56, 61; 28:1; Mk 15:40, 47; 16:1, 9; Lk 8:2; 24:10; Jn 19:25; 20:1, 18.

[4] Alban Butler, *Butler's Lives of the Saints*, new ed., ed. Peter Doyle (Collegeville, Minn.: Liturgical Press, 2000), 3:165.

separately, "with feastdays on March 21 (the unnamed sinner), March 18 (Mary of Bethany), and July 22 (Mary Magdalene)".[5]

In *The Da Vinci Code*, which draws heavily from recent esoteric works about the "goddess" Mary Magdalene,[6] readers are not told about the two traditions; in fact, there is no mention of Eastern Orthodoxy, the ancient Oriental Churches, or Protestant Christianity. Instead, readers are told that the Catholic Church, alarmed by Mary's position as chief apostle, slandered and "defamed" her by labeling her a prostitute (244). Attempts to destroy her reputation with insidious lies were made by "the Vatican" in the fourth century (254). All of this, Brown asserts (in his novel and in interviews), was due to the Church's desire to silence the truth about Mary Magdalene, including her marriage to Jesus and her position of authority in the early Church.

This tale of conspiracy and misogyny has attracted those who question the stance of the Catholic Church on the role of women in the Church and the Church's teachings about sexual mores. A December 2003 *Newsweek* article, "The Bible's Lost Stories", notes, "For Roman Catholics in particular, Mary Magdalene has emerged as a role model for women who want a greater church presence after the wave of sexual abuse scandals."[7] A college student, raised

---

[5] Ibid., 3:166.

[6] The novel prominently mentions Margaret Starbird's *Goddess in the Gospels: Reclaiming the Sacred Feminine* (Rochester, Vt.: Bear, 1998) and *The Woman with the Alabaster Jar: Mary Magdalen and the Holy Grail* (Rochester, Vt.: Bear, 1993) as well as *Holy Blood, Holy Grail* (1982; New York: Dell, 1983), written by Michael Baigent, Richard Leigh, and Henry Lincoln.

[7] Barbara Kantrowitz and Anne Underwood, "The Bible's Lost Stories", *Newsweek*, December 8, 2003. Accessed at www.msnbc.msn.com. *The Da Vinci Code* makes mention of the sex scandals, with Teabing stating that Catholic leaders have been lying to cover up the sexual abuse of children by priests (266). He follows these remarks by saying that the "Church's version of the Christ story" is a lie—the "greatest story ever *sold*" (266–77).

Catholic but now attending a Baptist church, states that *The Da Vinci Code* "raised troubling questions" about how women were treated in the early Church and suppressed by Church leaders.[8] An article in *Time* magazine, "Mary Magdalene: Saint or Sinner", describes the influence that these claims have had on women, including Ellen Turner, a Catholic who did not learn that Mary Magdalene "was not a whore" until she was nearly fifty. She is now active in "the liberal Catholic groups Call to Action and Futurechurch. . . . She was happy to find that the two organizations, which see Magdalene's recovered image as an argument for their goal of a priesthood open to all those who feel called, coordinate celebrations around the world on [Mary Magdalene's] feast day."[9]

The Church, the Pope, and the Magdalene

Are these accusations against the Church grounded in historical fact? Was Mary Magdalene's name "forbidden by the Church" (254) and her memory suppressed for hundreds of centuries? Was she called a prostitute so that her position as Jesus' wife and head apostle would be undermined? Was she the victim of an orchestrated plot to change her from the "apostle to the apostles" to a "redeemed whore" and "a manageable, controllable figure, and effective weapon and

---

[8] Kantrowitz and Underwood, "Bible's Lost Stories".

[9] David Van Biema, "Mary Magdalene: Saint or Sinner?" *Time*, August 11, 2003. Accessed at www.danbrown.com. Turner also states that Mary Magdalene "got the shaft" from the Catholic Church. "From the beginning, her view has been ignored, unappreciated. The first to see the risen Lord—those with more power have sought to marginalize her. Yet she is faithful. She remains. She cannot be silenced."

instrument of propaganda against her own sex", as one author has claimed?[10]

If the early Christians were as intent upon destroying the memory of Mary Magdalene as *The Da Vinci Code* claims, they did a poor job of it. Langdon tells Sophie that "the Church outlawed" any talk of Mary Magdalene (261)—and yet Mary Magdalene is mentioned, not once or twice, but a dozen times in the Gospels. But if Brown is correct in insisting (via Teabing) that Constantine severely edited those Gospels in the early 300s in order to reshape the Church to meet his political ends, Church leaders seriously blundered.[11] For not only is Mary Magdalene mentioned, she is given a prominent role as witness to the Resurrection, a remarkable fact considering that the testimony of women had little value in first-century Jewish society. Yet these references are not enough for those who are convinced that the Magdalene was deliberately denied her rightful place at the right hand of Jesus as his head apostle. And although she is

---

[10] Susan Haskins, *Mary Magdalen: Myth and Metaphor* (New York: Riverhead Books, 1993), 94. Haskins speculates that Mary Magdalene's role in Church teaching has nothing to do with facts but was "the result of a political decision, whose precise form may never be known, to reduce the role of women" (52). Feminist scholar Karen King, a professor of ecclesiastical history at Harvard, is of the same opinion: " 'What they did is divide the tradition into orthodoxy and heresy,' she says. 'They associated orthodoxy with Mary the mother and heresy with Mary Magdalene as an apostle. But they saved Magdalene for the church by making her a repentant prostitute. That made women nonthreatening. They had to somehow undermine her as a female authority figure.' The facts, say King, are on Magdalene's side: 'She got a raw deal' " (quoted by Roxanne Roberts, "The Mysteries of Mary Magdalene: 'The Da Vinci Code' Resurrects a Debate of Biblical Proportions", *Washington Post*, July 20, 2003. Accessed at www.washingtonpost.com).

[11] Teabing claims that Constantine commissioned a new Bible that omitted the gnostic gospels and "embellished" the gospels that were allowed in the Bible (234).

mentioned several more times than many of the apostles,[12] feminist writers speak of her being marginalized by that work of propaganda known as the New Testament, written by "the anti-Magdalene party".[13]

This understanding of Mary Magdalene is based on general themes outlined in *The Da Vinci Code*: the Church dislikes and fears sexuality; Jesus was a feminist who was intent on creating an egalitarian community free from male authority (248); he fulfilled his humanity by being married; and global peace will be realized only when there is a return to the ancient worship of "the goddess" (238). A central and re-occurring theme in the works of authors such as Margaret Starbird, Lynn Picknett, Susan Haskins, and Elaine Pagels is that of sexuality and gender. For those writers, Mary Magdalene represents a woman who is freed from sexual repression, who is not dependant upon a male-only hierarchy, and who fulfills her desires through confident individualism, not repentance and submission. Put directly, it is about power, with the recognition that sexuality is a core element of that power. Haskins states that what the Church "feared and abhorred" the most was that which is "incarnated in the flesh of the woman, her sexuality"[14] and so made Mary Magdalene a repentant whore in order to rob her of that power.

The authors of *The Templar Revelation*—a work Brown mentions in his novel and draws from extensively—write that Mary Magdalene's image throughout history is a direct reflection of the Church's negative stance toward women and feminine sexuality. The Magdalene is allowed to be a saint only

---

[12] For example, Thaddaeus is mentioned only twice, and Bartholomew just three times (Mt 10:3; Mk 3:18; Lk 6:14).

[13] Lynn Picknett and Clive Prince, *The Templar Revelation: Secret Guardians of the True Identity of Christ* (1997; New York: Simon and Schuster, 1998), 64.

[14] Haskins, *Mary Magdalen*, 94.

The Magdalene   81

as a "repentant whore", and "the dissemination of her legend depends upon her penitence and uncomfortable, solitary lifestyle. Her sainthood rests on her self-abnegation."[15] Not surprisingly, this statement is immediately linked to women's ordination: "Not unnaturally, being the only significant woman in the Jesus story apart from his mother, [Mary Magdalene] is seized upon by many women activists with the modern Church as a potent symbol of their rights."[16] This is followed by a lengthy attack on the authority of the Catholic Church, followed by assertions of Mary's preeminent place in the Church, "second only to Jesus, ranked above both male and female followers".[17]

The villains of this story, Dan Brown states, were the early Church Fathers. When asked in an interview about his belief that Mary Magdalene was married to Jesus, he stated, "I was skeptical, but after a year and a half of research I became a believer. As soon as people understand that the few Gospels included in the Bible are not the only version of the Christ story, they begin to sense contradictions. Magdalene is most obvious." Mary Magdalene's role, Brown says, was deliberately distorted, "a smear campaign by the early church

---

[15] Picknett and Prince, *Templar Revelation*, 61.

[16] Ibid. Picknett and Prince believe Mary Magdalene is a "potent symbol" of the rights of women who wish to be ordained as priest, and they insist that her "profound and lasting significance" rests on her being the first witness of the Resurrection. Yet, the authors later deny that Jesus died on the Cross or was resurrected, claiming that Jesus' death and Resurrection were part of an elaborate hoax concocted by Jesus and "his inner circle" (290; see 289ff.). They cite Hugh J. Schonfield's book *The Passover Plot* (New York: Bantam, 1967), which purports to explain how this plot was planned and carried out. Thus, the gnostic/feminist Mary Magdalene's importance is squarely based on an event that many of her followers believe did not occur. In addition, *Templar Revelation* spends considerable time arguing that the Christian Gospels are historically inaccurate and untrustworthy (237–44)—even after making a case for Mary's "true" role in the life of Jesus that is dependant on those same writings.

[17] Picknett and Prince, *Templar Revelation*, 64–65.

fathers"—what one of his characters calls "the greatest cover-up in human history." [18] The prime suspect among the early Church Fathers in this crime against femininity was Pope Gregory the Great (ca. 540–604), a noted preacher after whom Gregorian chant was named. On September 21, 591, the pope preached a homily at the basilica of San Clemente of Rome. The passage of Scripture he spoke about was Luke 7:36–50—the story of the woman "who was a sinner" who anointed Jesus' feet with oil. Pope Gregory stated:

> She whom Luke calls the sinful woman, whom John calls Mary, we believe to be the Mary from whom seven devils were ejected according to Mark. And what did these seven devils signify, if not all the vices? . . . It is clear, brothers, that the woman previously used the unguent to perfume her flesh in forbidden acts. What she therefore displayed more scandalously, she was now offering to God in a more praiseworthy manner. She had coveted with earthly eyes, but now through penitence these are consumed with tears. She displayed her hair to set off her face, but now her hair dries her tears. She had spoken proud things with her mouth, but in kissing the Lord's feet, she now planted her mouth on the Redeemer's feet. For every delight, therefore, she had had in herself, she now immolated herself. She turned the mass of her crimes to virtues, in order to serve God entirely in penance, for as much as she had wrongly held God in contempt. [19]

Gregory would often preach on the approaching judgment and the need for repentance. At the time of his famous homily, Rome was undergoing famine and the turmoil of war, and so Gregory took every opportunity to encourage Christians to repent of their sins and do away with all attachment to evil. Katherine Jansen, author of *The Making of the*

[18] Roberts, "Mysteries of Mary Magdalene".
[19] *Hom.* 33, PL 76:1239.

Magdalen: Preaching and Popular Devotion in the Later Middle Ages, offers further reasons why Gregory linked the sinner of Luke 7 and Mary of Bethany with Mary Magdalene. The first is the most obvious—the textual proximity of Luke's Gospel (chapter 7 and 8). A second is that by the sixth century, the biblical city of Magdala had acquired "a reputation of depravity and godlessness." [20] Another is that John 11:1–2 identifies the woman who anointed Christ and dried his feet with her hair as Mary of Bethany, sister of Martha and Lazarus. But the most important reason was that Gregory's "preferred method of exegesis was by recourse to the tropological sense of the text, or its moral sense". [21] He believed that the seven demons that had once possessed Mary Magdalene were not only literal demons but also represented the seven deadly sins.

Many of the early Church Fathers and medieval theologians developed and employed a method of exegesis, or interpretation, based on the "four senses of Scripture". These are the literal, allegorical, moral, and anagogical senses. Although the preferred means of interpreting the Bible for hundreds of years, this method was mostly abandoned with the advent of modern biblical studies, which emphasized historico-critical methods over allegorical or moral connections between apparently unrelated texts. Pope Gregory was a masterful preacher who plumbed the depths of texts in search of pastoral wisdom and moral exhortation: "His mind is soaked in Scripture, like the rest of the fathers. Gregory analyzes and exegetes almost any biblical character or theme (e.g., the apostle Peter, creation *ex nihilo* in Genesis or the nature of the resurrected body) from a deep scriptural awareness honed

[20] Katherine Ludwig Jansen, *The Making of the Magdalen: Preaching and Popular Devotion in the Later Middle Ages* (Princeton, N.J.: Princeton University Press, 2000), 33.
[21] Ibid.

by the biblical mindset and exegetical tradition of the Christian community in which he had rooted himself." [22] Although brilliant, Gregory was not a biblical scholar; he "was first and foremost a pastor of souls". [23]

So what does this say about Gregory's interpretation of Luke 7:36–50? Most modern scholars believe Gregory's creation of a single Mary out of three different women was not supported by the text. (By changing her choice of readings in the 1969 revision of the Lectionary, the Church left open the question of whether or not Mary Magdalene and the woman who was a sinner are the same person.) While perhaps factually flawed, Gregory's homily was not an outrageous act, and it certainly was not malicious. As a pastor and a man of holiness, Gregory held up his Mary Magdalene as an exemplar of repentance, humility, and devotion. As Jansen notes, "Gregory the Great's Magdalen was a multifaceted figure whose pious ministry to Christ, witnessing of the risen savior, heralding of the resurrection, and contemplative nature rendered her worthy of veneration. But most important to Gregory was the Magdalen's symbolic aspect as an exemplar of 'hope and repentance' for all sinners. This aspect of her persona of course derived from her identification as Luke's repentant sinner whose sins were forgiven by the Lord." [24] Even if his facts might not have been accurate,

---

[22] Christopher A. Hall, *Reading Scripture with the Church Fathers* (Downers Grove, Ill.: InterVarsity Press, 1998), 129.

[23] Ibid., 131.

[24] Jansen, *Making of the Magdalen*, 34–35. Anglican sister and scholar Benedicta Ward writes, "A forgiven sinner, Mary Magdalene anointing the feet of the Lord with tears and becoming the first witness of the resurrection, was presented by St. Gregory in a homily concerned with conveying the moral and spiritual application of scripture to a congregation in Rome in the sixth century" (Benedicta Ward, S.L.G., *Harlots in the Desert* [Kalamazoo, Mich.: Cistercian Publications, 1987], 13). Regarding the "conflation" of Mary Magdalene with Mary the sister of Martha and Lazarus, Ward notes: "The

Gregory was attempting, not to destroy Mary Magdalene, but to praise her. "Gregory's composite saint ordained the agenda of Magdalen veneration for the entire Middle Ages and well beyond", writes Jansen. "So great was the pontiff's authority that the Roman Church accepted his Magdalen for almost fourteen hundred years, until the liturgical calendar reform of 1969." [25]

Yet, however great the authority of Pope Gregory, his teaching about Mary Magdalene was not infallible, nor was it issued in an encyclical or a papal bull. It was never defined as Catholic dogma or upheld as sacred doctrine by an ecumenical council. But *The Da Vinci Code* and many of its sources react as though the sole purpose for the existence of the Church was to destroy Mary Magdalene. "The Church needed to defame Mary Magdalene", Teabing tells Sophie (244). A few pages later he tells her that "the Vatican" tried to bury Mary and her secret marriage to Jesus in the fourth century (254). Not one to restrain himself, he informs the naïve heroine that Mary Magdalene's name "was forbidden by the Church" (254). It is a classic case of people making noise in order to complain that someone is disturbing their peace and quiet.

---

same kind of conflation takes place in the sermons of Augustine and the commentaries of Bede, where, as with Gregory, the spiritual and moral application of the text was the main concern and not the historical sense at all. It seems possible to conclude from the commentaries that the Fathers of the early Church saw in this composite Mary a figure of significance beyond her several parts. The central fact of the gospel is that 'Christ Jesus came into the world to save sinners' (1 Timothy 1:15) and here is the most dramatic of all examples of this action" (Ward, *Harlots*, 13). This raises an ironic point: Those angry that the Church allegedly changed Mary Magdalene's identity in order to keep her from her proper place of authority have no problem saying that Jesus was merely a mortal prophet, a shaman, or a high-minded, neo-pagan priest—anyone but the incarnate Son of God.

[25] Jansen, *Making of the Magdalen*, 34–35.

As Kenneth Woodward notes in his article "A Quite Contrary Mary", the fuss about Mary Magdalene comes from "a small cadre of feminist scholars", many of them from Harvard Divinity School.[26] Their claim is that Mary Magdalene was robbed of her position of authority by the dreaded Peter, derisively described in *The Templar Revelation* as "the Big Fisherman of legend, the martyr and founder of the Roman Catholic Church".[27] Peter and his all-male society then worked tirelessly to destroy all evidence of the Magdalene's position and ruin her reputation. Thus, Woodward remarks, "a sermon preached by Pope Gregory in 591 is frequently cited on the latter point [the destruction of Mary's position and reputation], as if he had invented an anti-woman tradition and sealed it with (retroactive) infallibility." He then hones in on the real issue: "Blaming the pope fits the feminist agenda here, injecting an anti-hierarchical, indeed, anti-papal note. In short, patriarchy is again the culprit." [28]

[26] Kenneth L. Woodward, "A Quite Contrary Mary". Accessed at www.beliefnet.com, November 2003. Woodward also writes: "Were I to write a story involving Mary Magdalene, I think it would focus on this: that a small group of well-educated women decided to devote their careers to the pieces of Gnostic literature discovered in the last century, a find that promised a new academic specialty within the somewhat overtrodden field of Biblical studies, on which they could build a career. They became experts in this literature, as others become experts in the biology of the hermit crab. But unlike those who study marine decapod crustaceans, some of them came to identify with the objects of their study—in some cases, perhaps, because they had no other religious community to identify with other than that formed by common academic pursuit; others perhaps because they were in rebellion against whatever authoritative religious community nurtured their interest in religion in the first place, still others because they found in the Gnostic texts the kind of affirmation of inner divinity that their own New Age inclinations led them to."

[27] Picknett and Prince, *Templar Revelation*, 65.

[28] Woodward, "Quite Contrary Mary".

Mary Magdalene and the Middle Ages

Any supposed attempts to rid the Church of Mary Magdalene or ban her name from being mentioned did not succeed, simply because they did not exist. In fact, many of the early Church Fathers remark about the Magdalene, and she is described by Hippolytus (ca. 170–ca. 236) as "the apostle to the apostles" in his commentary on the Song of Songs. Even feminist theologian Rosemary Radford Ruether, hardly a supporter of the Catholic hierarchy, scoffs at the notion of a conspiracy against Mary Magdalene, pointing to the positive treatment she received from the early Church Fathers:

> This high regard for Mary Magdalene continues in the fourth- and fifth-century Latin fathers of the church. Ambrose, bishop of Milan, associated Mary Magdalene with the New Eve who clings to Christ as the new Tree of Life, thereby reversing the unfaithfulness of the first Eve. Augustine maintains this view, pairing Mary Magdalene with Christ as symbol of the New Eve and the church in relation to Christ as the New Adam. Her faithfulness reversed the sin of the first Eve.[29]

By the eighth century the Western Church was celebrating a feast day for Mary Magdalene, the twenty-second day of July. By the ninth century there were specific prayers for her feast day, and by the eleventh century there was "a

---

[29] Rosemary Radford Ruether, "No Church Conspiracy against Mary Magdalene", *National Catholic Reporter*, February 9, 2001. Accessed at www.findarticles.com. Note Ruether's defense of Pope Gregory: "It is only at the end of the sixth century that Pope Gregory I confuses the sinful woman of Luke 7 and Mary Magdalene in Luke 8 and identifies her as a repentant prostitute, whose former sinfulness is contrasted with that of the Virgin Mary. But there is no evidence that he makes this mistake in order to remove her as a 'role model' for women's ministry. Such an idea is unknown to him. The misinterpretation seems to come about primarily from a rhetorical tendency to reduce the complexity of 'Marys' in the New Testament to a simple dualism: the ever virgin mother and the repentant sinner."

complete mass dedicated to the saint (with introit, gradual, offertory, communion, and lessons)".[30] It was also in the eleventh century that devotion to the Magdalene began noticeably to increase. The cult of Mary Magdalene was established at Vézelay, in a Romanesque church in Burgundy that had been founded in the ninth century and was originally dedicated to the Virgin Mary.[31] During the abbacy of Geoffrey (1037–1052) Mary Magdalene was recognized as the patron of that church in a papal bull dated April 27, 1050, by Pope Leo IX.[32] At the same time, relics of the Magdalene were being sought and gathered in earnest, and soon Vézelay became a major destination for pilgrimages.

Numerous stories, almost all of them fanciful and legendary in nature, were created to explain how Mary Magdalene's remains had arrived at Vézelay. A leading tradition in the West held that Mary Magdalene, Martha, and Lazarus were expelled from Palestine following the crucifixion of Christ. Floating in an oarless boat, they eventually arrived at the southern coast of France. In the East, a tradition stated that Mary Magdalene had been the companion of the apostle John and Mary, the Mother of Jesus, and that they had all settled in Ephesus. According to *The Golden Legend*, the Magdalene and John were betrothed.[33] Some legends depict Mary Magdalene living her final days in a cave in France, a hermit covered only by her long hair; these stories probably date back no farther than the ninth century.

During the late medieval era it was common to hear sermons about Mary Magdalene and how she fulfilled the apostolic life. She was also a model for Christians seeking to leave

---

[30] Jansen, *Making of the Magdalen*, 35.

[31] Ibid., 35–36.

[32] Patrick J. Geary, *Furta Sacra: Thefts of Relics in the Central Middle Ages* (Princeton, N.J.: Princeton University Press, 1978), 90.

[33] *Butler's Lives of the Saints*, 3:164.

behind a life of sensuality and luxury, an encouragement to monks and nuns, as well as an exhortation to prostitutes. "But most of all a Magdalen sermon was the vehicle by which preachers called people to penance and offered them the hope of salvation. . . . We must not forget that it is our own age that officially memorializes Saint Mary Magdalene as a disciple; it was the 'Dark Ages' that honored her as a preacher and apostle of the apostles." [34]

The Gnostic Mary Magdalene

Sober historical assessments have not, however, endeared themselves to those who believe Mary Magdalene was Jesus' head apostle, lover, wife, and mother of his children. She was all of that and more, says Brown, "She's a historical figure whose time has come. People sense that." [35] In fact, a revised, highly individualized feminist version of Mary Magdalene has been around for many years. *The Da Vinci Code* simply appropriated elements of it and placed them in the middle of a best-selling novel.

Brown's depiction of Mary Magdalene as the embodiment of the "sacred feminine" has been a common theme of recent neo-gnostic, feminist works seeking to rewrite early Church history based upon gnostic writings such as the *Gospel of Thomas*, the *Gospel of Philip*, the *Gospel of Mary*, and a handful of others. In addition to Pagels' work and *Holy Blood, Holy Grail*, there is the popular esoteric *The Templar Revelation*, by Picknett and Prince, and various titles by Margaret Starbird. [36] All of these are part of a rapidly growing interest

---

[34] Jansen, *Making of the Magdalen*, 336.
[35] Quoted by Roberts, "Mysteries of Mary Magdalene".
[36] There are numerous others, but these are highlighted and referred to throughout this book because they have direct ties to *The Da Vinci Code*, all of them having been named in the novel at some point.

in gnosticism and "alternative" forms of Christianity that are making overt appearances in popular media, including novels, television, and movies. In addition to books focused on Mary Magdalene, there are numerous works in print about the larger world of goddess worship. Books such as *When God Was a Woman*, by Merlin Stone, and Riane Eisler's best seller *The Chalice and the Blade: Our History, Our Future*[37] popularized more scholarly forms of feminist interpretations of history that had been written in the 1960s and 1970s. *The Chalice and the Blade* sold over a half-million copies and presented a feminist-friendly Jesus and a therapeutic approach that appealed to readers not quite comfortable with more strident forms of feminism. The interest in "the goddess" also involved a renewed interest in wicca, New Age practices, neo-paganism, and radical feminism, and it was often accompanied by a strong animosity toward Christianity and any perceived form of "patriarchalism".

These elements are obvious in Brown's claims that Emperor Constantine was responsible for a move from "matriarchical paganism to patriarchal Christianity by waging a campaign of propaganda that demonized the sacred feminine, obliterating the goddess from modern religion forever" (124). *Goddess Unmasked*, written by professor of religious studies Philip G. Davis, provides a detailed examination of both the history and purpose of the goddess movement. Davis states that the phenomenal growth of goddess books sales has become far more than just an academic theory (as it once was). "It

---

[37] Merlin Stone, *When God Was a Woman* (New York: Harcourt Brace Jovanovich, 1978), and Riane Eisler, *The Chalice and the Blade: Our History, Our Future* (Cambridge, Mass.: Harper and Row, 1987). For critical assessments of these books, see Bruce S. Thornton's *Plagues of the Mind: The New Epidemic of False Knowledge* (Wilmington, Del.: ISI Books, 1999), especially "The False Goddess and Her Lost Paradise" (177–214), and Philip G. Davis, *Goddess Unmasked: The Rise of Neopagan Feminist Spirituality* (Dallas, Tex.: Spence, 1998).

has been clear from the outset, however, that Goddess books are not simply about the history of religion and culture; they are, in and of themselves, expressions of a particular religious mindset which shapes both their presuppositions and conclusions.... Goddess books, accordingly, should be seen as professions of faith, and their authors as neopagan evangelists."[38]

The point of the goddess movement and books is not a revitalization or a renewal of Christianity, as proponents sometimes assert, but a complete transformation involving the removal and destruction of core beliefs about the nature of God, the person of Jesus, the mission of the Church, and the truth about sexuality and marriage. All of this flows from a highly individualistic and self-centered approach to spirituality. "The whole point, for many in the movement", Davis explains, "is to discover divinity within the self and to encounter it in female form."[39] This is readily apparent in the works of Margaret Starbird, whose books are prominently mentioned in *The Da Vinci Code*. Her book *The Goddess in the Gospels: Reclaiming the Sacred Feminine* is an emotionally charged and often overwrought retelling of her journey from orthodox Catholicism to a goddess-centered, narcissistic spirituality. Describing a particular moment in which she glanced upon a copy of a book by the abolitionist Harriet Tubman, Starbird writes that she suddenly realized that her newfound knowledge was meant to help set "prisoners free" and that she would not rest until she had done her part "in breaking the chains imposed on Western societies for centuries by the 'Holy' Inquisition.... Like Harriet Tubman, who returned to the South after she had won her own freedom and worked to help others escape from slavery, my job would be to help

[38] Davis, *Goddess Unmasked*, 86, 87.
[39] Ibid., 94.

make the waters of truth available by writing the story of the archetypal Bride. 'You shall know the truth, and the truth shall make you free.' " [40]

Starbird and other feminists are convinced that Christianity is a male-centered religion that needs to rid itself of historical, traditional beliefs, including those about the very nature and work of Jesus. This is succinctly captured by feminist theologian Delores Williams' comment, "I don't think we need folks hanging on crosses and blood dripping and weird stuff." [41] Despite its claims to historical viability, the goddess movement is about feelings, not facts. "Ancient prehistory and religion are not the issue in Goddess literature", writes Bruce S. Thornton, a professor of classics and humanities. "Validating individualist self-actualization by liberationist and utopian claims is." [42]

This is readily evident in the claims made by *The Da Vinci Code* about the gnostic Mary Magdalene and her alleged intimate relationship with Jesus. It is this topic, of course, that has generated the most media attention, including a full one-hour special, "Jesus, Mary, and Da Vinci", on ABC in November 2003. [43] A substantial portion of that prime-time program was dedicated to pondering the veracity of the *Gospel of Philip*, a late second-century or early third-century gnostic text containing this passage: "And the companion of . . . Mary Magdalene . . . loved her more than all the disciples, and used to kiss her often on her mouth. The rest of the disciples . . . said to him 'Why do you love her more than all

[40] Starbird, *Goddess in the Gospels*, 138–39.

[41] Susan Cyre, "Fallout Escalates over 'Goddess' Sophia Worship", *Christianity Today*, vol. 38, no. 4 (April 4, 1994), 74. Quoted by Thornton, *Plagues of the Mind*, 180.

[42] Thornton, *Plagues of the Mind*, 185.

[43] See Carl E. Olson, "Prime Time Fiasco: ABC Takes on Jesus, Mary, and Da Vinci", *National Catholic Register*, November 16–22, 2003.

of us?'"[44] In Brown's novel, the historian Teabing helpfully explains to Sophie that "the word *companion*, in those days, literally meant *spouse*" (246). Brown then describes Teabing showing Sophie several other passages that "clearly suggested Magdalene and Jesus had a romantic relationship" (246). All of this rests on shaky ground, as Brown's interpretation of the gnostic texts does not align with that of the vast majority of scholars working in the field. Antti Marjanen, author of the monograph *The Woman Jesus Loved: Mary Magdalene in the Nag Hammadi Library and Related Documents*,[45] writes that Mary Magdalene's role in the gnostic writings is not established but is different in many of the texts. "Not all of the writings are encratic, not all of them portray Mary Magdalene as the privileged disciple," he observes, "and only in the *Gospel of Philip* can the idea of her spiritual marriage with Jesus find support."[46] Most scholars agree that those attempting to construct a picture of early Christianity based on Mary Magdalene as Jesus' wife and head apostle must do so by subjectively picking and choosing elements from second- and third-century writings, then project them back to the first century.

As Marjanen makes clear, the passage from the *Gospel of Philip* is the only place in the gnostic writings where Mary Magdalene is introduced as the companion of Jesus. In addition, "Apart from *Pistis Sophia*, the *Gospel of Philip* is the only Gnostic writing where Mary Magdalene appears with the explicit characterization of her identity."[47] The phrase "the companion of the Lord" is unique and is not used in

---

[44] *Gospel of Philip*, 63:30—64:5. From James M. Robinson, general ed., *The Nag Hammadi Library*, 3rd rev. ed. (San Francisco: HarperSanFrancisco, 1988).

[45] Antti Marjanen, *The Woman Jesus Loved: Mary Magdalene in the Nag Hammadi Library and Related Documents* (Leiden and New York: E.J. Brill, 1996).

[46] Ibid., 14.

[47] Ibid., 147.

referring to any other disciple of Jesus. Starbird insists that the phrase refers to an intimate sexual relationship, writing that "the word used has specifically conjugal overtones."[48] As evidence, she cites Haskins, who states that the word for companion "is more correctly translated as 'partner' or 'consort,' a woman with whom a man has had sexual intercourse".[49]

Marjanen disagrees, showing that the word *koinonos* is used in different ways in many writings, including works of the New Testament. "Difficulty in interpreting the word is complicated by the fact that the Greek word [*koinonos*] may assume a wide range of meanings", he explains. "Basically, it denotes a person engaged in 'fellowship or sharing with someone or in something.' What a *koinonos* can share with his or her partner can take many forms, ranging from a common enterprise or experience to a shared business." In the Bible the term is used to describe a wide range of relationships, denoting a marriage partner (Mt 2:14), a companion in faith (Philem 17), a co-worker in proclaiming the gospel (2 Cor 8:23), and a business associate (Lk 5:10).[50]

The word *koinonos* is also used in Matthew 23:30, Luke 5:10, 1 Corinthians 10:20, and Hebrews 10:33, all passages that refer to relationships that are non-sexual. So the best interpretation of the word as used in the *Gospel of Philip* is a spiritual companion or consort. The passage that Brown, Starbird, Haskins, and others build the marital embrace of Jesus

---

[48] Starbird, *Goddess in the Gospels*, 119.

[49] Haskins, *Mary Magdalen*, 37.

[50] Marjanen, *Woman Jesus Loved*, 151. In biblical-era Greek, the usual verb for marry is *gameo*. The word for bride is *numphe* and *nymphios*. Virgin is *parthenos*, and wife is *gyne*. There are three Greek words used to describe a companion: *sunekdemos* (a fellow traveler), *koinonos* (a "partaker with you"), and *sunergos* (a fellow worker or "companion in labor"). See Vine's *Expository Dictionary of Biblical Words* (Nashville, Tenn.: Thomas Nelson, 1985), 115.

and Mary Magdalene upon is, at most, a presentation of Mary as the "earthly partner of Jesus with whom he forms a spiritual partnership".[51] In another passage of the *Gospel of Philip* where kissing occurs, the act is described as one of spiritual nourishment that leads to spiritual procreation, not an act of romantic love: "For it is by a kiss that the perfect conceive and give birth. For this reason we also kiss one another. We received conception from the grace which is in one another."[52]

When the disciples ask why Jesus loves Mary more than them, he does not speak of sexual motives but of Mary's spiritual insight into what he is conveying to her.[53] Another gnostic text, *The [Second] Apocalypse of James*, contains a notable parallel to the story in the *Gospel of Philip*, in which the risen Jesus imparts his secret mysteries to James by kissing him on the mouth and calling him, "My beloved!"[54] It is a non-sexual, symbolic act "which demonstrates James' privileged position. Moreover, it is through embracing the Lord that James receives the most important revelation, i.e., he comes to understand who the Hidden One is."[55] In the gnostic context, the kiss between Jesus and Mary Magdalene indicates her privileged position, a position due, not to her being married to Jesus, but to having spiritual insight into

---

[51] Marjanen, *Woman Jesus Loved*, 154.

[52] *Gospel of Philip*, 58:30—59:6.

[53] Ibid., 64:7.

[54] "And he kissed my mouth. He took hold of me, saying, 'My beloved! Behold, I shall reveal to you those things that (neither) the heavens nor their archons have known. Behold, I shall reveal to you those things that he did not know, he who boasted, ". . . there is no other except me. Am I not alive? Because I am a father, do I not have power for everything?" Behold, I shall reveal to you everything, my beloved. Understand and know them, that you may come forth just as I am. Behold, I shall reveal to you him who is hidden. But now, stretch out your hand. Now, take hold of me'" (*The [Second] Apocalypse of James*. Accessed at http://www.gnosis.org).

[55] Marjanen, *Woman Jesus Loved*, 159.

his teaching that exceeds that of the other disciples. "In fact, kissing may very well be understood as a means by which a special spiritual power is conveyed to her." [56] The key point is that for the gnostics, the relationship between the two is spiritual only, with Mary being understood to be Jesus' spiritual counterpart. [57]

Even when the *Gospel of Philip* is accepted on its own terms, it does not yield the results that *The Da Vinci Code* and its sources claim for it. If Jesus and Mary Magdalene were married, why would the gnostics not have made it even more obvious? A possible reply is that they were too afraid of orthodox persecution and so chose to be ambiguous and secretive in their communications. And yet the gnostic writings are full of teachings that are obviously incompatible with an orthodox understanding of Jesus Christ, his life on earth, and the Church he established. In the end, a couple of ambiguous second- or third-century gnostic texts read through the lens of feminist ideology do not provide proof, even modest proof, that Jesus and Mary Magdalene were married or were romantically involved.

Of course, the argument for Jesus and Mary being married does not rest exclusively on the gnostic writings. One popular argument is that since Jesus was a rabbi, he had to have been married since single rabbis were unheard of in first-century Palestine. But Jesus did not hold any official position, nor was he formally trained. In Mark's Gospel the

---

[56] Ibid., 159–60.

[57] "In Valentinian terms, Mary is also seen as Jesus' *syzygos*, i.e., she forms a spiritual consortium with Jesus. Together they provide the prototype of the union between Christ and his Church which materializes when the pneumatic elect are united with their pleromatic counterparts. The relationship between Mary and Jesus is purely spiritual. The mention of Jesus kissing Mary has no sexual implications but it is to be understood as a metaphorical expression for conveying special spiritual nourishment and power" (ibid., 219).

chief priests and the scribes ask Jesus, "By what authority are you doing these things, or who gave you this authority to do them?" (Mk 11:28), and John's Gospel depicts the Jews as marveling and asking, "How is it that this man has learning, when he has never studied?" (Jn 7:15). The term *rabbi* (literally, "my great one") was used honorifically, "but the title in pre-AD 70 Judaism was more loosely used than later on." [58] The use of the word as an official term for an official teacher or scholar "actually belongs to the period following the destruction of the temple" in A.D. 70. [59] With the loss of the Temple, the importance of the local synagogue increased, and with it the role of the rabbi. [60]

Scholars have speculated that Jesus' remark about people "who have made themselves eunuchs for the sake of the kingdom of heaven" (Mt 19:10–12) was made in response to criticisms about his own unmarried state. "He who is able to receive this," Jesus states, "let him receive it." This echoes a passage in Isaiah in which eunuchs who "keep my sabbaths" and "hold fast my covenant" will be blessed (Is 56:3–5). The state of celibacy was strongly endorsed by Paul in 1 Corinthians 7, in which he states that he wishes that "all were even as I myself am" (1 Cor 7:7), that is, unmarried. "But", he adds, "each has his own special gift from God, one of one kind and one of another." Although it was uncommon for men not to marry in Jesus' day, it was not unheard of. Celibacy was not forbidden and condemned, as Langdon claims (245).

---

[58] Raymond E. Brown, Joseph A. Fitzmyer, and Roland E. Murphy, eds., *The New Jerome Biblical Commentary* (Englewood Cliffs, N.J.: Prentice Hall, 1990), 1319.

[59] David Noel Freedman, ed., *Eerdmans Dictionary of the Bible* (Grand Rapids, Mich.: W. B. Eerdmans, 2000), 1106.

[60] See Barbara Geller, "Transitions and Trajectories: Jews and Christians in the Roman Empire", in *The Oxford History of the Biblical World*, ed. Michael D. Coogan (Oxford: Oxford University Press, 1998), 586–88.

It is speculated that the Nazarite vows of the Old Testament (Num 6:1–21; Judg 13:5, 7; 16:17) included celibacy, for they involved "days of separation". The prophet Jeremiah was commanded by God not to marry: "You shall not take a wife, nor shall you have sons or daughters in this place" (Jer 16:1–2).

In the Hellenistic world in the two centuries prior to Christ, celibacy became a precondition for entering into a sacred space and coming into contact with the gods. "Any literate Jew in touch with the major philosophical movements of the time would have been influenced by this rich body of tradition and practice." [61] And during the time of Christ, there were Jewish groups and movements embracing celibacy. "Traditions encouraging a dedicated single life also existed elsewhere in Judaism. Members of the ascetic Jewish sect of the Essenes were known for their emphasis on celibacy." [62]

The Bridegroom and the Bride

Ironically, many who argue that Jesus was a radical feminist—or "the original feminist", according to Teabing (248)—who had no qualms about overthrowing conventional notions of gender and sexuality also argue that Jesus would not dare go unmarried because of the negative attention it would bring him. A far better explanation is that offered by the Church: Jesus was not married to Mary Magdalene, but he is the Bridegroom (Mt 9:15; Mk 2:19) who has taken as his Bride the Church: "Let us rejoice and exult and give him the glory, for the marriage of the Lamb has come, and

[61] Freedman, *Eerdmans Dictionary of the Bible*, 227.
[62] Darrell L. Bock, "Was Jesus Married?" Accessed at www.beliefnet.com, January 2004. Bock refers to Josephus, *Antiquities* 18.1.5.21; *Jewish War* 2.8.2.121–22; Philo, *Hypothetica* 11.14–18.

his Bride has made herself ready; . . . And I saw the holy city, new Jerusalem, coming down out of heaven from God, prepared as a bride adorned for her husband; . . . Then came one of the seven angels who had the seven bowls full of the seven last plagues, and spoke to me, saying, 'Come, I will show you the Bride, the wife of the Lamb'" (Rev 19:7; 21:2, 9). The *Catechism of the Catholic Church* summarizes this key Christian belief in this way:

> The theme of Christ as Bridegroom of the Church was prepared for by the prophets and announced by John the Baptist [Jn 3:29]. The Lord referred to himself as the "bridegroom" [Mk 2:19]. The Apostle speaks of the whole Church and of each of the faithful, members of his Body, as a bride "betrothed" to Christ the Lord so as to become but one spirit with him. [Cf. Mt 22:1–14; 25:1–13; 1 Cor 6:15–17; 2 Cor 11:2.] The Church is the spotless bride of the spotless Lamb. [Cf. Rev 22:17; Eph 1:4; 5:27.] "Christ loved the Church and gave himself up for her, that he might sanctify her" [Eph 5:25–26]. He has joined her with himself in an everlasting covenant and never stops caring for her as for his own body. [Cf. Eph 5:29.] [63]

This is, not surprisingly, unacceptable to those feminists who insist that Jesus was married to Mary Magdalene. It might seem odd that proponents of sexual liberation who often have a palpable dislike for the masculine are so adamant about this point. After all, marriage routinely has been dismissed by feminists as a means of controlling and dominating women and suppressing their full sexuality. But the point of the mythical marriage of Jesus and Mary Magdalene is not to advance a better understanding of marriage or deeper appreciation for the feminine; it is to destroy the truth about

---

[63] *Catechism of the Catholic Church* (CCC), 2nd ed. (Washington, D.C.: United States Catholic Conference—Libreria Editrice Vaticana, 1997), no. 796.

the covenantal union between God and man that has taken place in the marriage between Jesus and his true Bride, the Church.

The writings of Margaret Starbird are instructive in this regard, filled as they are with tortured explanations of how Mary Magdalene fulfills the Old Testament promises of the beloved Bride and how humanity must "rediscover" the sacred feminine and abandon the destructive notion of "the celibate male image of God".[64] The "male Logos", Starbird fumes, must give way for "Eros, the bridal aspect of divinity".[65] These beliefs rest on an unabashed narcissism and dislike for the suffering Christ. Starbird states that humanity has been "duped for centuries" into accepting suffering in a patient, docile manner that reflects the teachings and example of Jesus. This mentality, she writes, has allowed the Church to maintain control over the majority of people and have kept those people from being able to shape their own "wholeness and well-being". But those repressed will no longer allow themselves to be "children", Starbird proclaims, for they are "partners" who are able to set their own "goals and standards". She then states, "I would climb down from the Logos-oriented cross and redesign my life based on the blueprint for balance ... I had been shown."[66]

In many ways this helps to explain the dislike that many feminists have for the Virgin Mary, described in *The Templar Revelation* as "non-sexual and remote".[67] She is perceived as weak, docile, and submissive, the embodiment of subordination. According to one feminist theologian, this "linkage of femininity and subordination" in the Virgin Mary "remains

---

[64] See Starbird, *Goddess in the Gospels*, 145–53.
[65] Starbird, *Woman with the Alabaster Jar*, 163.
[66] Starbird, *Goddess in the Gospels*, 103.
[67] Picknett and Prince, *Templar Revelation*, 61.

fundamental in ecclesiology and Mariology".[68] Again, the vital link between one's understanding of the Church and of sexuality comes to the fore. The radical feminist Mary Daly, a former nun, derisively depicts the Virgin Mary as a "domesticated" goddess who was sexually violated: "The catholic Mary is not the Goddess creating parthenogenetically on her own, but rather she is portrayed/betrayed as Total Rape Victim—a pale derivative symbol disguising the conquered Goddess."[69] Daly continues by sneering that "despite all the theological minimizing of Mary's 'role,' the mythic presence of the Goddess was perceivable in this faded and reversed mirror image."[70]

In her study *Mary Magdalen: Myth and Metaphor*, Susan Haskins suggests that the restoration of Mary Magdalene to her rightful place will lead to a "radical revision" of Christianity's view of woman. The resistance of the Catholic Church to female priests, she believes, "derives from deeply entrenched responses" that have been shaped and conditioned by the many centuries of dogma upholding the image of the Virgin Mary. "It is perhaps time to recognise the true feminine model" of Mary Magdalene, she writes, which "embodies strength, courage and independence, all feminine qualities which the Church has attempted to suppress by subordinating women to the model it has created, the passive virgin and mother".[71] And so, as Manfred Hauke notes, for feminists Mary Magdalene is far superior to the Mother of Jesus for she "is not tied to any notions of order. Hence,

---

[68] Kari Børreson, quoted by Manfred Hauke, *God or Goddess? Feminist Theology: What Is It? Where Does It Lead?* (San Francisco: Ignatius Press, 1995), 186–87.

[69] Mary Daly, *Gyn-Ecology:The Metaethics of Radical Feminism* (Boston: Beacon Press, 1978), 84.

[70] Ibid., 85.

[71] Haskins, *Mary Magdalen*, 386, 387.

for women who are becoming more independent, the model is not Mary but Mary Magdalen." [72]

Magdalene and Benjamin

The Da Vinci Code contains a number of remarks that are apparently essential to the story but whose meaning and importance are never explained—they simply hang on the page, without any rhyme or reason. A good example is the novel's curious claim that Mary Magdalene was from the "House of Benjamin", was of royal descent, and that by marrying Jesus she helped fuse "two royal bloodlines, creating a potent political union" that had the potential to restore the dynasty of kings under Solomon (248–49).

Two serious problems can be found with these assertions. First, they are without any historical basis; secondly, even if there were some validity to them, what would it matter? Why would Solomon's kingship have any purpose or meaning today? And if Jesus were a mere "mortal prophet" (233), why would a royal goddess have any interest in him or need to rely upon him? As Francis Cardinal George, archbishop of Chicago, remarked upon reading the novel, "Jesus isn't God but Mary Magdalene is a goddess? I mean, what does that mean? If he's not God, why is he married to a goddess?" [73] Also, having Davidic blood in Jesus' day would not have been very unusual or unique since all of his stepfather Joseph's relatives had it. And there would have been quite a few of them, with twenty generations of kings of Judah, in

---

[72] Hauke, *God or Goddess?* 187.

[73] Cathleen Falsani, "Cardinal Takes a Crack at *The Da Vinci Code*", *Chicago Sun-Times*, January 9, 2004. Accessed at www.suntimes.com.

addition to the generations from the six centuries between the Babylonian Exile and the birth of Jesus.[74]

The reference to the house of Benjamin comes from *Holy Blood, Holy Grail*, which takes its information from *Dossier secrets*, the alleged secret papers of the Priory of Sion: "Among the genealogies in the *Dossier secrets*, for example, there were numerous footnotes and annotations. Many of these referred specifically to one of the twelve tribes of ancient Israel, the Tribe of Benjamin."[75] The authors claim that since Israel's first king, Saul, was from the tribe of Benjamin, that tribe has a right to the throne. "But Saul was eventually deposed by David, of the Tribe of Judah. And David not only deprived the Benjamites of their claim to the throne. By establishing his capital at Jerusalem he deprived them of their rightful inheritance as well."[76] The argument is made that if Jesus married a Benjamite woman, he would solidify his status as "King of the Jews": "Such a marriage would have constituted an important dynastic alliance and one filled with political consequence."[77]

The first king of Israel, Saul, was a Benjamite (1 Sam 9–10), but he was rejected by God as king because of his disobedience and was replaced by David (see 1 Sam 16:1ff). Although the Benjamites were renowned as a fierce, fighting tribe,[78] they were not considered "rightful" heirs to the throne; it

[74] The kingdom of Judah lasted from ca. 1000 B.C. until the Babylonian Exile of 586 B.C.

[75] Baigent, Leigh, and Lincoln, *Holy Blood, Holy Grail*, 271. See 271–79 and 346–47. For more on the Priory of Sion, see chap. 8 of this book, "The Priory of Sion Hoax".

[76] Baigent, Leigh, and Lincoln, *Holy Blood, Holy Grail*, 347.

[77] The authors of *Holy Blood, Holy Grail* believe that Jesus' crucifixion and Resurrection were an elaborate hoax, a common belief in popular esoteric literature. See ibid., 352–59.

[78] John L. McKenzie, S.J., *Dictionary of the Bible* (New York: Touchstone, 1965, 1995), 89.

was not a royal line. Ironically, the tribes of Benjamin and Judah would be closely linked during the monarchic and post-exilic periods: "Despite ancient connections with the house of Joseph (Ps 80:2) and support for a favorite son, Saul, earlier (2 Sam 2:9; 16:5–8), Benjamin sided with Judah following the split of the monarchy (1 Kings 12:21). For the rest of the monarchic period and into the postexilic period, Benjamin, along with Judah, made up the nation of Judah and later the Persian province of Yehud (Neh 11:4)."[79]

Holy Blood, Holy Grail admits that in the New Testament there is "no indication of the Magdalene's tribal affiliation".[80] However, it is unlikely she was of the tribe of Benjamin; Magdala was located on the northwestern shore of the Sea of Galilee, in northern Israel, whereas the tribes of Judah and Benjamin resided in the south, on the west side of the Dead Sea. The proof offered by *Holy Blood, Holy Grail* is that "subsequent legends" and "other traditions"[81] state she was of the tribe of Benjamin, though none of them is mentioned or cited. Most likely this is a reference to the work of medieval preachers and hagiographers of the tenth to twelfth centuries. Humbert of Romans in the eleventh century had preached a sermon identifying the Magdalene as "descended from *stirpe regia*", or royal stock. A tenth-century sermon from Cluny makes her an heiress, and a twelfth-century Cistercian text says that Mary Magdalene's "mother Eucharia came from the royal house of Israel, while her father Theophillus descended from noble satraps and was governor of Syria". *The Golden Legend*, one of the most famous works of medieval hagiography, named Syrus as Mary's father, stated that Mary owned Magdala,

---

[79] Freedman, *Eerdmans Dictionary of the Bible*, 166.
[80] Baigent, Leigh, and Lincoln, *Holy Blood, Holy Grail*, 347.
[81] Ibid.

named Lazarus as lord of part of Jerusalem, and Martha's domain as Bethany—all of which makes for great legend but not viable history.[82]

Not only is there a lack of evidence for a political alliance resulting from Jesus and Mary Magdalene being married, there would have been no reason for such an alliance. Jesus made it known on more than one occasion that he had not come to establish an earthly kingdom or to overthrow the local Roman government. His kingdom was not of this world, and he came to conquer sin and death, not governments and emperors. At his trial, interrogated by Pilate, Jesus explained the nature of his kingdom:

> Pilate entered the praetorium again and called Jesus, and said to him, "Are you the King of the Jews?" Jesus answered, "Do you say this of your own accord, or did others say it to you about me?" Pilate answered, "Am I a Jew? Your own nation and the chief priests have handed you over to me; what have you done?" Jesus answered, "My kingship is not of this world; if my kingship were of this world, my servants would fight, that I might not be handed over to the Jews; but my kingship is not from the world." (Jn 18:33–36)

Once again, an argument has been offered that seeks to undermine a key Christian belief: the nature of Jesus' mission and of his kingdom. If Jesus were just a mortal prophet who married to re-establish an earthly, political kingdom, then he failed and Christianity is a lie and a farce. Yet, as before, those offering esoteric and convoluted theories about the "real" Jesus fail to offer proof, fact, or historical evidence. Once again, ideology fails to overcome reality.

[82] Jansen, *Making of the Magdalen*, 149.

Where There Is Smoke, There Is . . . Smoke

There is no credible evidence that Jesus was married, that
Mary Magdalene was of royal blood, or that the two created
a dynastic alliance together. But there is plenty of evidence
that those promoting these beliefs are willing to do so without any proof or logical explanation.

In *The Woman with the Alabaster Jar*, Margaret Starbird
explains the methodology behind her research into the supposed marriage of Jesus and Mary Magdalene. In collecting
material for her book, she writes, "I have operated under
the assumption that where there is smoke, there is fire."[83]
There is much diverse evidence for her theories, she argues,
and so there are good reasons to take them seriously. There
must be some truth, she reasons, otherwise why would
movies such as *Godspell*, *Jesus Christ Superstar*, and *The
Last Temptation of Christ* "depict the relationship of Jesus
and Mary Magdalene as one of special intimacy and
significance"?[84]

Other proof offered in that book and *The Goddess in the
Gospels* includes contorted appeals to pagan religions, esoteric and occult artwork, gnostic texts, tarot cards, and
numerology. "Of course", she admits, "I cannot prove that
the tenets of the Grail heresy are true—that Jesus was married or that Mary Magdalene was the mother of his child. I
cannot even prove that Mary Magdalene was the woman with
the alabaster jar who anointed Jesus at Bethany." This is not,
however, a problem. "But I can verify that these are tenets of
a heresy widely believed in the Middle Ages; that fossils of
the heresy can be found in numerous works of art and literature; that it was vehemently attacked by the hierarchy of

---

[83] Starbird, *Woman with the Alabaster Jar*, xxi.
[84] Ibid.

the established Church of Rome; and that it survived in spite of relentless persecution." [85]

Yet falsehoods and heresies often do survive, and they are often revived in later times in different ways. The question is that of truth. There is far more evidence that Jesus was not married, and far more people have believed it throughout history. If smoke is the test of truth, the historical, orthodox Christian claims are a blazing fire engulfing the solitary match struck by modern-day feminists, wiccans, and neo-pagans. Either Jesus was married, or he was not. Either Mary Magdalene was the victim of a vicious smear campaign, or she was not. Either she was a goddess, or she was not. Either *The Da Vinci Code* is accurate and factual in its presentation of Jesus and Mary Magdalene, or it is not. The evidence says, "Not!"

[85] Ibid.

Chapter 3

The Christ and the *Code*

[Jesus was] a mortal prophet . . . a great and powerful man,
but a *man* nonetheless. A mortal.

—Leigh Teabing, fictional historian

The Jesus of the Gospels and of established Christianity is
ultimately incomplete.

— *Holy Blood, Holy Grail*

To this day, millions of Christians ignore the evidence for
the New Testament being a mixture of myth, fabrication,
garbled versions of eyewitness accounts and material taken
from other traditions.

— *The Templar Revelation*

If *The Da Vinci Code*'s depiction of Jesus Christ is correct,
Christians might as well play golf on Sunday mornings and
put their Bibles in storage. Although Dan Brown claims to
be a Christian of some untraditional sort, his novel takes great
pains to assure readers that Christ is not someone worthy of
the sort of worship, attention, and adoration he has received
for two thousand years. The novel's claim that Jesus was merely
a man and nothing more is not a new one, of course, this
notion having been around since the time of Jesus himself.

"He was in the world," the apostle John states of the incarnate Word in the prologue of his Gospel, "and the world was made through him, yet the world knew him not" (Jn 1:10). But Brown apparently is not satisfied with calling Jesus' divinity into question. About halfway through *The Da Vinci Code*, in the course of Sophie and Langdon's lengthy conversation with Leigh Teabing at the English historian's home, an important exchange—lecture, really—takes place (233). In it, Teabing makes the following assertions:

1. The divinity of Jesus was first raised and established at the Council of Nicaea in A.D. 325.
2. Prior to that time, no one—not even Jesus' followers—believed Jesus was anything more than a "mortal prophet" and great man. No one believed that Jesus was the Son of God until that momentous event.
3. This belief was proposed and voted into existence (by a "relatively close vote") at the Council of Nicaea, endorsed by Emperor Constantine for the purpose of solidifying his power and the power of the "new Vatican power base" of the Catholic Church.
4. This meant that those claiming to be Christian could "redeem themselves" only through the "established sacred channel" of the Catholic Church.

We will examine the role of Emperor Constantine and the Council of Nicaea in more detail in subsequent chapters.[1] This chapter will examine the basic claim that no one believed that Jesus is divine prior to A.D. 325 and that this idea was created out of thin air by a pagan Roman emperor. The importance of this topic is self-evident: if Brown is correct, Christianity and the Catholic Church are shams because both

[1] See chap. 4 below, "Constantine, Paganism, and Nicaea".

are based on the doctrine of Jesus' divinity. Likewise, if Brown is incorrect, it is further proof that *The Da Vinci Code* and Brown's claims that it is historically accurate and thoroughly researched are shams.

So what about Teabing's claim that until A.D. 325—nearly three centuries following Jesus' time on earth—nobody believed that Jesus was anything more than "a mortal prophet" and "a great and powerful man"? Notice that Teabing does not personally reject the divinity of Jesus (many people do reject it) or claim that certain modern-day scholars deny that Jesus was somehow divine (many scholars do deny it); rather, he claims that the early followers of Jesus—the Christians of the first three centuries following Jesus' time on earth— believed that he was not divine at all but merely "a mortal". For one thing, this seriously undermines the credibility of Teabing's character, for any historian, whether Christian or not, knows that the early Christians most definitely believed that Jesus of Nazareth was somehow divine, being the "Son of God" and the resurrected Christ. In fact, the central issue at the Council of Nicaea in A.D. 325 was *not* whether Jesus was merely human or something more, but how exactly his divinity—which even the heretic Arius acknowledged—was to be understood: Was he fully divine? Was the Son equal to the Father? Was he a lesser god? What did it mean to say that the Son was "begotten", as the Gospel of John states in several places (Jn 1:14, 18; 3:16, 18)?

Even *Holy Blood, Holy Grail* and *The Templar Revelation*,[2] two of Brown's main sources for his statements about Jesus, Constantine, paganism, and the Council of Nicaea, do not

[2] Michael Baigent, Richard Leigh, and Henry Lincoln, *Holy Blood, Holy Grail* (1982; New York: Dell, 1983), and Lynn Picknett and Clive Prince, *The Templar Revelation: Secret Guardians of the True Identity of Christ* (1997; New York: Simon and Schuster, 1998). Both are mentioned on p. 253 of *The Da Vinci Code*, and Brown's reliance upon them is evident throughout the novel.

propose that prior to A.D. 325 nobody believed Jesus was divine. In fact, the authors of *Holy Blood, Holy Grail* do not even deny the possibility that Jesus was divine; their main interest is insisting that Jesus was married to Mary Magdalene: "And while we ourselves cannot subscribe to Jesus' divinity, our conclusions do not preclude others from doing so. Quite simply there is no reason why Jesus could not have married and fathered children while still retaining his divinity." [3]

The authors of *The Templar Revelation* have a different perspective; although they admit that Jesus was called the "Son of God" by his early followers, they write that this was a mistake and that "Jesus was not so much the Son of God as a devoted son of the Goddess." [4] Their central thesis is that Jesus was "essentially an Egyptian missionary" intent on promoting the pagan religion of the Isis/Osiris mystery cult of Egypt. "Christianity was not the religion founded by the unique Son of God who died for all our sins", they write; "it was the worship of Isis and Osiris repackaged. However, it rapidly became a personality cult, centered on Jesus." [5] Both books agree that Jesus' main goal was the establishment of political power, that he did not die on the Cross, and that his Resurrection was a clever and elaborate hoax, all of which is either stated directly or hinted at in *The Da Vinci Code*.

The essential point is that Teabing's statements, which apparently reflect Brown's beliefs as well, are not only false, but they are not even supported by Brown's main sources. What *The Da Vinci Code* does share with *The Templar Revelation* and *Holy Blood, Holy Grail* is the conviction that historical, creedal Christianity is a lie, an elaborate ruse born

---

[3] Baigent, Leigh, and Lincoln, *Holy Blood, Holy Grail*, 408.

[4] Picknett and Prince, *Templar Revelation*, 297.

[5] Ibid., 301. See chap. 4 below, "Constantine, Paganism, and Nicaea", for a response to the charge that Christianity was reliant upon pagan mystery religions for its central doctrines and practices.

out of the thirst for power and a violent desire to suppress the truth about Jesus: that he was a mere mortal or a married man with lofty political goals or the high priest of an Egyptian mystery religion. In their own ways, each denies the death and Resurrection of Jesus, his salvific work, and the establishment of a unique people—the Church—bound, not by ethnicity or sex or social status, but by the unique work of Jesus Christ, the God-man. "For in Christ Jesus you are all sons of God, through faith", the apostle tells the Christians in Galatia, "For as many of you as were baptized into Christ have put on Christ. There is neither Jew nor Greek, there is neither slave nor free, there is neither male nor female; for you are all one in Christ Jesus" (Gal 3:26–28).[6]

The Divinity of Jesus: The Testimony of the New Testament

There is clear and copious evidence that the early Christians, dating back to Jesus' time on earth, believed that Jesus of Nazareth was divine. In his seminal study *Early Christian Doctrines*, noted scholar J. N. D. Kelly writes that "the all but universal Christian conviction [in the centuries prior to the Council of Nicaea] had been that Jesus Christ was divine as well as human. The most primitive confession had been 'Jesus

---

[6] There is not room in this book for a thorough explanation and defense of Christian belief in Christ's death and Resurrection. Some popular books on the topic include William Lane Craig, *The Son Rises: Historical Evidence for the Resurrection of Jesus* (Chicago: Moody Press, 1981) and *Knowing the Truth about the Resurrection* (Ann Arbor, Mich.: Servant Books, 1988); Norman L. Geisler, *The Battle for the Resurrection* (Nashville: Thomas Nelson, 1992); Peter Kreeft and Ronald K. Tacelli, *Handbook of Christian Apologetics* (Downers Grove, Ill.: InterVarsity Press, 1994); C. S. Lewis, *Mere Christianity* (1942; New York: Macmillan, 1978) and *Miracles: A Preliminary Study* (1947; New York: Macmillan, 1967); and Lee Strobel, *The Case for Christ: A Journalist's Personal Investigation of the Evidence for Jesus* (Grand Rapids, Mich.: Zondervan, 1998).

is Lord' [Rom 10:9; Phil 2:11], and its import had been elaborated and deepened in the apostolic age." [7] Jesus was indeed a prophet, explains German theologian Karl Adam, but the Gospels depict him as uniquely more: "There can be no doubt: the Canonical Gospels see in the person of Jesus Jahve [*Yahweh* = God] himself. According to them, Jesus thinks, feels, and acts in the clear consciousness that he is not simply one called like the rest of the prophets, but rather the historical manifestations and revelation of God himself." [8]

Explicit and implicit evidence that Jesus and his followers knew he was more than a mere mortal is found throughout the New Testament. The infancy narrative in Matthew's Gospel contains a quote from the Old Testament prophet Isaiah: "'Behold, a virgin shall conceive and bear a son, and his name shall be called Emmanuel' (which means, God with us)" (Mt 1:23). In that same Gospel there is an account of the baptism of Jesus; as Jesus comes up out of the water "the heavens were opened and he saw the Spirit of God descending like a dove, and alighting on him; and lo, a voice from heaven, saying, 'This is my beloved Son, with whom I am well pleased'" (Mt 3:16–17).

John's Gospel contains some of the strongest statements about the divinity of Jesus. The densely theological prologue proclaims: "In the beginning was the Word, and the Word was with God, and the Word was God. He was in the beginning with God; all things were made through him, and without him was not anything made that was made" (Jn 1:1–3); the Word is Jesus, the incarnate Son: "And the Word became flesh and dwelt among us, full of grace and truth; we have beheld his glory, glory as of the only Son from the Father"

---

[7] J. N. D. Kelly, *Early Christian Doctrines*, 5th rev. ed. (San Francisco: Harper and Row, 1978), 138.

[8] Karl Adam, *The Christ of Faith* (Pantheon Books: New York, 1957), 59.

(Jn 1:14). Later, after upsetting some of the Jewish authorities because of his activities on the Sabbath, Jesus' life is threatened, "because he not only broke the sabbath but also called God his Father, making himself equal with God" (Jn 5:18).

The eighth chapter of John's Gospel contains another firm affirmation of Jesus' divinity. After having a debate about Abraham with some of the religious leaders, Jesus declares: "Your father Abraham rejoiced that he was to see my day; he saw it and was glad" (Jn 8:56). Indignant, the leaders respond, "You are not yet fifty years old, and have you seen Abraham?" (v. 57). "Truly, truly, I say to you," Jesus replies, "before Abraham was, I am" (v. 58). This is met with hostility; the crowd attempts to kill him, recognizing that he has applied to himself the name of God—"Yahweh", or "I AM"—revealed to Moses in the burning bush (Ex 3:14).

Not only did Jesus makes statements and perform acts (for example, raising people from the dead and curing illnesses) that are tantamount to claims of divinity, his Resurrection was a divine validation of his ministry and message—including his claims to divinity. Jesus' emphatic insistence that he is divine can mean only one of two things: "Either to believe that in him God encounters us, or to nail him to the cross as a blasphemer. There is no third way." [9] For Jesus' followers, his Resurrection was solid and life-changing proof that he was who he said he was—the Son of God. This is captured in John's Gospel in the story of the apostle Thomas. After his crucifixion and Resurrection, Jesus appears to the disciples (Jn 20:19–23), but "Thomas, one of the twelve, called the Twin, was not with them when Jesus came" (Jn 20:24).

---

[9] Theologian Horst George Pöhlmann, quoted by William Lane Craig in *Will The Real Jesus Please Stand Up? A Debate between William Lane Craig and John Dominic Crossan* (Grand Rapids, Mich.: Baker Books, 1998), 26.

Eight days later Jesus appears to the disciples again; this time Thomas is among them. Upon seeing Jesus and touching his pierced hands and side, "Thomas answered him, 'My Lord and my God!'" (Jn 20:28).

Numerous other examples from the four Gospels could be given, including over *forty* passages where Jesus is called the "Son of God" (see Mt 11:27; Mk 12:6; 13:32; 14:61–62; Lk 10:22; 22:70; Jn 10:30; 14:9), is ascribed the power to forgive sins (Mk 2:5–12; Lk 24:45–47), claims unity and oneness with the Father (Jn 10:30; 12:45; 14:8–10), and performs many miracles, including raising Lazarus from the dead (Jn 11). Even if readers believe the disciples were mistaken or that Jesus was a charlatan, there is little doubt that *they* believed he was divine and far more than a mortal prophet.

Similar affirmations of Jesus' divinity are found throughout the canonical writings of Paul and the other New Testament authors. In his first letter to the Church at Corinth, written within a generation of Jesus' crucifixion, Paul declares that "no one can say 'Jesus is Lord,' except by the Holy Spirit" (1 Cor 12:3). In his letter to the Philippians, he writes that "though [the Son] was in the form of God, [he] did not count equality with God a thing to be grasped" (Phil 2:6). The Son's willingness to become man will, paradoxically, lead to the universal confession "that Jesus Christ is Lord, to the glory of God the Father" (Phil 2:11). Paul's first letter to his young son in the Christian faith, Timothy, contains the emphatic declaration that the "Lord Jesus Christ . . . [is] the blessed and only Sovereign, the King of kings and Lord of lords, who alone has immortality and dwells in unapproachable light, whom no man has seen or can see. To him be honor and eternal dominion. Amen" (1 Tim 6:15–16).

The final book of the Bible, the Book of Revelation (or the Apocalypse) presents Jesus as the eternal, conquering, and resurrected King and Savior—another far cry from a "mortal prophet". When John sees Jesus, he falls "at his feet as though dead." "But he laid his right hand upon me, saying, 'Fear not, I am the first and the last'" (Rev 1:17). The title of "the First and the Last" is one of titles used in the Old Testament to describe *Yahweh*, the one true God: "Thus says the LORD, the King of Israel and his Redeemer, the LORD of hosts: 'I am the first and I am the last; besides me there is no god'" (Is 44:6; see Is 41:4; 48:12). This title is applied to Jesus two more times in the Book of Revelation, including 2:8 and 22:12–13. The latter passage, at the conclusion of the book, identifies Jesus as "the Alpha and the Omega, the first and the last, the beginning and the end" (Rev 22:13). This is the same language used by the Lord God at the opening of the book (Rev 1:8), making an overt and intentional connection between God and the divinity of Jesus Christ.[10]

The Testimony of Early Christian Writers

The testimony of the New Testament books alone—all written by early second century at the latest[11]—clearly refutes Teabing's statement that prior to Constantine and the Council of Nicaea none of Jesus' followers believed he was anything more than a mortal. But there is also the testimony of numerous Christian writers between A.D. 100 and the fourth century to the belief in Jesus' divinity. In addition to proving what Christians really did believe about Jesus in the first three

[10] Popular works examining the biblical, historical, and logical evidences for Jesus' divinity include Karl Adam, *The Son of Man* (New York: Image, 1960); Kreeft and Tacelli, *Handbook of Christian Apologetics*; Peter Kreeft, *Fundamentals of the Faith* (San Francisco: Ignatius Press, 1988); Lewis, *Mere Christianity* and *Miracles*; Frank J. Sheed, *What Difference Does Jesus Make?* (New York: Sheed and Ward, 1971); and Strobel, *Case for Christ.*

[11] See Raymond E. Brown, Joseph A. Fitzmyer, Roland E. Murphy, eds., *New Jerome Biblical Commentary* (Englewood Cliffs, N.J.: Prentice Hall, 1990), 1043–54.

centuries of Christianity, these writings also provide an invaluable context for the theological issues and battles that would eventually be addressed, at least in part, by the Council of Nicaea.

Ignatius of Antioch (ca. 50–ca. 117) was the bishop of Antioch; it has been speculated that he, just like the apostle Paul, may have been a persecutor of the Christians prior to his conversion.[12] Captured by the Roman army and en route to Rome to be executed, he wrote a series of seven letters to churches at Ephesus, Magnesia, Tralles, Rome, Philadelphia, and Smyrna, and one to Polycarp (ca. 69–ca. 155), the bishop of Smyrna. In his letter to the Ephesians, he writes: "There is one Physician who is possessed both of flesh and spirit; both made and not made; God existing in flesh; true life in death; both of Mary and of God; first possible and then impossible, even Jesus Christ our Lord."[13]

Later, in the same letter, he tells his readers that they must "do everything as if he [Jesus] were dwelling in us. Thus we shall be his temples and he will be within us as our God—as he actually is."[14] He then states, "For our God, Jesus Christ, was, according to the appointment of God, conceived in the womb by Mary, of the seed of David, but by the Holy Ghost. He was born and baptized, that by His passion He might purify the water." Further, in his letter to the Smyrnaeans, Ignatius refers to Jesus as "the Christ God".[15]

Justin Martyr (ca. 100–ca. 165) was born into a pagan family and became a Christian around the age of thirty. He was a Christian philosopher who taught in Ephesus and then later

[12] F. L. Cross and E. A. Livingstone, eds., *The Oxford Dictionary of the Christian Church*, 3rd ed. (New York: Oxford University Press, 1997), 817.

[13] Ignatius of Antioch, *Letter to the Ephesians*, chap. 7.

[14] Ibid., 15.

[15] Ignatius of Antioch, *Letter to the Smyrnaeans* 10.

in Rome, where he had a school. Justin was one of the leading apologists for the Christian faith in the second century; he defended Christian teachings—including the belief that Jesus was divine—against pagan philosophers. He and several of his disciples were arrested, beaten, and then beheaded by the Romans for their refusal to worship pagan gods. In his *First Apology*, he writes, "Jesus Christ is the only proper Son who has been begotten by God, being His Word and first-begotten, and power; and, becoming man according to His will, He taught us these things for the conversion and restoration of the human race." [16] In his *Dialogue with Trypho*, Justin provides a lengthier defense of his belief that Jesus is God:

> "But if you knew, Trypho," continued I, "who He is that is called at one time the Angel of great counsel, and a Man by Ezekiel, and like the Son of man by Daniel, and a Child by Isaiah, and Christ and God to be worshipped by David, and Christ and a Stone by many, and Wisdom by Solomon, and Joseph and Judah and a Star by Moses, and the East by Zechariah, and the Suffering One and Jacob and Israel by Isaiah again, and a Rod, and Flower, and Corner-Stone, and Son of God, you would not have blasphemed Him who has now come, and been born, and suffered, and ascended to heaven; who shall also come again, and then your twelve tribes shall mourn. For if you had understood what has been written by the prophets, you would not have denied that He was God, Son of the only, unbegotten, unutterable God." [17]

Melito of Sardis (d. ca. 190) was the bishop of Sardis; little else is known of him, and most of his works have come down as fragments or are taken from quotes of other Christian

---

[16] Justin Martyr, *First Apology*, par. 23.
[17] Justin Martyr, *Dialogue with Trypho*, chap. 126.

writers. Melito affirms the belief that Jesus was both God and man:

> It is no way necessary in dealing with persons of intelligence to adduce the actions of Christ after his baptism as proof that his soul and his body, his human nature, were like ours, real and not phantasmal. The activities of Christ after his baptism, and especially his miracles, gave indication and assurance to the world of the deity hidden in his flesh. Being God and likewise perfect man, he gave positive indications of his two natures: of his deity, by the miracles during the three years following after his baptism, of his humanity, in the thirty years which came before his baptism, during which, by reason of his condition according to the flesh, he concealed the signs of his deity, although he was the true God existing before the ages.[18]

Irenaeus (ca. 130–ca. 200), the bishop of Lyons, was one of the most important of the pre-Nicaean Christian writers and an ardent opponent of the gnostic theologian Valentinus (d. ca. 165). His major work was *Adversus haereses*, commonly known as *Against Heresies*. In arguing against the gnostic dualism of the Valentinians, Irenaeus spends much time developing a thorough explanation of the Christian belief that Jesus is God. This includes lengthy statements such as this one, which condemns those who believe that Jesus was a mortal only:

> But again, those who assert that He [Jesus] was simply a mere man, begotten by Joseph, remaining in the bondage of the old disobedience, are in a state of death having been not as yet joined to the Word of God the Father, nor receiving liberty through the Son. . . . Now, the Scriptures would not have testified these things of Him, if, like others, He had been a mere man. But that He had, beyond all others, in

[18] Melito of Sardis, fragment in Anastasius of Sinai's *The Guide*, 13.

Himself that pre-eminent birth which is from the Most High Father, and also experienced that pre-eminent generation which is from the Virgin, the divine Scriptures do in both respects testify of Him: also, that He was a man without comeliness, and liable to suffering; that He sat upon the foal of an ass; that He received for drink, vinegar and gall; that He was despised among the people, and humbled Himself even to death and that He is the holy Lord, the Wonderful, the Counsellor, the Beautiful in appearance, and the Mighty God, coming on the clouds as the Judge of all men;—all these things did the Scriptures prophesy of Him.[19]

Clement of Alexandria (ca. 150–ca. 215) was a Greek theologian and the author of several works, including *Exhortation to the Greeks*. In that work he teaches that "He [Jesus] alone is both God and man, and the source of all our good things";[20] he also states: "Despised as to appearance but in reality adored, [Jesus is] the expiator, the Savior, the soother, the divine Word, he that is quite evidently true God, he that is put on a level with the Lord of the universe because he was his Son."[21] Similar remarks are made by the great African Church Father **Tertullian** (ca. 160–ca. 225). He wrote that "God alone is without sin. The only man who is without sin is Christ; for Christ is also God."[22] In another work he discusses the relationship of the divine and human natures of Jesus Christ: "The origins of both his substances display him as man and as God: from the one, born, and from the other, not born."[23] The Alexandrian scholar and theologian **Origen** (ca. 185–ca. 254), who authored hundreds of books, stated around A.D. 225 that "although [the Son] was God, he took

[19] Irenaeus, *Against Heresies*, bk. 3, chap. 29:1, 2.
[20] Clement of Alexandria, *Exhortation to the Greeks* 1:7:1.
[21] Ibid., 10:110:1.
[22] Tertullian, *The Soul* 41:3.
[23] Tertullian, *The Flesh of Christ*, 5:6–7.

flesh; and having been made man, he remained what he was: God." [24] Writing at nearly the same time, the theologian **Hippolytus** (ca. 170–ca. 236) stated, "Only [God's] Word is from himself and is therefore also God, becoming the substance of God." [25]

There are many other examples, but we will conclude this section with a passage from **Gregory Thaumaturgus** (or the **Wonderworker**) (ca. 213–ca. 270), bishop of Pontus, in part because it ties in well with the Council of Nicaea and the Niceno-Constantinopolitan Creed. Gregory was a Greek Church Father who came from a pagan family and became Christian under the guidance of Origen. In his *Declaration of Faith*, a creedal statement, he states:

> There is one God, the Father of the living Word, *who is His* subsistent Wisdom and Power and Eternal Image: perfect Begetter of the perfect *Begotten*, Father of the only-begotten Son. There is one Lord, Only of the Only God of God, Image and Likeness of Deity, Efficient Word, Wisdom comprehensive of the constitution of all things, and Power formative of the whole creation, true Son of true Father, Invisible of Invisible, and Incorruptible of Incorruptible, and Immortal of Immortal and Eternal of Eternal. And there is One Holy Spirit, having His subsistence from God, and being made manifest by the Son, to wit to men: Image of the Son, *Perfect* Image of the Perfect; Life, the Cause of the living; Holy Fount; Sanctity, the Supplier, *or Leader*, of Sanctification; in whom is manifested God the Father, who is above all and in all, and God the Son, who is through all. There is a perfect Trinity, in glory and eternity and sovereignty, neither divided nor estranged. . . . And thus neither was the Son ever wanting to the Father, nor the Spirit to the Son; but

---

[24] Origen, *The Fundamental Doctrines* I, Preface, 4.
[25] Hippolytus, *Refutation of All Heresies* 10:33.

without variation and without change, the same Trinity *abideth* ever.[26]

Heavenly God-Man or Hijacked Prophet?

These patristic quotes (and so many others like them) demonstrate that prior to the Council of Nicaea there were plenty of Jesus' followers who believed he was divine. As we will see, these quotes and the beliefs they articulate also form a sturdy, logical bridge between Jesus and the Creed that was formulated in the fourth century, first at Nicaea (A.D. 325) and then at Constantinople (A.D. 381).

In addition to that patristic bridge, the teachings of the New Testament and the early Christian writers also help to answer two interrelated claims made in Brown's novel. One is that the early Church "stole" Jesus from his true followers, turning him into an unreal, supernatural creature; the other is that history has been written by the "winners"—that is, by Christians and the Church. In the midst of his lengthy lecture, Teabing tells Sophie that Constantine deified Jesus in order to maintain power and that Jesus as Messiah, not a mere mortal, was vital to the success of both the Church and the state. Scholars believe, he continues, that "the early Church literally *stole* Jesus from His original followers" and covered Jesus' gospel in "an impenetrable cloak of divinity", cementing and expanding their power (233).

As we saw in the chapter on gnosticism,[27] this depiction of the early Christians as hijacking the truth about Jesus and making him God while the gnostics emphasized Jesus' humanity is completely incorrect. In fact, it is the exact opposite of the actual case, for the depictions of Jesus in the four Gospels

[26] Gregory Thaumaturgus, *Declaration of Faith*.
[27] See chap. 1 above, "Gnosticism: The Religion of the *Code*".

are filled with concrete, historical details, social and political information, and logical narrative, qualities sorely lacking in most gnostic writings. This is not to say that everything said about Jesus in the New Testament can be historically corroborated, but the historical evidence that does exist upholds and supports what the New Testaments describes.[28]

This key point should be kept in mind when considering Brown's belief—made known both through the character Teabing and in his own statements—that history has been written by the winners. Teabing makes that very remark before telling Sophie that "the loser is obliterated" and that "by its very nature, history is always a one-sided account" (256).[29] An article in the *Washington Post* reports that Brown has the same conviction.

> History [Brown says] is written by the "winners", those societies and belief systems that conquered and survived. Even with that bias, we still measure the accuracy of an idea by examining how well it concurs with our existing historical record. "Many historians now believe that in gauging the historical accuracy of a given concept, we should first ask ourselves a far deeper question: 'How historically accurate is history itself?'"[30]

[28] "One cannot give historical evidence to support all of the details about the person and work of Jesus recorded in the canonical Gospels. Nevertheless, the historical evidence that is available supports the presumption of at least the general trustworthiness of particularly the Synoptic tradition. When sources repeatedly prove trustworthy where they can be tested, they should be given the benefit of the doubt where they cannot. This is what is frequently referred to as placing the burden of proof on the skeptic when it comes to Gospel historicity" (Craig L. Blomberg, "The Jesus of History and the Christ of Faith: Harmony or Conflict?" in Craig, *Will The Real Jesus Please Stand Up?*, 114).

[29] Yet Teabing immediately adds that the secret Sangreal documents "tell the other side of the Christ story", which means that the losers must not have been obliterated and that history is not a one-sided account.

[30] Roxanne Roberts, "The Mysteries of Mary Magdalene: 'The Da Vinci Code' Resurrects a Debate of Biblical Proportions", *Washington Post*, July 20,

Once again, Brown's confused thinking comes to the fore. On one hand, history cannot be trusted or accepted as true; on the other, we gauge truth by using history as a measuring stick. Such an approach cannot lead to any proper understanding of historical events because it is rooted in a suspicion of anything contrary to personal ideology. The fact that Brown refers to the "winners" indicates that he has already made a judgment based on his beliefs, not on the historical facts as they can best be understood. It is similar to saying to someone, "I don't trust you because I don't like you", and also saying, "I don't like you because I don't trust you." For whatever reason, Brown does not like Christianity and the Catholic Church; therefore history must be rigged and wrong because it supports the claims of Christianity and the Catholic Church. He does not like the Church's portrayal of Jesus Christ, and so any evidence for that depiction must be tainted by the "winners".[31] Of course, for the first three hundred

---

2003. Accessed at www.washingtonpost.com. Brown adds: "'I'm not entirely convinced history is unknowable.' ... 'We're entering an age, he says, when we've started to question everything. In the past, knowledge was something that was handed down by authority figures; now we seek and discover for ourselves.'" This is just another way of saying two things: I am the only trustworthy authority, and I am much smarter than anyone from a previous era of history. Both beliefs are endemic within a postmodern culture that believes in nothing except the right to believe in nothing.

[31] In more technical terms, Brown's approach is a variation on the "hermeneutic of suspicion" utilized by many feminist biblical scholars. This means that texts such as the New Testament writings should not and cannot be taken at face value but must be interpreted with the knowledge that they are strongly biased against women. Thus, feminist scholar Elisabeth Schüssler Fiorenza advocates a "hermeneutics of imagination", meant to free readers from the confines of a patriarchal perspective. See Philip Jenkins, *Hidden Gospels: How the Search for Jesus Lost Its Way* (New York: Oxford University Press, 2001), 88. Jenkins summarizes this perspective this way: "From a postmodern view, texts in themselves lack authority, and have value only insofar as they speak to their readers" (88–89). The issue, in the end, is not truth but whether something is true *for me*.

years of its existence, Christianity was not a "winner" in relation to the pagan, Roman world. If anything, the Christians were "losers", having to endure almost continual persecution, derision, and, in many cases, death. For those three centuries, Christians did not have the support of the emperor or the instruments of the state to help them.

Brown is hardly alone in low regard for the Church and her true history, and his beliefs about Jesus have much in common with the speculations of the Jesus Seminar and men such as Robert W. Funk, John Dominic Crossan, and Marcus Borg—some of the more extreme and fringe scholars of the so-called search for the "historical Jesus". Most of the members of the Jesus Seminar would agree, at least in general, with Teabing's and Brown's comments. Robert Funk, the founder of the Jesus Seminar, has stated, "We want to liberate Jesus. The only Jesus most people want is the mythic one. They don't want the real Jesus. They want one to worship. The cultic Jesus." [32] The real Jesus, Marcus Borg states, has little to do with the Jesus presented in the Gospels: "Most (perhaps all) of the 'exalted titles' by which Jesus is known in the Christian tradition do not go back to Jesus himself. He did not speak of or think of himself as 'the Son of God,' or as 'one with the Father,' or as 'the light of the world,' or as 'the way, the truth, and the life,' or as 'the savior of the world.' " [33]

As Borg's remark indicates, in order to "liberate" Jesus from the clutches of the Catholic Church and "fundamentalist" Protestants, Funk and Company claim that most of what is found in the Gospels is made up or has been radically revised, with only a small percentage directly traceable to

---

[32] Quoted in Douglas Groothuis, *Searching for the Real Jesus in an Age of Controversy* (Eugene, Ore.: Harvest House, 1996), 17–18.

[33] Marcus J. Borg, "Me and Jesus—The Journey Home: An Odyssey", *The Fourth R*, vol. 6, no. 4. (July/August 1993). Accessed at www.westarinstitute.org.

the "real" Jesus. The introduction to *The Acts of Jesus: The Search for the Authentic Deeds of Jesus*, written by Funk and the Jesus Seminar (and just one of the seemingly endless volumes published by that organization), states:

> During the second phase of the Jesus Seminar, which lasted from 1991 to 1996, the Fellows examined 387 reports of 176 events, in most of which Jesus is the principal actor, although occasionally John the Baptist, Simon Peter, or Judas is featured. Of the 176 events, only ten were given a red rating (red indicates that the Fellows had a relatively high level of confidence that the event actually took place). An additional nineteen were colored pink (pink suggests that the event probably occurred). The combined number of red and pink events (29) amounts to 16% of the total (176). That is slightly lower than the 18% of the sayings—primarily parables and aphorisms—assigned to the red and pink categories in The Five Gospels.[34]

The Jesus Seminar was a media favorite in the 1990s, a clever mixture of public relations (the group voted on the authenticity of sayings and stories by using colored beads) and iconoclastic scholarship—or pseudo-scholarship, as many critics of the Seminar believed it to be. Luke Timothy Johnson, author of *The Real Jesus: The Misguided Quest for the Historical Jesus and the Truth of the Traditional Gospels* and *Living Jesus: Learning the Heart of the Gospel*,[35] sarcastically stated that the Seminar

[34] Robert Walter Funk, *The Acts of Jesus: The Search for the Authentic Deeds of Jesus* (San Francisco: HarperSanFrancisco, 1998). Accessed online at www.westarinstitute.org/Jesus_Seminar/jesus_seminar.html.

[35] Luke Timothy Johnson, *The Real Jesus: The Misguided Quest for the Historical Jesus and the Truth of the Traditional Gospels* (San Francisco: HarperSanFrancisco, 1996) and *Living Jesus: Learning the Heart of the Gospel* (San Francisco: HarperSanFrancisco, 1999). Johnson's books are good places to start for a critique of the Jesus Seminar. Also see Ben Witherington III, *The Jesus Quest* (Downers Grove, Ill.: InterVarsity Press, 1997), 42–57, and N. T. Wright, *Jesus and the Victory of God* (Minneapolis: Fortress Press, 1996), 29–35.

created a Jesus who was "a sort of faculty lounge lizard. . . . He's multicultural; he's inclusive; he's politically correct; he's not embarrassingly divine; he doesn't talk about suffering and sacrifice. He's kind of a neat guy who invites everybody to the table and doesn't make any demands." [36] In other words, he sounds very much like the Jesus described in *The Da Vinci Code*—a Jesus who is agreeable to twenty-first-century Americans and who will not demand too much of them.

In remarks made at the opening of the Jesus Seminar in 1985, Funk stated, "What we are about takes courage, as I said. We are probing what is most sacred to millions, and hence we will constantly border on blasphemy. We must be prepared to forebear the hostility we shall provoke. At the same time, our work, if carefully and thoughtfully wrought, will spell liberty for other millions. It is for the latter that we labor." [37] As is so often the case (and as *The Da Vinci Code* mimics), those who work to undermine the teaching of the established Christian faith consider themselves to be freedom fighters and even martyrs for the truth (although most do not believe that any firm truth can be found). Meanwhile, those who uphold traditional Christian doctrine are portrayed as fundamentalists, zealots, and narrow-minded bigots. In Brown's world this means that the Catholic Church

[36] Allison O. Adams, "The Gospels according to Luke", *Emory Magazine*, Fall 1996. Accessed online at www.emory.edu/EMORY_MAGAZINE/fall96/johnson.html. It should be noted that although Funk, Crossan, Borg, and Co. are regarded by many secularists as "leading scholars" in the field of biblical studies, their position is a minority one among New Testament scholars studying the historical Jesus. Scholars including Raymond E. Brown, Joseph Fitzmyer, Luke Timothy Johnson, Richard B. Hays—hardly fundamentalists or archconservative scholars—have been highly critical of both the methods and conclusions of the Jesus Seminar.

[37] The opening remarks of Jesus Seminar founder Robert Funk, presented at the first meeting held March 21–24, 1985, in Berkeley, California. Accessed at www.westarinstitute.org.

is full of lies, deception, and insidious schemes to suppress the truth. Thus Teabing informs Sophie of the Church's knack for coercion, threatening, hiding, lying, and misleading. "The Church may no longer employ crusaders to slaughter non-believers," he states "but their influence is no less persuasive. No less insidious" (407).

The "liberty" created by the Seminar has essentially become the freedom to create Jesus in whatever image each scholar desires and a "freedom" from the confines of creed and dogma—the same sort of freedom that is lauded throughout *The Da Vinci Code.* This same idea is taken up in a more scholarly form in Elaine Pagels' *The Gnostic Gospels* and *Beyond Belief.*[38] The jacket for the latter best seller states, "Pagels shows that what matters about Christianity involves much more than any one set of beliefs" and that "the impulse to seek God overflows the narrow banks of a single tradition." As different as they are in some respects, *The Da Vinci Code,* the Jesus Seminar, and *Beyond Belief* all claim to locate the truth about Jesus that exists behind the wall of dogma and doctrine erected by the Church; all believe that "ortho-doxy" is narrow and confining—even dull and disingenu-ous. Each insists that its approach is one of freedom and excitement. This approach is hardly new; it was in vogue a hundred years ago when the young G. K. Chesterton, him-self once an atheist, wrote his classic book *Orthodoxy* and pointed out the dangers of abandoning the adventure of orthodoxy for the insanity of error:

> People have fallen into a foolish habit of speaking of ortho-doxy as something heavy, humdrum, and safe. There never was anything so perilous or so exciting as orthodoxy. It was

[38] Elaine Pagels, *The Gnostic Gospels* (1979; New York: Vintage Books, 1989) and *Beyond Belief: The Secret Gospel of Thomas* (New York: Random House, 2003).

sanity: and to be sane is more dramatic than to be mad. . . .
To have fallen into any of those open traps of error and exaggeration which fashion after fashion and sect after sect set
along the historic path of Christendom—that would indeed
have been simple. It is always simple to fall; there are an infin-
ity of angles at which one falls, only one at which one stands.
To have fallen into any one of the fads from Gnosticism to
Christian Science would indeed have been obvious and
tame. But to have avoided them all has been one whirling
adventure." [39]

The Nature and Meaning of Heresy

Those seeking to restore the "losers" to their proper place in
history know they must revise the common understanding
of heresy. Pagels rehabilitates the gnostic heretics by describing them as seekers, not believers—people who "seek for
God".[40] From this perspective, true faith is all about seeking
and choice—not certainty and dogma. Heresy is described
as choosing differently from orthodox Christianity, as choosing correctly over the falsehoods foisted upon history by hierarchy, structure, and dogma.

In *The Da Vinci Code*, Langdon informs Sophie that anyone choosing the "forbidden" gnostic gospels instead of Constantine's supposedly sanitized edition "was deemed a heretic"
(234). He claims that the word *heretic* originated at that
moment in time, in the years immediately following the
Council of Nicaea. "The Latin word *haereticus* means
'choice'", he remarks. "Those who 'chose' the original history of Christ were the world's first *heretics*" (234).

[39] G. K. Chesterton, *Orthodoxy*, in *The Collected Works of G. K. Chesterton*,
vol. 1 (San Francisco: Ignatius Press, 1986), 305–6.
[40] Pagels, *Beyond Belief*, 28–29.

Brown apparently relies on a section of *The Templar Revelation*, which notes, "in fact, the word heresy originally just meant choice" and then implies that this originated at the Council of Nicaea.[41] But the term "heresy" actually dates back several centuries prior to Constantine, even before the time of Christ. For example, "Josephus applies the name (*airesis*) to the three religious sects prevalent in Judea since the Machabean period: the Sadducees, the Pharisees, the Essenes (Bel. Jud., II, viii, 1; Ant., XIII, v, 9)."[42] The word comes from the ancient Greek αἱρέσις (*hairesis*), which does indeed mean "choice", "thing chosen", or "an opinion". In antiquity, including the first and second centuries after Christ, the term often referred to the beliefs or tenets of a specific philosophical school or "sect"; it is used this way in Acts 5:17; 15:5; 24:5, 14; 26:5; 28:22.[43] But the New Testament also uses the word to describe groups or parties who caused division and discord within the early Church. Paul uses it in speaking of "factions" in 1 Corinthians 11:19 and Galatians 5:20, and of a "factious" man in Titus 3:10. It also appears in the second epistle of Peter: "But false prophets also arose among the people, just as there will be false teachers among you, who will secretly bring in destructive heresies, even denying the Master who bought them, bringing upon themselves swift destruction" (2 Pet 2:1).

Ignatius of Antioch, writing around A.D. 110, also refers to heretics: "Keep off foreign fare", he writes to the Trallians, "by which I mean heresy."[44] In his letter to the Ephesians he refers to "sectarianism", by which he means speaking lies

---

[41] Picknett and Prince, *Templar Revelation*, 237–38.

[42] "Heresy", in *The Catholic Encyclopedia*. Accessed online at www.newadvent.org.

[43] See *Oxford Dictionary of the Early Church*, 3rd ed. (Oxford: Oxford University Press, 1997), 758, and *Vine's Expository Dictionary of Biblical Words* (Nashville: Thomas Nelson, 1985), 303.

[44] Ignatius of Antioch, *Letter to the Trallians* 6.

about Jesus Christ.[45] Both are most likely references to the Docetists, who did not acknowledge the humanity of Jesus but believed he only seemed, or appeared, to be human.[46] Irenaeus wrote his classic work *Adversus haereses* around A.D. 180, stating that he intended "to the best of my ability, with brevity and clearness to set forth the opinions of those who are now promulgating heresy".[47] Those included "Valentinus, who adapted the principles of the heresy called 'Gnostic' to the peculiar character of his own school".[48] And so, some 150 years prior to Constantine and the Council of Nicaea, gnostic leaders and their teachings were being denounced as heretical, choosing beliefs contrary to that of the Church established by Jesus and his apostles.

Finally, Tertullian wrote *De praescriptione haereticorum* ("The Prescription against Heretics") around A.D. 200; it appears to be the first time the word "heresy" is used in Latin:

> The character of the times in which we live is such as to call forth from us even this admonition, that we ought not to be astonished at the heresies (which abound) neither ought their existence to surprise us, for it was foretold that they should come to pass; nor the fact that they subvert the faith of some, for their final cause is, by affording a trial to faith, to give it also the opportunity of being "approved." [49]

Contrary to *The Da Vinci Code*'s claim that those "who 'chose' the original history of Christ were the world's first *heretics*", the heretics specifically condemned at the time of Constantine were Arians—not gnostics, as Brown has implied.[50]

---

[45] Ignatius of Antioch, *Letter to the Ephesians* 6.
[46] Gr., *doceo* = "I seem".
[47] Irenaeus, *Adversus haereses*, bk. 1, pref., 2.
[48] Ibid., bk. 1, 11.1.
[49] Tertullian, *De praescriptione haereticorum* 1.
[50] See chap. 4 below, "Constantine, Paganism, and Nicaea".

Chapter 4

Constantine, Paganism, and Nicaea

> The state religion of Rome under Constantine was, in fact, pagan sun worship; and Constantine, all his life, acted as its chief priest.
>
> —*Holy Blood, Holy Grail*

> The Eastern Orthodox Church calls Constantine a saint and "the Peer of the Apostles." ... Sometimes Christianity needs hard men, and it benefited greatly from Constantine.
>
> —H. W. Crocker III, *Triumph: The Power and Glory of the Catholic Church*

Constantine the Great. The name conjures up a host of images, often conflicting and usually controversial: patron of the Church, convert, pagan, true Christian, pagan conniver. The debate about Constantine, his exact beliefs, his relationship with the Catholic Church, and his influence upon Christianity has raged for decades. For many Christians, he represents all that was wrong with Church-state relations in the ancient and medieval worlds. For some, he stands for courage under fire, a convert willing to take a risk for the fledgling Christian faith.

Although a completely clear picture of Constantine may never be possible, most historians acknowledge that he was a complex man and a powerful and sometimes cruel emperor (he executed a wife and a son under mysterious circumstances). His apparent—and apparently authentic—passion for Christianity was not always guided by theological knowledge or godly wisdom. There is also no doubt that the course of Christianity was substantially influenced and changed by Constantine. The real issue, of course, is what sort of influence the emperor exerted and whether or not it was appropriate.

In *The Da Vinci Code*, Constantine's reign is presented as a key turning point in the history of Christianity and Christendom. Far more controversial is its portrayal of the emperor as a power-hungry pretender and Machiavellian prince ("a very good businessman", Teabing cracks) whose only interest in the Catholic Church was political. The historian Teabing describes Constantine as "a lifelong pagan" (232) and makes these claims:

1. Constantine was baptized on his deathbed against his wishes.
2. He was the head priest of the cult of *Sol Invictus*, or the Invincible Sun, for the official religion of Rome was "sun worship".
3. Constantine's sole purpose was to unify Rome by means of a single religion; he was not a believing Christian.
4. He converted the pagans of Rome and the Empire to Christianity by creating a "hybrid religion" that was a mixture of pagan "symbols, dates, and rituals" and Christianity.
5. Constantine transformed Jesus from a mere mortal man to the "Son of God" and thus cemented the

Catholic Church's control of the person of Jesus
(232–33).[1]

Constantine's Childhood and Conversion

The date of Constantine's birth is unknown but was likely
between A.D. 273 and 275.[2] He was born into a difficult
time, with the Roman Empire shaken by civil wars, the inva-
sion of barbarians, famine, and plagues. Numerous men
declared themselves emperor, and leadership was unstable,
with assassinations and mutinies being a regular part of political life along with financial instability and social unrest. His
father, Flavius Constantius, was a Roman officer, possibly
the governor of a province. Constantius was eventually made
a Caesar in the West under Diocletian, and Constantine spent
twelve years traveling with the emperor as a member of his
retinue, "the migratory capital of the empire".[3]

Initially Christians enjoyed freedom and relative peace during the rule of Diocletian. That changed in A.D. 303, when
the emperor's oracles proclaimed that Christians—"the just"—
were somehow preventing them from performing their
soothsaying duties. An edict was posted on February 23, 303,

---

[1] Most, if not all, of these statements are taken directly from *Holy Blood,
Holy Grail* (1982; New York: Dell, 1983), written by Michael Baigent, Richard Leigh, and Henry Lincoln. In some cases the phrases and order of ideas
used are identical. For example, Constantine's interest in the Catholic Church
is described as "primarily a matter of expediency" (365). Constantine did not
convert to Christianity, the authors state; he "does not seem to have been
Christian at all but unabashedly pagan" (366). "In the interests of unity", the
authors continue, "Constantine deliberately chose to blur the distinctions among
Christianity, Mithraism and Sol Invictus—deliberately chose not to see any
contradictions among them" (367). The Council of Nicaea decided that "Jesus
was a god, not a mortal prophet" (368).

[2] A. H. M. Jones, *Constantine and the Conversion of Europe* (Toronto: University of Toronto Press, 1978), 13.

[3] Ibid., 25.

ordering the destruction of the Christian Scriptures and churches and the prohibition of all Christian meetings for worship; Christians in the military were also stripped of their rank. Christians were essentially reduced to the level of slaves. Christian leaders were required to sacrifice to pagan gods or else be executed. In 305 a seriously ill Diocletian abdicated, and Constantius was named Augustus of the West. A year later, while fighting in Britain, Constantius died, and his son, who was in his early- to mid-twenties, was named Constantine Augustus. Constantine had, Jones writes, demonstrated both an ambitious hunger for power and a decisive manner of leadership. "By temperament he was authoritarian, generous to a fault, explosive of anger, but easily mollified. In his crude fashion he was strongly religious—he believed, that is, that success depended on the favour of higher powers." [4]

Constantine's passion for religion was based, in part, "on his political intuition that the unity of the empire restored by him could be maintained only with the help of a Church united in belief and government and subordinated to the state". [5] But it would be incorrect to portray Constantine as simply a calculating leader who merely used the Church for his political ends. Historian Hugo Rahner explains that Constantine's religious motives were deeper than a mere desire for more power. "Even before he became involved with the Church, Constantine was obsessed with a superstitious religious conviction that revealed itself in his strange personal cult of the invincible sun, in the worship, influenced by Stoicism and Platonism, of the supreme Divinity, in a misty feeling that 'Providence' had bestowed on him a mission as its herald and miraculous instrument." [6]

[4] Ibid., 58.
[5] Hugo Rahner, *Church and State in Early Christianity* (San Francisco: Ignatius Press, 1992), 41.
[6] Ibid., 41–42.

In A.D. 313, Constantine and his fellow-emperor Licinius issued the Edict of Milan, which recognized Christianity as a legal religion. It stated that "Christians and all others should have the freedom to follow the kind of religion they favored; so that the God who dwells in heaven might be propitious to us and to all under our rule.... Moreover, concerning the Christians, we before gave orders with respect to the places set apart for their worship. It is now our pleasure that all who have bought such places should restore them to the Christians, without any demand for payment." [7] The Edict, Paul Johnson writes, "was one of the decisive events in world history. Yet the story behind it is complicated and in some ways mysterious." [8]

Historians will likely never know for certain what happened in A.D. 312 at the Battle of the Milvian Bridge, where "a most incredible sign appeared to [Constantine] from heaven." [9] Having seen the Cross of Christ in the sky, Constantine underwent a conversion. But, as Johnson notes, "there is a conflict of evidence about the exact time, place and details of this vision, and there is some doubt about the magnitude of Constantine's change of ideas. His father had been pro-Christian. He himself appears to have been a sun-worshipper, one of a number of late-pagan cults which had observances

---

[7] *Edict of Milan*, March 313, par. 3, 7.

[8] Paul Johnson, *A History of Christianity* (New York: Atheneum, 1976), 67.

[9] "A most incredible sign appeared to him from heaven.... He said that about noon, when the day was already beginning to decline, he saw with his own eyes the trophy of a cross of light in the heavens, above the sun, and an inscription, CONQUER BY THIS attached to it.... He said, moreover, that he doubted within himself what the import of this portent might be.... Then in his sleep the Christ of God appeared to him with the sign which he had seen in the heavens, and he commanded him to make a likeness of that sign and to use it as a safeguard in all engagements with his enemies" (Eusebius, *Life of Constantine* 1.28).

in common with the Christians." [10] Here Johnson refers in part to the fact that the Christians had been celebrating their weekly liturgy on Sunday, the first day of the week, since the time of Paul and the other apostles. Sunday was also the feast day of the *Sol Invictus* (Invincible Sun) cult, whose worship of the pagan sun god had appeared in the Roman world around the middle of the second century and had been strongly supported by Emperor Aurelian (A.D. 270–275).[11] It should also be noted that Rome's *official* religion was *not* sun worship. "Rome's official religion", states Dr. Margaret Mitchell, associate professor of New Testament and Early Christian Literature in the Divinity School at the University of Chicago, "was the cult of Roma—the goddess—and of her deified emperors, and the Capitoline trio Jupiter, Juno and Minerva".[12]

As noted, Teabing's remarks are taken directly (nearly verbatim) from *Holy Blood, Holy Grail* (365–68), but that book's account is more accurate than what is found in Brown's novel. For instance, all evidence, including the writings of Bishop Eusebius, indicates that Constantine did become a sincere and believing Christian and sought to renounce his former worship of pagan gods. Yet it is also evident that he did struggle with reconciling his attachment to the *Sol Invictus* cult with his belief in the God of the Christians. Part of this was due to his position as emperor, the fact that the majority of the population was pagan, and likely his own inner decision to be a ruler before being a Christian. It would be a gross oversimplification to think that Constantine could only benefit

---

[10] Johnson, *History of Christianity*, 67.

[11] Chas S. Clifton, *Encyclopedia of Heresies and Heretics* (New York: Barnes and Noble, 1992), 121.

[12] Dr. Margaret M. Mitchell, "An Expert Opinion", a sidebar to a review of *The Da Vinci Code* by Denis DeClue, *Lake* magazine. Accessed at http://lakemagazine.com, September 2003.

from becoming a Christian and publicly supporting the Church. "The Christians were a tiny minority of the population," states A. H. M. Jones in *Constantine and the Conversion of Europe*,

> and they belonged for the most part to the classes of the population who were politically and socially of the least importance, the middle and lower classes of the towns. The senatorial aristocracy of Rome were pagan almost to a man; the higher grades of the civil service were mainly pagan; and above all the army officers and men were predominantly pagan. The goodwill of the Christians was hardly worth gaining, and for what it was worth it could be gained by merely granting them toleration.[13]

From Paganism to Christianity

Constantine's move from paganism to Christianity was not immediate or always consistent. But over the course of several years he increased his support of the Church and implemented laws against certain pagan practices and activities. "For a time it seemed as if merely tolerance and equality were to prevail", states the *Catholic Encyclopedia*. "Constantine showed equal favour to both religious [sic]. As *pontifex maximus* he watched over the heathen worship and protected its rights. The one thing he did was to suppress divination and magic; this the heathen emperors had also at times sought to do. Thus, in 320, the emperor forbade the diviners or haruspices to enter a private house under pain of death."[14]

Some scholars argue that the chasm between the monotheism of Christianity and the cult of *Sol Invictus* was not as

---

[13] Jones, *Constantine and the Conversion of Europe*, 73.

[14] "Constantine the Great", in *The Catholic Encyclopedia*. Accessed at www.newadvent.org/cathen/04295c.htm.

wide as it might initially appear. The cult of *Sol Invictus* was not polytheistic or even pantheistic but monotheistic; it was "the worship of the divine spirit by whom the whole universe was ruled, the spirit whose symbol is the sun; a symbol in which this spirit in some way specially manifests itself. . . . The whole cult is penetrated with the idea of an overruling divine monarchy. Moreover, the cult was in harmony with a philosophical religion steadily growing, in the high places of the administration, throughout this same [fourth] century, the cult of *Summus Deus*—the God who is supreme." [15]

For Constantine—a man without concern for theological precision—there was probably little, if any, distinction between the pagan and Christian notions of God (even though he surely recognized the differences in worship and morality). "The transition from solar monotheism (the most popular form of contemporary paganism) to Christianity was not difficult", writes Henry Chadwick. "In Old Testament prophecy Christ was entitled 'the sun of righteousness'[Mal. 4:2]. Clement of Alexandria (c. A.D. 200) speaks of Christ driving his chariot across the sky like the Sun-god. . . . Tertullian says that many pagans imagined the Christians worshipped the sun because they met on Sundays and prayed towards the East." [16]

The Da Vinci Code implies that Constantine was baptized against his wishes (232). This was not the case. He had desired to be baptized in the waters of the Jordan River, where Jesus had been baptized, but it was not to be. Not long after the Easter of 337 he called together some bishops, removed his purple robe, and put on the white garments of a catechumen, then was baptized by Eusebius, the bishop of

---

[15] Philip Hughes, *The Church in Crisis: A History of the General Councils, 325–1870* (New York: Image, 1964), 29–30.

[16] Henry Chadwick, *The Early Church* (1967; Harmondsworth, U.K.: Penguin Books, 1973), 126.

Nicomedia.[17] He died a few days later. It was common for Christians at the time to put off baptism until their deathbed. Serious sins committed after baptism would require severe penance, so some considered it safer to wait until the end of life to be baptized. This practice was mentioned by Augustine in his *Confessions*; as a child he nearly died of illness and his mother considered having him baptized. Augustine writes that once he recovered, however, "my cleansing was deferred, as if it were inevitable that, if I should live, I would be further polluted; and, further, because the guilt contracted by sin after baptism would be still greater and more perilous." [18] This approach to baptism would have fit Constantine's case since he undoubtedly understood that many of his actions were considered grave sins by the Church: "It was common at this time (and continued so until about A.D. 400) to postpone baptism to the end of one's life, especially if one's duty as an official included torture and execution of criminals. Part of the reason for postponement lay in the seriousness with which the responsibilities were taken." [19]

Constantine did see Christianity as a unifying force—and he was correct in his assessment that Christianity, not paganism, had the moral core and theological vision to change society for the better. He may not have been a saint, but neither was he simply a political operator without concern for truth and goodness. Will Durant, hardly partial to the Catholic Church, writes, "His Christianity, beginning as policy, appears to have graduated into sincere conviction. He became the most persistent preacher in his realm, persecuted heretics faithfully, and took God into partnership at every step. Wiser than Diocletian, he gave new life to an aging

---

[17] See Jones, *Constantine and the Conversion of Europe*, 195–200.
[18] Augustine of Hippo, *Confessions*, bk. 1, chap. 10.17.
[19] Chadwick, *Early Church*, 127.

Empire by associating it with a young religion, a vigorous organization, a fresh morality."[20] Constantine was not a lifelong pagan or a cynical manipulator, as *The Da Vinci Code* suggests. "[Dan] Brown has turned him into a cartoonish villain", states Dr. Mitchell. "That Constantine the emperor had 'political' motives (*The Da Vinci Code*, p. 234) is hardly news to anyone! The question is how religion and politics (which cannot be separated in the ancient world) were interrelated in him."[21] The "answers" that Brown gives to that question are less than satisfying as we shall see in his explanation of how Constantine supposedly "created" a "hybrid religion" of paganism and Christianity.

Pagan Roots or Modern Myths?

Brown is especially adamant that Constantine was at the heart of the move from "matriarchal paganism to patriarchal Christianity" by "waging a campaign of propaganda that demonized the sacred feminine, obliterating the goddess from modern religion forever" (124). This is puzzling, since his novel also states that all of the pagans of the time were sunworshippers, or worshippers of a male deity, *Sol Invictus* (232). Also clouding the matter is that paganism is presented

[20] Will Durant, *Caesar and Christ: The Story of Civilization*, pt. 3 (New York: Simon and Schuster, 1944), 664. Elaine Pagels echoes Durant in her recent best seller, *Beyond Belief*, stating that "the simplistic view often expressed by historians in the past—namely, that catholic Christianity prevailed only because it received imperial patronage, or that people participated because their leaders somehow succeeded in coercing them" cannot be supported. Constantine did not "simply use Christianity for cynical purposes. We do not know his motives, but his actions suggest that he believed he had found in Christ an all-powerful divine patron and the promise of eternal life; and during the thirty years he ruled after that, he legislated, to the extent he considered practical, the moral values he found in biblical sources" (*Beyond Belief: The Secret Gospel of Thomas* [New York: Random House, 2003], 179–80).

[21] Mitchell, "An Expert Opinion".

throughout *The Da Vinci Code* as a monolithic body, a unified phenomenon of pre-Christian beliefs. Early in the novel Langdon tells Fache, the French policeman, "Nowadays, the term *pagan* had become almost synonymous with devil worship—a gross misconception" (36). However dubious that might be, Brown's blanket statements about what "the ancients" or the "pagans" (36–37, 238) believed are even more misleading, since there were numerous pagan religions in the ancient world. "'Pagan' was a term of colloquial usage whose first written record can be found in Christian inscriptions from the fourth century", notes Karen King. "There pagan referred to persons who had not been baptized, in short, to non-Christians. Classical historians invented the derivative, 'paganism,' primarily to describe the cultic aspects of ancient Mediterranean religious practices. The term covers a wide geographical area and an enormous diversity of beliefs, practices, and material goods (temples, cultic implements, statuary, and so forth). If anything, paganism encompasses phenomena much more varied than either Judaism or Christianity."[22]

Responding directly to Brown's depiction of ancient paganism, Margaret Mitchell writes: "'Pagan' is just the Christian term for 'not-Christian.' The religions of the Mediterranean world were multiple and diverse, and cannot be all boiled down to 'sun-worshippers' (232)."[23] She refers here to Teabing's claim that Constantine was able to convert "sun-worshipping pagans to Christianity". This was supposedly accomplished by cleverly mixing paganism and Christianity into a "hybrid religion" that appealed to both groups (232). However, this remark actually contradicts an earlier state-

[22] Karen L. King, *What Is Gnosticism?* (Cambridge, Mass.: Belknap Press of Harvard University Press, 2003), 48.
[23] Mitchell, "An Expert Opinion".

ment by Langdon—even though the two men apparently agree on these issues. While at the Louvre at the beginning of the novel, Langdon had told Fache that "the Vatican" had worked to destroy pagan religions. This was accomplished, Langdon said, with "a smear campaign" against pagan deities, "recasting their divine symbols as evil. . . . In the battle between the pagan symbols and Christian symbols, the pagans lost" (37). So, according to Teabing, the Church allowed Constantine to take pagan symbols and create a "hybrid religion" (232). But according to Langdon, the Church never considered such a concession; rather, she sought to eliminate by force all vestiges of pagan worship and belief.

Neither account comes close to doing justice to the complex and difficult relationship that Christianity had with the many varieties of paganism that existed in the third and fourth centuries. One thing is evident: the early Christians had proven that they were not willing to compromise with paganism, which is why so many of them were persecuted and killed by the Romans at various times in the first three centuries of the Church's history. Why would Christians who had suffered just a few years earlier under Diocletian for refusing to renounce their unique beliefs about God, Jesus, and salvation willingly compromise those same beliefs without so much as a whimper?

Brown is following the popular, but long discredited, argument developed in the late nineteenth century by rationalists (most of them antagonistic to Christianity) attempting to undermine the historical claims of Christianity. As Ronald Nash explains, "During a period of time running roughly from about 1890 to 1940, scholars often alleged that primitive Christianity had been heavily influenced by Platonism, Stoicism, the pagan mystery religions, or other movements in the Hellenistic world." A number of scholarly books and papers were written rebutting those claims, and today, Nash notes, "most Bible scholars regard the question as a dead issue." [24]

Secondly, the depiction of a "hybrid religion" that mixed together Christian and pagan elements misrepresents how Christians took certain symbols and feast days and Christianized them—cleansing them of those elements not compatible with their doctrines and practices but keeping what could be used for good ends. It also fails to acknowledge the actual sources for Christian beliefs such as the Virgin Birth, the deity of Christ, and the Passion and Resurrection. As we shall see, these beliefs are rooted in historical claims, not mythological stories, and most—if not all—predate those pagan ideas that appear, at least superficially, to have similar features.

The Da Vinci Code drags out several of the standard lines— many again taken nearly verbatim from *Holy Blood, Holy Grail*[25]—about how everything in Christianity was taken from pagan sources. Langdon describes this as "transmogrification" and provides the following examples of this alleged process (232):

1. Catholic halos coming from "Egyptian sun disks".
2. Pictograms of the Egyptian goddess Isis nursing her son Horus are transformed into images of Mary nursing the baby Jesus.
3. Catholic elements such as "the miter, the altar, the doxology, and communion, the act of 'God-eating'" all come from earlier pagan mystery religions.

Teabing adds:

4. Jesus is based on the pre-Christian pagan god Mithras, who was called "Son of God" and "Light of the World", was born on December 25, died and was

---

[24] Ronald H. Nash, *The Gospel and the Greeks: Did the New Testament Borrow from Pagan Thought?* 2nd ed. (Phillipsburg, N.J.: P and R Press, 2003), 1.

[25] See Baigent, Leigh, and Lincoln, *Holy Blood, Holy Grail*, 367–68.

buried "in a rock tomb, and then resurrected in three days".

5. December 25 is also the birthday of the pagan deities "Osiris, Adonis, and Dionysus".

6. The Hindu deified hero Krishna was given gifts of "gold, frankincense, and myrrh" shortly after birth.

7. Sunday was "stolen from the pagans".

Unfortunately for Brown and the authors of *Holy Blood, Holy Grail*, there is little or no evidence that most pagan mystery religions such as the Egyptian cult of Isis and Osiris or the cult of Mithras existed in the forms described in their books *prior to the mid-first century*. This is a significant point, for much of the existing evidence indicates that the third- and fourth-century beliefs and practices of certain pagan mystery religions are read back into the first-century beliefs of Christians—without support for such a presumptive act. It is not until at least the second century, if not the third century A.D., that there is sufficient source materials to reconstruct a reliable semblance of the pagan mystery religions. "Far too many writers use this late source material (after A.D. 200) to form reconstructions of the third-century mystery experience and then uncritically reason back to what they think must have been the earlier nature of the cults", writes Ronald Nash. "Information about a cult that comes several hundred years after the close of the New Testament canon must not be read back into what is presumed to be the status of the cult during the first century A.D. The crucial question is not what possible influence the mysteries may have had on segments of Christendom after A.D. 400, but what effect the emerging mysteries may have had on the New Testament in the first century." [26]

[26] Ronald Nash, "Was the New Testament Influenced by Pagan Religions?" *Christian Research Journal*, Winter 1994. Accessed online at www. equip.org.

Rather than Christian borrowing from pagan mystery religions, there is evidence that some of the pagan mystery religions may have taken and incorporated elements of Christian belief in the second and third centuries, especially as the strength and appeal of Christianity became steadily apparent. "It must not be uncritically assumed", states historian Bruce Metzger, "that the Mysteries always influenced Christianity, for it is not only possible but probable that in certain cases, the influence moved in the opposite direction." [27] Unfortunately, many works written on a popular level do make that uncritical assumption and do not consider the possibility that the influence may have traveled *from* Christianity, not to it.

A host of scholars, including Nash, E. O. James, Bruce Metzger, Günter Wagner, and Hugo Rahner point out that the pagan mystery religions were quite different from Christianity in significant ways. Those pagan mystery religions, which flourished in the third and fourth centuries, were based on an annual vegetation cycle; they stressed esoteric (hidden) knowledge; they emphasized emotional ecstasy over doctrine and dogma; and their central goal was mystical experience. They were also very syncretistic, taking elements from other pagan movements and shedding beliefs with little regard for any established teaching or belief system—completely contrary to the apostolic tradition so intensely guarded by Christians. [28] There is a sharp contrast between the mythological character of pagan mystery religions and the historical character of the Gospels and the New Testament writings. "In the nature of the case a most profound difference between Christianity and the Mysteries was involved in the historical

[27] Bruce M. Metzger, *Historical and Literary Studies: Pagan, Jewish, and Christian* (Grand Rapids, Mich.: W. B. Eerdmans, 1968), 11. Accessed online at http://www.frontline-apologetics.com/mystery_religions_early_christianity.htm.

[28] See Nash, *Gospel and the Greeks*, 105–20.

basis of the former and the mythological character of the latter", writes Metzger in his study *Historical and Literary Studies: Pagan, Jewish, and Christian.*

> Unlike the deities of the Mysteries, who were nebulous figures of an imaginary past, the Divine Being whom the Christian worshipped as Lord was known as a real Person on earth only a short time before the earliest documents of the New Testament were written. From the earliest times the Christian creed included the affirmation that Jesus "was crucified under Pontius Pilate." On the other hand, Plutarch thinks it necessary to warn the priestess Clea against believing that "any of these tales [concerning Isis and Osiris] actually happened in the manner in which they are related." [29]

With this in mind, here is a brief examination of some of the pagan religions from which *The Da Vinci Code* claims Constantine and the Church borrowed or stole key beliefs in the fourth century.

The Mithraic Maze

The pagan religion of Mithraism was one of the most important—and intriguing—of the ancient mystery religions. Although there has been much scholarly dispute over the exact origins of the Mithraic religion, it is generally agreed that Mithra was originally a Persian god who was depicted as a bucolic deity who watched over cattle. Mithraism was not introduced to the West and the Mediterranean world until the first century at the earliest, where it "emerged as one of the most striking religious syntheses in antiquity: in the first four centuries of the Christian era it swept across the Roman world, becoming the favoured religion of the Roman legions

[29] Metzger, *Historical and Literary Studies*, 13.

and several Roman emperors." [30] This second form, con-
temporaneous with Christianity, was for men only—it has
"often been described as a type of Roman Freemasonry" [31]
and is commonly called "Roman Mithraism". In the early
third century A.D., this form would result in Mithras being
elevated to the status *Sol Invictus* (Invincible Sun). While scholars distinguish between the earlier Iranian Mithraism and the
later Roman Mithraism, most popular works straining to con-
nect Mithras to Jesus do not.

This failure (intentional or not) to distinguish between
the two usually results in later beliefs being read back into
the earlier, pre-Christian form of Mithraism. But the Mithraic beliefs and practices that Christianity is accused of "steal-
ing" did not come into vogue until the end of the first century
at the earliest, far too late to shape the Gospels and their
depiction of Jesus. Although there are numerous theories
about how Mithraism moved from Persia to Rome and how
it changed along the way, the physical evidence indicates that
"the flowering of [Roman] Mithraism occurred after the close
of the New Testament canon, much too late for it to have
influenced anything that appears in the New Testament.
Moreover, no monuments for the cult can be dated earlier
than A.D. 90–100, and even this dating requires us to make
some exceedingly generous assumptions." [32] David Ulansey
substantiates Nash's assessment:

> The earliest physical remains of the cult date from around
> the end of the first century A.D., and Mithraism reached its
> height of popularity in the third century. In addition to sol-

[30] Yuri Stoyanov, *The Other God: Dualist Religions from Antiquity to the Cathar
Heresy* (New Haven: Yale University Press, 2000), 75.

[31] Ibid., 75.

[32] Nash, "Was the New Testament Influenced?" See Manfred Clauss, *The
Roman Cult of Mithraism: The God and His Mysteries* (New York: Routledge,
2001), 21–32.

diers, the cult's membership included significant numbers of bureaucrats and merchants. Women were excluded. Mithraism declined with the rise to power of Christianity, until the beginning of the fifth century, when Christianity became strong enough to exterminate by force rival religions such as Mithraism.[33]

Mithraism was highly syncretistic, absorbing and borrowing an eclectic range of beliefs and religious ideas. By the time it became popular in the Roman Empire it had changed from a public religion for the many to a mystery religion meant for a few elite. "Ultimately", Yuri Stoyanov writes, "the novel and composite form of Mithra-worship that developed and became widely diffused in the Roman world was virtually a new mystery religion, in which the old Irano-Babylonian core seems to have been refashioned and recast into a Graeco-Roman mould tinged with astrological lore and Platonic speculation." [34]

A central rite of Roman Mithraism was the *taurobolium*— the slaughtering of a bull over the head of an initiate (who was usually in a pit beneath a grate), drenching him in blood. Some have suggested that the apostle Paul's theology of redemption by Christ's blood and his language in Romans 6 of death and resurrection are taken from this bloody pagan rite. But Gunter Wagner, in his book *Pauline Baptism and the Pagan Mysteries*, discounts this theory: "The *taurobolium* in the Attis cult is first attested in the time of Antoninus Pius for A.D. 160. As far as we can see at present it only became a personal consecration at the beginning of the third century A.D. The idea of a rebirth through the instrumentality of the *taurobolium* only emerges in isolated instances towards the

[33] David Ulansey, "The Cosmic Mysteries of Mithras". Accessed online at www.well.com/user/davidu/mithras.html. Ulansey is the author of *The Origins of the Mithraic Mysteries* (New York: Oxford University Press, 1991).

[34] Stoyanov, *Other God*, 77–78.

end of the fourth century A.D.; it is not originally associated with this blood-bath." [35]

Other serious differences exist between the myth of Mithras and the Gospel accounts of Jesus. The Roman Mithras is "born" from a rock; he is called "the rock-born god". "The most common representation of the birth shows Mithras naked," writes Manfred Clauss, "his sole clothing the phrygian cap; and wielding a torch and a dagger." [36] In the Persian legends, he was born of a virgin mother, Anahita (once worshipped as a fertility goddess), who swam in Lake Hamun in the Persian province of Sistan where Zoroaster / Zarathustra had left sperm four hundred years earlier. Christians, of course, believe Jesus is born of a virgin Jewish girl, by the power of the Holy Spirit (see Lk 1:35).

The central feat of Mithras' life on earth was the capturing and killing of a stolen bull at the command of the god Apollo, symbolizing the annual spring renewal of life. While Mithras was subduing the bull, other animals joined in the fray. After Mithras finished his appointed task, he and Apollo quarreled but eventually reconciled and feasted together. [37] The central accomplishments of Jesus' life were his death and Resurrection, which Christians believe were historical events that took place in first-century Palestine—not in a nebulous mythic netherworld.

Mithraism did not originally have a concept of a god who died and was then resurrected. [38] Despite the claims

---

[35] Gunter Wagner, *Pauline Baptism and the Pagan Mysteries* (Edinburgh: Oliver and Boyd, 1963), 266. Quoted by Edwin M. Yamauchi, "Easter: Myth, Hallucination, or History?" *Christianity Today* (March 15 and 29, 1974). Accessed online at http://www.leaderu.com/everystudent/easter/articles/yama.html.

[36] Clauss, *Roman Cult of Mithraism*, 64. See 62–71, "Rock-birth".

[37] Peter Clark, *Zoroastrianism: An Introduction to an Ancient Faith* (Brighton, U.K.: Sussex Academic Press, 1998), 157–58.

[38] Nash, *Gospel and the Greeks*, 136–37. Also, E. O. James, *Comparative Religion* (New York: University Paperbacks, 1961), 246–49.

made in *The Da Vinci Code*, there is no ancient account of Mithras dying, being buried "in a rock tomb, and then resurrected in three days" (232). Reputable scholarship holds that Mithras is born from rock in an underground cavern but not resurrected. That assertion apparently is taken (either directly or from a second-generation source) from Kersey Graves' *The World's Sixteen Crucified Saviors*,[39] a work of pseudo-scholarship and anti-Christian polemics that is so shoddy that many atheists and agnostics disavow it. Graves writes that several pagan deities, including "'Mithra the Mediator' of Persia did, according to their respective histories, rise from the dead after three days' burial."[40] However, Graves provides no documentation, as was his common practice (or non-practice). E. O. James, who was professor of history and philosophy of religion at the University of London, references an ancient work by Pseudo-Dionysius when he notes that "in contrast to the other Graeco-Oriental mystery divinities, the Persian saviour-god [Mithras] did not himself pass through death to life, though by his sacrificial act [killing a bull] he was a life-giver."[41] James later observes that Mithraism—which was a strong adversary of Christianity in the third and fourth centuries—was overcome by Christianity, not by being absorbed, "but because the Church was able to meet its adversary on the sure ground of historical fact". Christianity went far beyond "the ancient seasonal drama with its polytheistic background" and offered initiates a "renewal of spiritual life and regeneration of outlook ... to a degree unknown and unattainable in any rival system. Therefore, Christianity

---

[39] Kersey Graves, *The World's Sixteen Crucified Saviors* (Publisher unknown, 1875). Available online at www.infidels.org.
[40] Ibid., chap. 19.
[41] James, *Comparative Religion*, 247.

ultimately prevailed because it provided a different gift of life from that bestowed in the pagan cults."⁴²

Christmas Gifts, Halos, the Nursing Christ, and Other Details

The story of the Hindu deity Krishna's birth and the presents of gold, frankincense, and myrrh also apparently comes from Graves' *The World's Sixteen Crucified Saviors*. In the seventh chapter of that work, Graves writes:

> Other Saviors at birth, we are told, were visited by both angels and shepherds, also "wise men," at least great men. Chrishna, the eighth avatar of India (1200 B.C.) (so it is related by the "inspired penman" of their pagan theocracy) was visited by angels, shepherds and prophets (avatars). "Immediately after his birth he was visited by a chorus of *devatas* (angels), and surrounded by shepherds, all of whom were impressed with the conviction of his future greatness." We are informed further that "gold, frankincense and myrrh" were presented to him as offerings.⁴³

Again, Graves conveniently provides no sources or citations, which is one of many reasons his book has been long discredited by scholars working in the field of comparative religion. But that does not keep this popular idea from appearing on numerous web sites and in many popular esoteric books, with few (if any) providing sources or citations. There is a good reason for this absence of evidence. The *Bhagavad-Gita* (first century A.D.) does not mention Krishna's childhood, and the stories of Krishna's childhood recorded in the *Hari-vamsa Purana* (ca. A.D. 300) and the *Bhagavata Purana* (ca. A.D. 800–900) do not mention the gifts at all. Even if they did,

---

⁴² Ibid., 248–49.

⁴³ Graves, *World's Sixteen Crucified Saviors*, chap. 7.

those works were written well after the birth of Christ, making such a claim pointless.

The halo, or nimbus, employed in Christian art was used by a number of pre-Christian cultures, including Greek and Roman, to distinguish figures who were gods or demigods.[44] Roman emperors, for example, were depicted on coins with radiant heads. This is a good example of Christianity gradually appropriating a cultural element and using it in a way totally in keeping with Christian theology and belief. For Christians to take over this attribute is about as scandalous as later artists depicting Jesus in the robes of a philosopher or in the clothing of a later age. The use of a halo would have been a natural choice for Christian art since both Moses and Jesus are described in the Bible as having shining faces after significant events. Moses' face radiated light after he came down from Mount Sinai and the presence of God (Ex 34:29–35), and at the Transfiguration, Jesus' "face shone like the sun, and his garments became white as light" (Mt 17:2). The use of halos in Christian iconography is simply a case of Christians recognizing the usefulness of an artistic motif and appropriating it for their specific needs.

Langdon claims that artwork of Isis nursing her son Horus formed "the blueprint for our modern images of the Virgin Mary nursing Baby Jesus" (232). It is a curious statement since any sensible person recognizes that the image of a nursing mother is hardly unique to one religion or culture. Christian artists undoubtedly copied the poses of figures depicted in pagan art, including mothers (or goddesses) nursing children. One of the earlier renderings of Mary is a late second-century or early third-century fresco found on a wall of the

---

[44] F. L. Cross and E. A. Livingstone, eds., *The Oxford Dictionary of the Christian Church* 3rd ed. (New York: Oxford University Press, 1997), 732.

catacombs of Priscilla in Rome[45] mentioned by Pope John Paul II in a general audience on May 23, 1990. The Madonna and Child have been depicted in numerous ways throughout history, often reflecting the culture of the respective painters and sculptors.[46]

The real issue is, not of similarity, but of dissimilarity— recognizing that the differences between Christianity and pagan mystery religions are far greater than any similarities. Take, for instance, the Isis cult of Egypt. The Egyptian goddess Isis was part of a polytheistic fertility cult. After her husband Osiris was assassinated and dismembered, Isis searched and found all the parts of his body and then restored him— not to life on earth, but to life in the underworld, as a "dead god".[47] Originally, Isis was one of several goddesses (Nut, Neith, and so on), and Horus, her son, was one of the eight gods "of the Ennead".[48] Worship of Isis was established in Greece around the fourth century B.C., where she remained a goddess of fertility and became a popular deity whose temples were established in numerous cities. In this Hellenistic form, the Isis cult was a pagan mystery religion in which adherents underwent esoteric, occult rites.[49]

Langdon claims that "the miter, the altar, the doxology, and communion, the act of 'God-eating'" were all borrowed or stolen from pagan mystery religions (232). As we

[45] Andre Grabar, *La Premier Art chrétien* (Éditions Gallimard, 1996), 99, figure 95.

[46] See Caroline Ebertshäuser et al., *Mary: Art, Culture, and Religion through the Ages*, trans. Peter Heinegg (New York: Crossroad, 1998).

[47] See E. O. James, *Cult of the Mother-Goddess* (New York: Barnes and Noble, 1994), 241ff.

[48] Ibid., 57.

[49] Nash, *Gospel and the Greeks*, 126–28. For more on Isis, see "Isis as Saviour Goddess", in *The Savior God: Comparative Studies in the Concept of Salvation*, ed. C. J. Bleeker and S. G. F. Brandon (Manchester, U.K.: Manchester University Press, 1963), 1–16.

have noted, however, the "mystery religions" did not come into existence until the end of the first century at the earliest, making it difficult for Christians to take, borrow, or steal anything from them. The *miter*, or *mitre*, is a word derived from the Greek *mitra*, meaning "turban" or "headband". It is the liturgical headdress and part of the insignia of the bishop.[50] It did not appear in the West until the middle of the tenth century and was not used by bishops in the East until after the fall of Constantinople in 1453. In the East it seems to have been derived from the crowns worn by Byzantine emperors; in the West it appears to have been a variation of the unofficial hat, the *camelaucum*, worn by the pope in processions. In both cases, the mitre has no connections with pagan mystery religions.

Altars are a common element in most religions, and there are over three hundred references to altars in the Old Testament. The first Christians, who were all Jewish, would hardly be new to the concept of an altar, especially when the altar in the Temple was a focal point of the Jewish religion. Not surprisingly, there are several references to altars in the New Testament, including references in the Gospels to the altar in the Temple (Mt 5:23–24; 23:18–20; Lk 1:11) and references in the book of Revelation to the heavenly altar in the throne room of God (Rev 6:9; 8:3–5; 9:13; 11:1; 14:8; 16:7). There is also this passage in the epistle to the Hebrews: "We have an altar from which those who serve the tent have no right to eat" (Heb 13:10). It is likely a reference to the eucharistic table of the Christians, and a similar use of language was common among the early Church Fathers. For example, Ignatius of Antioch, writing to the Church at Philadelphia, states, "Take care, then, to partake of one Eucharist; for, one is the Flesh of Our Lord Jesus Christ, and one the cup to unite us

---

[50] Cross and Livingstone, *Oxford Dictionary of the Christian Church*, 1096.

with His Blood, and one altar, just as there is one bishop assisted by the presbytery and the deacons, my fellow servants. Thus you will conform in all your actions to the will of God." [51] Other references to a Christian altar appear in the writings of Tertullian and Cyprian.

A doxology is simply a hymn or ascription of praise and glory (*doxa* = glory; *logos* = word). Almost all religions have statements about the glory and power of a deity, reflecting the natural human desire to recognize what is sacred and Other. Traditionally, in historic Christianity, there are three types of doxology: the Great Doxology, the Less Doxology, and the Metrical Forms. Langdon is probably referring to the Great Doxology, which has a key place in the first part of the Mass and begins with these statements of praise:

> Glory to God in the highest and on earth peace, good will to men.
> We praise You; we bless You; we worship You; we glorify You; we thank You, for Your great glory.
> O Lord King, God in Heaven, the Father Almighty. O Lord, Only-Begotten Son, Jesus Christ and Holy Spirit.
> O Lord God, Lamb of God, the Son of the Father, Who take away the sin of the world, have mercy on us; You, Who take away the sins of the world;
> Receive our prayers, You, Who sit at the right hand of the Father, and have mercy on us.
> For You alone are Holy; You alone are the Lord, Jesus Christ, to the glory of God, the Father. Amen.

All of this language is taken directly from passages in the New Testament; all of it reflects the unique beliefs of the Christians. Such language did not, of course, come from

[51] Ignatius of Antioch, *Epistle to the Philadelphians*, par. 4.

pagans, who for the most part were polytheistic and did not believe in the Trinity or the divinity of Jesus Christ.

Langdon's reference to "God-eating" is likely an appeal to Mithraism, for it was the only mystery religion that celebrated anything resembling communion;[52] many of the mystery religions, such as the Orphic cult, had no sacred meal at all. However, the "offering of bread and wine is known in virtually all ancient cultures," states Clauss, "and the meal as a means of binding the faithful together and uniting them to the deity was a feature common to many religions."[53] But did these actions mean the same things to Christians and followers of Mithras? In his work on comparative religion, E. O. James writes that the Christian's sacramental understanding differed from that of the pagan mystery religions in several significant respects: "So far as we know, initiates in those cults were neither baptized into the name of the saviour-god or goddess, nor were they the recipients of a pneumatic gift as a result of lustration." James goes on to note that the Christian Eucharist was strongly connected to a life of holiness and purity, while "normally in a Mystery cult initiation was an end itself irrespective of any ethical considerations."[54] Metzger also emphasizes this point, noting that pagan sacraments, although oriented toward the hereafter, operated with "no effective change of the moral self for the purposes of living",[55] an approach at odds with the Christian understanding of the sacraments.

In the myth of Mithras, the god does not even die but is a savior-god by virtue of killing a bull; initiates into the Mithraic cult would dramatize this mythical event, and the blood

---

[52] See Nash, *Gospel and the Greeks*, 148–49.

[53] Clauss, *Roman Cult of Mithraism*, 108.

[54] James, *Comparative Religion*, 239.

[55] Metzger, *Historical and Literary Studies*, 14. Here Metzger quotes from A. D. Nock, "Mystery", *Encyclopedia of the Social Sciences* (1937), 11:274.

of a slain bull would be ceremoniously poured over initiates. At the higher stages of the cult, members participated in a sacred meal of bread and water (or wine, a detail that is still being debated); there is no indication that those participating believed they were engaging in "God-eating". Little is known of that meal, so a fuller comparison with Christian communion is difficult to make. Regardless, the Jewish character and context of the Passover meal, the Last Supper, and the Christian Eucharist are the essential elements that shape the Christian sacrament and ritual—not pagan rites. "[O]n almost any view of this matter," Metzger writes, "the Jewishness of the setting, character, and piety expressed in the rite is overwhelmingly pervasive in all the accounts of the origin of the Supper." [56] The fullness of this Jewish character is described by Jean Daniélou in his important study *The Bible and the Liturgy*. "The Eucharist is the fulfillment of the meal of Jewish worship; It signifies, then, as did these [Jewish communal] meals, participation in the blessings of the Covenant...." Daniélou explains, "In fact, the meal in the course of which Christ instituted the Eucharist seems to have been a ritual meal, a *chaboura*, such as was customarily celebrated by the Jewish communities.... It was, then, in this framework of a sacred Jewish meal that Christ instituted the meal of the New Covenant, as it was in the framework of the Jewish commemoration of the Pasch that He died on the Cross." [57]

Sunday and Christmas Day

Was Sunday "stolen from the pagans" as Teabing states (232)? And what about Langdon's statement that Constantine moved

[56] Metzger, *Historical and Literary Studies*, 16.

[57] Jean Daniélou, S.J., *The Bible and the Liturgy* (Notre Dame, Ind.: University of Notre Dame Press, 1956), 160; see 142–90.

the Christian day of worship from Saturday—the Jewish Sabbath—to Sunday "to coincide with the pagan's veneration day of the sun"? How to respond to his gleeful remark that Christians in church on Sunday morning have "no idea that they are there on account of the pagan sun god's weekly tribute—*Sunday*" (232–33)?

The implication of Teabing and Langdon's remarks is that for over two hundred years, until the time of Constantine, the Christians worshipped on Saturday. Not so. Christians of the New Testament era were already worshipping on Sunday, or the "Lord's day", as it is described in Revelation 1:10. This was to honor the day that Jesus rose from the dead; having been crucified on a Friday, Jesus rose from the dead on the third day (see Mk 16:2)—the day after the Sabbath, or Sunday.[58] This practice is referred to in Acts 20:7: "On the first day of the week, when we were gathered together to break bread, Paul talked with them, intending to depart on the morrow; and he prolonged his speech until midnight." The apostle Paul mentions in his First Letter to the Corinthians (1 Cor 16:2) that tithes and offering should be set aside on the first day of the week, another indication that the early Christians viewed the day after the Jewish Sabbath as the most important day of the week.

There are numerous references by the early Church Fathers to Christians worshipping on "the day of the Lord" (or *Dies Domini*, as it came to be known in the West). Ignatius of Antioch writes around A.D. 110, "How, then, shall we be able to live apart from Him, seeing that the prophets were His disciples in the Spirit and expected Him as their Master, and that many who were brought up in the old order have come to the newness of hope? They no longer observe the

---

[58] Sabbath was the only day of the week named by Jews; the other days were simply numbered: "first day", "second day", etc.

Jewish Sabbaths, but keep holy the Lord's day, on which, through Him and through His death, our life arose." [59] The *Epistle of Barnabas*, which was probably written before the end of the first century, states, "This is why we also observe the eighth day with rejoicing, on which Jesus also rose from the dead, and having shown himself ascended to heaven." [60] There are many references to the "eighth day" in the writings of the Church Fathers, as Daniélou details in *The Bible and the Liturgy*.[61] Daniélou also flatly states that "the Lord's Day is a purely Christian institution; its origin is to be found solely in the fact of the Resurrection of Christ on the day after the Sabbath." [62] Another early, non-canonical reference to the Lord's Day is found in *The Didache*: "And on the Lord's Day, after you have come together, break bread and offer the Eucharist, having first confessed your offences, so that your sacrifice may be pure." [63] Justin Martyr, writing in the middle of the second century, makes the first known reference by a Christian author to "Sunday"; all prior references had been to the "day of the Lord".

Brown apparently thinks—mistakenly so—that since the observance of Sunday as a day of rest was not sanctioned by civil authorities until the fourth century then it must not have been observed prior to that time. But over one hundred years earlier, around A.D. 200, Tertullian writes about Sunday as a day of rest: "We, however (just as tradition has taught us), on the day of the Lord's Resurrection ought to guard not only against ... every posture and office of solicitude, deferring even our businesses lest we give any place to

[59] Ignatius of Antioch, *Epistle to the Magnesians*, chap. 9.

[60] *Epistle of Barnabas*, chap. 15.

[61] See Daniélou, *Bible and the Liturgy*, chap. 15, "The Lord's Day" (242–61), and chap. 16, "The Eighth Day" (262–86).

[62] Daniélou, *Bible and the Liturgy*, 242.

[63] *The Didache* 14.1.

the devil."[64] The Council of Elvira, a local Spanish council that convened around A.D. 303, decreed that Sunday was to be a special day of worship and rest, stating, "If anyone in the city neglects to come to church for three Sundays, let him be excommunicated for a short time so that he may be corrected."[65] Two decades later, in 321, Constantine officially declared Sunday a day of rest in the Roman Empire, "commanding abstention from work, including legal business, for townspeople, though permitting farm labour".[66] Since Christians considered Jesus to be the "Sun of Righteousness" (see Mal 4:2) and "the light of the world" (Jn 8:12; 9:5), they thought it fitting that the true God would supersede the old Roman Sun-god. St. Jerome (ca. 345–420) wrote, "The Lord's day, the day of Resurrection, the day of Christians, is our day. It is called the Lord's day because on it the Lord rose victorious to the Father. If pagans call it the 'day of the sun,' we willingly agree, for today the light of the world is raised, today is revealed the sun of justice with healing in his rays."[67]

Did Christians take December 25, the "birthday of Osiris, Adonis, and Dionysus" (232), and use it for their celebration of the birth of Jesus? Most Christian scholars have essentially agreed with this statement and have argued that the Christians appropriated this important pagan holy day as a way of showing the superiority of the true God-man, Jesus. And if that is the case, it simply tells us that the early Christians saw a chance to make a statement about Jesus and his divinity by

[64] Tertullian, *De orat.* 23; cf. *Ad nation.* I, 13; *Apolog.* 16.

[65] Council of Elvira, canon 21.

[66] Cross and Livingstone, *Oxford Dictionary of the Christian Church,* 1558.

[67] St. Jerome, *Pasch.,* CCL 78, 550. *Catechism of the Catholic Church* (CCC), 2nd ed. (Washington, D.C.: United States Catholic Conference—Libreria Editrice Vaticana, 1997), no. 1166.

taking an important day from the pagan calendar and using it to celebrate his birth.

However, some have argued that December 25 was not taken from pagans by Christians, but vice versa. In an article in *Touchstone* magazine titled "Calculating Christmas",[68] William J. Tighe, associate professor of history at Muhlenberg College, argues that the belief that December 25 was taken from pagans by Christians goes back to two scholars living in the late seventeenth and early eighteenth centuries, Paul Ernst Jablonski and Dom Jean Hardouin. Jablonski was a German Protestant who "wished to show that the celebration of Christ's birth on December 25th was one of the many 'paganizations' of Christianity that the Church of the fourth century embraced, as one of many 'degenerations' that transformed pure apostolic Christianity into Catholicism." Hardouin was a Benedictine monk who sought to demonstrate that the Catholic Church adopted pagan festivals without paganizing the gospel. Tighe points out that none of the Roman cults had major celebrations on December 25. It was Emperor Aurelian (A.D. 270–275) who "appears to have promoted the establishment of the festival of the 'Birth of the Unconquered Sun' as a device to unify the various pagan cults of the Roman Empire around a commemoration of the annual 'rebirth' of the sun." By creating the new feast, Aurelian hoped that "the beginning of the lengthening of the daylight, and the arresting of the lengthening of darkness, on December 25th to be a symbol of the hoped-for 'rebirth,' or perpetual rejuvenation, of the Roman Empire, resulting from the maintenance of the worship of the gods whose tutelage (the Romans thought) had brought Rome to greatness and world-rule."

---

[68] William J. Tighe, "Calculating Christmas", *Touchstone*, December 2003. Accessed online at www.touchstonemag.com.

Once Christianity had separated from Judaism (especially after the destruction of the Temple in Jerusalem in A.D. 70) and emerged as a unique religion, it sought to calculate the exact day of Jesus' death. There was much confusion due to different calendars; after much debate and difficulty, the Eastern Christians chose April 6 and the Western Christians chose March 25 as the date of Jesus' crucifixion. At this point the ancient and obscure notion of an "integral age" comes into play; this was the belief that the Old Testament prophets died on the same date of either their birth or conception. Most Christians accepted April 6 or March 25 as the date of Jesus' conception, thus arriving at January 6 (in the East) and December 25 (in the West) as the date of his birth. Although these dates would not be made "official" until the late fourth century, they were held long before both Aurelian and Constantine.

Tighe argues that the pagan feast instituted by Emperor Aurelian on December 25, 274, was an attempt to use the winter solstice to make a political statement, "but also almost certainly an attempt to give a pagan significance to a date already of importance to Roman Christians. The Christians, in turn, could at a later date re-appropriate the pagan 'Birth of the Unconquered Sun' to refer, on the occasion of the birth of Christ, to the rising of the 'Sun of Salvation' or the 'Sun of Justice.' " [69] Although Tighe's thesis is still relatively new, it offers more compelling evidence that the early Christians were not nearly as reliant upon pagan feast days as has often been assumed.

The Biased Pagan-Christian Connection

Nash presents several arguments against Christian dependence on pagan mystery religions; together they constitute a

[69] Ibid. Also see "The Christian Mystery of Sun and Moon", in Hugo Rahner, S.J., *Greek Myths and Christian Mystery* (London: Burns and Oates, 1957), 89–176.

strong rebuttal to the belief, taken up in *The Da Vinci Code*, that Christianity is essentially an imitation of older, pagan belief systems.[70]

1. Coincidence does not prove causal connection, and similarity does not prove dependence. It should not surprise anyone that there would be some general similarities between ancient pagan religions and Christianity. "An aptitude for religion is a human datuum", notes Jean Daniélou, acclaimed for his studies of ancient pagan, Jewish, and Christian beliefs.[71] Man is a religious creature; he is also a limited creature, with only so many options for the physical expression of his beliefs. "Man actually has at his disposal only a limited number of ideas, ritual forms, and religious images", writes Louis Bouyer in his study of natural religion and Christianity. "That they are found perceptibly the same in religions that are near to one another in time and space should not deceive us; they are also found the same in religions between which it would be fantastic to postulate any historical connection. But what is essential to each is not in this material but in the way it is arranged." [72]

A look at various religions indicates this is so. They share many outward elements: sacred spaces and building, sacred books, sacred rites and practices, individual and communal acts of worship, rituals, holy days, hierarchy, structures of authority, and individuals who are recognized for unique talents or acts. For example: Islam, Mormonism, and ancient Greek paganism all have these elements. Yet they hold to very different views of God, salvation, and so on. General

---

[70] Nash, "Was the New Testament Influenced?"

[71] Jean Daniélou, S.J., *God and the Ways of Knowing* (reprt., San Francisco: Ignatius Press, 2003), 10.

[72] Louis Bouyer, *Rite and Man: Natural Sacredness and Christian Liturgy* (Notre Dame, Ind.: University of Notre Dame Press, 1963), 36.

similarities between certain pagan mystery religions and Christianity may or may not be significant; the real issues are the focus, theology, and purpose of those religions.

Unfortunately, books such as *The Da Vinci Code* take the approach of throwing together a convenient mixture of religions (that is, sun-worshipping paganism; Mithraism; the cults of Isis, Osiris, Adonis, and Dionysus; and Hinduism's Krishna) that contain some parallels and similarities and then declare: "See the similarities? Obviously Christianity is derived directly from paganism." Usually ignored is that for every general similarity (for instance, Mithras born of a virgin) there are serious differences (the virgin became pregnant by swimming in water containing four-hundred-year-old sperm).

2. **Describing pagan rituals in Christian verbiage is misleading and careless and leads to faulty conclusions.** This commonly occurs in the case of Christian baptism and the Eucharist, which some writers claim were derived directly from the esoteric rites of pagan mystery religions. One problem is that those religions came into existence much too late to influence the beliefs of first-century Christians. Another is that the pagan rites were focused on emotion and magic, not on historical fact and the objective work of God through physical sacraments. Another serious problem is that these claims ignore the obvious and very important Jewish character of the Christian sacraments, rooted in both the events of Jesus' life and the Old Testament context of worship and sacrifice.

3. **The dates do not add up.** The mystery religions that supposedly influenced Christianity often do not have physical evidence for existing prior to the second century. This is the consistent finding of reputable scholars in the fields of comparative religion and archaeology.

4. **Paul, who was raised as a devout Jew and had one of the great rabbis as a teacher, would not have borrowed from mystery religions.** "He would have known something", Fr. Raymond E. Brown notes in *An Introduction to the New Testament*, "about the religion of the Gentiles among whom he lived, e.g., have had some awareness, probably prejudiced and unsympathetic, of Pagan myths and Greco-Roman civic religions. [But] the idea that he borrowed many ideas from the mystery religions is overdone."[73] Albert Schweitzer stated, "Paulinism and Hellenism have in common their religious terminology, but, in respect of ideas, nothing. The Apostle did not Hellenize Christianity. His conceptions are equally distinct from those of Greek philosophy and from those of the Mystery-Religions."[74]

5. **Early Christianity was exclusive in nature.** One reason the early Christians were persecuted so harshly by the Romans was their exclusive claims for Jesus. For the most part, Rome was willing to accommodate a variety of religious beliefs, as long as they took a syncretistic approach to other religions and paid special favor to the cult of the emperor. The Christians refused, insisting that Jesus, not the emperor, was God. As A. H. M. Jones notes, Christianity

> had one great difference from the other cults. Its adherents refused to worship the other gods, and even abhorred them as demons. Hence they tended to be exclusive and clannish. They would not attend public festivals or athletic sports or theatrical shows.... They avoided joining the army, either because they might, in the course of their military duties, have to attend pagan worship, or because as soldiers of the

[73] Raymond Brown, *An Introduction to the New Testament* (New York: Doubleday, 1996), 425.

[74] Albert Schweitzer, *Paul and His Interpreters*, 238. Quoted by Nash, *Gospel and the Greeks*, 172.

Lord they could not give their allegiance to a power which they sometimes equated with the Prince of Darkness.[75]

For this reason, Jones explains, the Christians were disliked by pagans and accused of bizarre activities at their liturgies and gatherings. It is also why the Roman government eventually persecuted and killed large numbers of the early Christians.

6. **The Christian faith taught by Paul was grounded in real, historical events, not mythic or allegorical stories without historical basis.** The pagan myths were not meant to be historical narratives; rather, they were dramatic renderings of what initiates into a mystery religion supposedly went through in their initiation. Those stories, as we have seen in several cases, would often change—even dramatically so—as elements were set aside and others were taken from other religions. The historical claims of Christianity about the person of Jesus of Nazareth are based on historical narratives (the Gospels and the Acts of the Apostles), the witness of the early Church, and an increasing amount of archaeological and scholarly evidence. The historically verifiable nature of Christianity indicates that it could not have been taken whole cloth or even partially from pagan myths.

7. **Parallels that do exist may reflect the influence of Christian beliefs on pagan systems—not vice versa.** This option is usually not considered by opponents of Christianity; it is assumed that the Christian-pagan relationship was a one-way street. There is no doubt that early Christians, who lived in a pagan culture, were influenced by paganism and sometimes used the same terms and motifs as their pagan neighbors in describing their beliefs. But the success of the Christian faith was impossible for pagans to ignore, and some of them

---

[75] Jones, *Constantine and the Conversion of Europe*, 43–44.

sought to borrow Christian ideas, or at least terminology, in their rituals and practices. In responding to claims that pagan beliefs were a basis for Christian belief, as found in *The Da Vinci Code*, Dr. Margaret Mitchell writes:

> It is absolutely true that "The vestiges of pagan religion in Christian symbology are undeniable" (p. 232). But the conclusion drawn from that—"Nothing in Christianity is original"—is not, and, from the point of view of the history of religions, [is] an old, long-disqualified claim. . . . Current scholarship recognizes that the relationship between the Christian cult and the world around it, and the ways in which it was culturally embedded in that world—sometimes unreflectively, sometimes reflexively, sometimes in deliberate accommodation, sometimes in deliberate cooptation—are far more complicated than noted here.[76]

The Emperor and the Council and Heresy

The historian Leigh Teabing, lecturing to Langdon and Sophie, claims that it was at the Council of Nicaea that Jesus was first declared divine (233). A full history and background to the Council of Nicaea, which convened in A.D. 325, is impossible here; there are several popular and scholarly works that provide that information.[77] But a brief over-

---

[76] Mitchell, "An Expert Opinion". Mitchell also states: "Conspiracy theories sell books, but they do not explain complex human phenomena which are both local and more wide-spread—and hardly could have been instituted as a wide-spread, Stalinesque program of cultural totalitarianism as Brown has conjured up for Constantine."

[77] See Msgr. J. D. Conway, *Times of Decision: Story of the Councils* (Notre Dame, Ind.: Fides, 1962); Hughes, *Church in Crisis*; John Henry Cardinal Newman, *The Arians of the Fourth Century* (repr., Eugene, Ore.: Wipf and Stock, 1996); Basil Struder, *Trinity and Incarnation: The Faith of the Early Church* (Collegeville, Minn.: Liturgical Press, 1993); Kenneth D. Whitehead, *One, Holy, Catholic, and Apostolic: The Early Church Was the Catholic Church* (San Francisco: Ignatius Press, 2000).

view of the basic facts will show that the claims made in *The Da Vinci Code* are wide of the mark on a number of counts.

The Council of Nicaea was the first ecumenical council of the Church, made possible by the patronage of Constantine and his desire to end the disunity and controversy being caused by the Arian heresy. Arius (b. ca. 260–280; d. 336) was a priest from Alexandria who was noted for his preaching and ascetic life-style. Around 319 or so he began to gain attention for his teaching that Jesus was not fully divine but was less than the Father. Arius held that the Son had not existed for all of eternity past but was a created being who was begotten by the Father as an instrument of, first, creation and then, later, salvation. Put another way, Arius believed that Jesus, the Son of God, was not God by nature but was a lesser god.

This belief was condemned by the bishop Alexander at a local synod held in Alexandria around 320, with ninety-eight of a hundred bishops voting against Arius' views. But the priest's teachings attracted interest and were spreading quickly, partially due to his clever use of catchy songs proclaiming his doctrinal beliefs and also due to the patronage of Eusebius, the bishop of Caesarea and one of the greatest scholars of his time. Arius' beliefs were proving so popular and disruptive that Constantine decided to bring together the bishops and put an end to the controversy; his primary interest was most likely in unity rather than in precise theological clarity, but he realized the former would depend in large part upon the latter.

On May 20, 325, a number of bishops, the vast majority of them from the East, convened at Nicaea (modern day Iznik, north of Constantinople); the Council lasted until July 25 of the same year. The number of bishops in attendance has traditionally been listed as 318, likely a symbolic number; the

actual number was probably around 220 to 250.[78] Due to poor
health, the pope did not attend but sent two deacons to represent him. "The great bulk of the Council came from the
Greek-speaking provinces of the empire . . .", writes A. H. M.
Jones. "The bulk of the gathering were simple pastors, who
would naturally resent any innovation on the faith which they
had learned and would have little sympathy with the intellectual paradoxes of Arius. Many could boast of the proud title of
confessor, having endured imprisonment, torture, and penal
servitude for the sake of their faith."[79] This rugged and tried
character of most of the bishops is completely contrary to *The
Da Vinci Code*'s implication that the bishops meekly accepted
whatever the emperor told them (233). Many of the bishops
at Nicaea were veterans of the persecution of Diocletian. Is it
reasonable to think that they would quietly allow Constantine to change the faith for which they had already suffered and
were willing to die? Constantine, while actively involved in the
Council, knew that his place was, not to be a theologian or
scholar, but to help facilitate as structured and productive a
gathering as possible. After all, one of the strengths of Roman
culture was organization; the Greeks, on the other hand, were
more attuned to theological nuance and detail.

In *The Da Vinci Code*, Teabing states that at the Council of
Nicaea Jesus was established as "the Son of God" (233). This
false statement is taken from *Holy Blood, Holy Grail*, which
states, "Most important of all, the Council of Nicaea decided,
by vote, that Jesus was a god, not a mortal prophet."[80] As

---

[78] "The traditional number, which goes back to a late writing of Athanasius (*Ep. ad Afros*, 2) is 318, probably a symbolic figure based on the number of
Abraham's servants (Gen 14:14)." Cross and Livingstone, *Oxford Dictionary of
the Christian Church*, 1144.

[79] Jones, *Constantine and the Conversion of Europe*, 131.

[80] Baigent, Leigh, and Lincoln, *Holy Blood, Holy Grail*, 368. The irony is
that Arius believed that Jesus was a god, but not equal to God.

already noted, the Gospels alone refer to Jesus as the "Son of God" twenty-five times. The term occurs over forty times in the New Testament, and this description is used often by the early Church Fathers. However, in Jesus' time the term "Son of God" did not refer to a divine person; it was a messianic title that "referred to the king as Israel's representative".[81] As time went on and the early Christians recognized the divinity of Jesus, the title naturally took on a deeper meaning—a meaning that the Council of Nicaea would ratify, clearly and definitively, as the consistent belief of the Church. As we have already seen, the belief in Jesus' divinity and Godhead goes back to the earliest days of Christianity. The Council of Nicaea focused on clarifying the unique relationship between the Father and the Son and condemning those ideas of Arius that would imply, or assert outright, that the Son was less than the Father, was a created being, and was a lesser god. The *Catechism of the Catholic Church* ably summarizes the basic issue: "The first ecumenical council of Nicaea in 325 confessed in its Creed that the Son of God is 'begotten, not made, of the same substance (*homoousios*) as the Father,' and condemned Arius, who had affirmed that the Son of God 'came to be from things that were not' and that he was 'from another substance' than that of the Father."[82]

As for the "relatively close vote", it is a figment of Teabing's and Brown's imagination. Only two bishops out of

---

[81] N. T Wright, *Jesus and the Victory of God* (Minneapolis, Minn.: Fortress Press, 1996), 486. Karl Adam writes that during the time of Jesus "popular devotion gave to the awaited Christ (the Messias) the additional name of Son of God—but in a theocratic, not a metaphysical, sense. This theocratic understanding included the idea of particular endowment with Grace by God, but excluded the essential divinity of Christ" (*The Christ of Faith: The Christology of the Church* [New York: Pantheon Books, 1957], 124).

[82] CCC 465.

some 220 to 250 voted in favor of Arius' position—over 99 percent of the bishops upheld the belief that the Son was equal with the Father and of the same substance. Even *Holy Blood, Holy Grail*, which apparently provided much of Brown's material for his comments on this topic, gets it right, acknowledging in a terse footnote: "218 for, 2 against." [83] Once again, Brown's embellished version of the facts is not only incorrect, it is completely contrary to the truth.

Teabing also states that at the Council there were "many aspects of Christianity" that were "debated and voted upon". The wording implies that these "aspects" were somehow new and unique; they are listed as "the date of Easter, the role of the bishops, the administration of sacraments, and, of course, the *divinity* of Jesus" (233).[84] The twenty canons—or laws— of the Council were actually rather mundane and were, "in great part, a repetition of measures enacted eleven years earlier in the Latin council held at Arles, in Gaul".[85] Five of the canons addressed the sensitive subject of those Christians who had fallen away from the Church during the recent persecutions, providing guidelines for penance, readmission to Holy Communion, and other directives. Two other canons dealt with the readmission of heretical schismatics: the Novatians and the followers of Paul of Samosata, the former bishop of Antioch who had been deposed in 268 for criminal actions and teaching heresy. Some ten canons addressed issues having to do with the clergy: "No one is to be ordained who has had himself castrated, nor anyone only recently admitted to the faith.... No clerics—bishops, priests, or deacons—

---

[83] Baigent, Leigh, and Lincoln, *Holy Blood, Holy Grail*, 473. It also adds, "The Son was then pronounced identical with the Father" (473). Not quite— the Son was pronounced "one in substance"; he is a separate Person from the Persons of the Father and the Holy Spirit.

[84] Compare to ibid., 368.

[85] Hughes, *Church in Crisis*, 36.

are to move from one diocese to another. Clerics are forbidden to take interest for money loans, and for this offence they must be deposed."[86] Other canons involved matters of jurisdiction pertaining to the three most famous sees of the ancient Church: Alexandria, Antioch, and Jerusalem.

The issue of Easter and its dating was quite complicated—it was addressed at the Council because of the emperor's desire for unity in important matters of religious observance. At the time, churches in different regions celebrated Easter on different days; the confusion was partially the result of the lunar calendar of the Jews and of the antagonism of some Christians toward the Jews—they refused to celebrate Easter on the same day as the Jewish Passover. The Council sought to enforce a uniform date, but the results were mixed, and the controversy would continue on for many centuries. In this instance, and in the instances of the canons, there were no issues of dogma addressed; all were matters of discipline, made necessary by the real life issues and concrete pastoral problems faced by the Church in the midst of confusion, rapidly changing conditions, and cultural shifts.

Constantine and the New Testament Canon

Not content to misrepresent Constantine's attitude toward Christianity and actual role at the Council of Nicaea, Brown also makes a number of unsubstantiated and outrageous claims about the emperor's role in the formation of the New Testament canon. These claims include the following:

1. At the time of Constantine, "thousands of documents" depicting Jesus' life as a "*mortal* man" were in existence (234).

[86] Ibid., 38.

2. Constantine rewrote history in order to deify Jesus, and he "upgraded" his status (234).

3. Constantine commissioned and financed a "new Bible" that left out "those gospels that spoke of Christ's *human* traits and embellished those gospels that made him godlike" (234).

4. "More than *eighty* gospels were considered for the New Testament", but only four were chosen, supposedly because they presented a more "godlike" Jesus (231).

5. This Bible "was collated by the pagan Roman emperor Constantine the Great" (231).

6. Hundreds, if not thousands, of other "earlier gospels were outlawed, gathered up, and burned" (234).

Most of this material is taken from Brown's favorite source, *Holy Blood, Holy Grail*, and Brown cannot resist taking that book's dubious theories to an even greater level of historical revisionism. *Holy Blood, Holy Grail* describes Constantine's commissioning and financing of new copies of the Bible as "one of the single most decisive factors in the entire history of Christianity",[87] whereas Teabing, in *The Da Vinci Code*, describes it as "the most profound moment in Christian history" (234). Important, yes, but hardly the most profound moment in the history of Christianity; even the first Council of Nicaea would have to rank higher than Constantine's involvement in producing fifty copies of the Christian Scriptures.

The claim that "thousands of documents" that chronicled Jesus' life were in existence is spurious and is far off the mark. Many of the gnostic writings referred to have been lost, but the actual number was probably several dozen. Bart D.

---

[87] Baigent, Leigh, and Lincoln, *Holy Blood, Holy Grail*, 368.

Ehrman's *Lost Scriptures*, which offers selections from a large number of gnostic and heretical texts, contains a total of seventeen "non-canonical gospels", including *The Gospel of Mary, The Gospel of Philip*, and the *Gospel of Thomas*.[88] As noted before, few of these works provide any concrete details about the "mortal prophet" Jesus, but they instead portray a gnostic Jesus who has little to do with the mundane, concrete world and who possesses few discernible "human traits". Once again, Brown has it backward, or upside down: the four Gospels of the Bible are full of details about the human qualities of the incarnate Word, while the writings of the various gnostic groups are mostly devoid of such descriptions.

The reference to a "new Bible" is misleading, implying that Constantine created a canon that had not existed before. Although some details have been lost to ancient history, the main outlines of the emperor's actions are well known, as Bruce Metzger explains:

> About the year 332 the Emperor Constantine, wishing to promote and organize Christian worship in the growing number of churches in his capital city, directed Eusebius to have fifty copies of the sacred Scriptures made by practiced scribes and written legibly on prepared parchment. At the same time the emperor informed him, in a letter still preserved to us, that everything necessary for doing this was placed at his command, among other things two public carriages for conveying the completed manuscripts to the emperor for his personal inspection.[89]

Eusebius refers to those manuscripts as "bound volumes of a threefold and fourfold form",[90] a term that has been debated

---

[88] Bart D. Ehrman, *Lost Scriptures* (New York: Oxford University Press, 2003), 7–90.

[89] Bruce Metzger, *The Canon of the New Testament* (Oxford: Clarendon Press, 1987), 206.

[90] Eusebius, *Vita Const* IV.36.37.

and interpreted in different ways. Most scholars agree that the editions produced under the patronage of Constantine contained nearly all, if not all, of the twenty-seven books that now make up the New Testament, with the possible additions of the *Epistle of Barnabas* and the *Shepherd of Hermas*.[91]

Constantine had nothing to do with the selection of the books within these editions, or with their collation. He relied on the Church, which had firmly established the four Gospels and the majority of the New Testament long before the fourth century. The Christian canon was largely set by the late 200s. Different regions had slightly different lists of books that they used in liturgy, but Christians generally agreed on what books did or did not belong in the New Testament canon, with the exception of books such as Hebrews and the Apocalypse. Finally, in the late 300s and early 400s, a series of regional councils settled the issue of the canon in the West, while some debate continued in the East. "Nevertheless," Philip Jenkins notes, "the Great Church had substantially decided its canon of approved gospels no later than the early third century. Neither Constantine nor Athanasius had anything to do with those decisions."[92]

Finally, in the midst of accusing Constantine of destroying "gospels" and creating a new version of the Bible, *The Da Vinci Code* insinuates that the Dead Sea Scrolls contained some of the works that the emperor was unable to destroy. It does this by simply dropping in a free-floating sentence on the heels of Teabing's claim that some gnostic gospels had survived. The Dead Sea Scrolls, readers are told, were discovered in a cave near Qumran in the 1950s (234). What are they to make of it? It is apparently meant to make readers

---

[91] Metzger, *Canon of the New Testament*, 207.

[92] Philip Jenkins, *Hidden Gospels: How the Search for Jesus Lost Its Way* (New York: Oxford University Press, 2001), 87.

think that the Dead Sea Scrolls contain gnostic writings and hidden truths about Jesus' life. However, although this idea is sometimes floated in popular circles, it is not true. There are more than eight hundred manuscripts in the Qumran collection, with about two hundred scrolls containing Old Testament works, including selections from almost every single Old Testament book. There are numerous manuscripts of the Psalms, Deuteronomy, and the prophet Isaiah, which happen to be the three most quoted books in the New Testament. However, the Qumran community had been destroyed before most of the New Testament was put to paper, and none of the scrolls contain New Testament texts. Nor is there any mention of Jesus, John the Baptist, or any known Christians.[93]

[93] David Noel Freedman, ed., *Eerdmans Dictionary of the Bible* (Grand Rapids, Mich.: W. B. Eerdmans, 2000), 325–29.

Chapter 5

Myths of the Holy Grail

> The Grail itself is the symbol of God's grace. At once the
> dish of the Last Supper, the vessel which received the effu-
> sion of Christ's blood when His side was pierced, and in
> the text both chalice and ciborium, its "secrets" are the
> mystery of the Eucharist unveiled.
>
> —P. M. Matarasso, *The Quest of the Holy Grail*

Dan Brown inverts the ancient insight that a woman's body
is symbolically a container and makes a container symbolically a woman's body. And he gives that container a name
every Christian will recognize, for he claims that the Holy
Grail was really the body of Mary Magdalene. She was the
figurative vessel that carried the holy blood of Christ in her
womb while bearing his offspring. Her breasts, however, go
unremarked as vessels of milk to nourishing children, her
own body fluids being merely royal as opposed to holy. Besides
equating the Magdalene with the Grail, Brown also calls her
the Chalice and the Rose, making her a manifestation of the
"divine feminine" (238). Grail quests in medieval literature
were really coded searches for lost sacred femininity suppressed by the murderous Church. Around the Magdalene-
Grail he clusters other supposed goddess associations including
the number five, pentagrams, pentacles, poetic pentameter,
five-petalled flowers, apples, rose windows, and the compass

rose of navigation. (Somehow his rosy list overlooks less glamorous concepts such as hose nozzles and the malady rose fever, among twelve pages of words and meanings related to "rose" in the *Oxford English Dictionary*.)

The Most Enduring Legend of All Time?

The object of a successful Grail quest is "to kneel before the bones of Mary Magdalene" (257), something Brown's hero—but not his heroine—actually gets to do at the novel's sodden climax (454). On the other hand, the villainous Vatican's Grail quests were secret missions to kill the Magdalene's descendants, who continue the holy blood of Jesus (257). The hierarchy has always tried to destroy the Grail to keep its ill-gotten patriarchal power (268). As another negative example, Brown's villain Teabing is a quester so murderously obsessed that the Grail has become his spiritual mistress, and therefore he fails for unworthiness.

Brown's version of the Priory of Sion not only guards the secret of the Magdalene-Grail equation but also her relics, her bloodline, and four huge chests full of documents verifying the same. Significantly, he adds another feature to the society, goddess worship, which had not featured at all in the program of the modern Priory.

To this degree Brown fuses the principal tenets of *Holy Blood, Holy Grail* with *The Templar Revelation*'s emphasis on the goddess and the mystical feminism of Margaret Starbird. Brown's characters worship the fusion of masculine and feminine divinity through the ancient pagan rite of *hieros gamos* ("sacred marriage"), but he does not specifically identify Jesus and Mary Magdalene as lovers who performed this ritual. They are properly wed, just like his heroine Sophie's grandparents in *The Da Vinci Code*, and their cultic functions are discreetly unmentioned. Starbird has the Magdalene as Christ's bride in *The Woman with the Alabaster Jar,* but Picknett and Prince have Jesus and Mary Magdalene unmarried—and uncongenial—participants in the sexual worship of the Egyptian goddess Isis. Picknett's recent solo book, *Mary Magdalene: Christianity's Hidden Goddess,* depicts her as a Jewish-Ethiopian goddess-worshipping priestess-preacher of Johannite Christianity. Whatever happened to the signature red hair? Perhaps Brown realized that he had better stick to prettier theories.

Brown makes large claims for the Grail story, calling it "the most enduring legend of all time" (249). Never mind that it was unknown until the late twelfth century. He wonders why none of the other Passion relics have attracted such a mystique, apparently unaware of the stories of the True Cross, which are more than seven centuries older and connected with widely dispersed visible relics. Brown says that the Grail has been the object of wars and quests—as if these were real and not literary events.

To universalize the Grail, Brown connects it with a V-shaped figure called the "chalice". It is supposed to be the most ancient symbol of femininity, while the reversed figure termed the "blade" represents masculinity. Turned into triangles and superimposed, they become the familiar Star of David or Seal of Solomon, which supposedly means a conjunction of gender principles. Brown is taking these ideas from Riane Eisler's *Chalice and the Blade,*[1] which neo-pagan writer Margot Adler calls "a provocative, feminist reinterpretation of history".[2] Dipping a blade into a chalice is in fact a detail in Gardnerian wiccan ritual.

[1] Riane Eisler, *The Chalice and the Blade* (San Francisco: Harper and Row, 1988).

[2] Margot Adler, *Drawing Down the Moon: Witches, Druids, Goddess-Worshippers, and Other Pagans in America Today,* rev. ed. (New York: Penguin-Arkana, 1997), 537.

Incidentally, one paragraph of Adler's own summary of common neo-pagan beliefs would not have sounded out of place in *The Da Vinci Code*: "In our culture which has for so long denied and denigrated the feminine as negative, evil or, at best, small and unimportant, women (and men too) will never understand their own creative strength and divine nature until they embrace the creative feminine, the source of inspiration, the Goddess within." [3] The incompatibility of these notions with Christianity should be obvious.

The Star (more properly the Shield) of David was not used by Jews in biblical times but entered Jewish culture as a protective sign via Islamic magic practices around the tenth century. It became a heraldic symbol in early modern Prague and finally emerged as the universal emblem of Jewishness among nineteenth-century Zionists, hence its use on the Israeli flag. [4] Granted that anything concave is "feminine" and anything convex is "masculine" in a Freudian sense, if the so-called chalice and blade were as primordial and universal as Brown claims, they would be easy to detect in the most ancient human societies. But an examination of a work by pagan-friendly archeologist Marija Gimbutas, *The Goddesses and Gods of Old Europe*, on Neolithic divine imagery reveals many kinds of sexual symbols but no chalices or blades. [5] Going farther back in time to Ice Age Europe, two pages of Paleolithic signs reproduced by Alexander Marshak

[3] Ibid., ix.

[4] "Magen David", in *The Oxford Dictionary of the Jewish Religion*, ed. R.J. Zwi Werblowsky, Geoffrey Wigoder, et al. (New York: Oxford University Press, 1997).

[5] Marija Gimbutas, *The Goddesses and Gods of Old Europe*, new ed. (Berkeley, Calif.: University of California Press, 1982). Gimbutas' interpretations are immensely popular in the goddess movement but not universally accepted by non-pagan scholars.

in *The Roots of Civilization* show a variety of female and male signs but only one possible chalice.[6]

On the other hand, recognition of the female body as a container is a basic mythological insight simply extrapolated from observing the functions of breast and womb as vessels. *The Great Mother* by Erich Neumann is a notable analysis of the worldwide maternal archetype from a Jungian perspective. Neumann connects the Grail with the breast as an "open" symbol of nourishment, transformation, and fertility.[7]

These traits will be met in the legendary Holy Grail. But it is worth noting that Mary Magdalene is essentially a *transformed* rather than a *transforming* person: in the Bible she goes from possessed to free; in tradition she goes from sinner to saint. In neither the canonical nor the gnostic gospels is she physically fertile; her impact is spiritual only. The Grail-as-Magdalene is a poor fit. Our Blessed Lady as Virgin and Mother—Neumann analyzes her in both roles—makes the perfect living Grail because she is the "container" par excellence of Christ's own blood. The contrast between Mary Magdalene and Mary of Nazareth will be explored below.

The Birth of the Grail

The word *grail* was first mentioned in English in 1330 according to the *Oxford English Dictionary*. It has also been spelled *greal*, *graal*, and *graile* with earlier Old French renderings as *graal*, *greal*, *greel*, and *greil*, ultimately *Le Saint Graal*. Sir Thomas Malory, whose *Le Morte d'Arthur* (1470) includes the best English telling of the Grail story, calls it the Sankgreall and

<hr />

[6] Alexander Marshak, *The Roots of Civilization* (New York: McGraw-Hill, 1972), 198–99.

[7] Erich Neumann, *The Great Mother: An Analysis of the Archetype*, trans. Ralph Mannheim (1955; Princeton, N.J.: Princeton University Press, 1972), 47, 61, 89.

the Holy Grayle. "Grail" is derived ultimately from the Latin *gradale*, meaning "by degree or stages", referring to a type of deep platter from which foods were served course by course at a medieval banquet.

This usage as a common noun predates all references to the *Holy Grail*. Therefore, Brown's division of *sangreal* as "sang real", supposedly French for "royal blood" (249) is wrong, since "royal blood" in French would be *le sang royal*. Sangreal is properly "Holy Grail" and would be divided "Sangreal". Neither can Brown's borrowing from *Holy Blood, Holy Grail* be justified by an appeal to an occasional mistaken usage by Malory that makes "the Sankgreal" refer to "the blessed bloode of our Lorde Jhesu Cryste" rather than the vessel holding it.[8] Malory clearly means our Lord's own blood and not his alleged bloodline. Take away this false construction of "sang real" and the argument for a divine lineage collapses.

The Grail debuts in medieval literature even before it has become "the Holy Grail".[9] In *Perceval* or the *Conte del Graal*, a French poem by Chrétien de Troyes from the second half of the twelfth century, the *graal* is a large jeweled dish containing a single Mass wafer that a beautiful maiden carries at a banquet. The maimed king who presides over the gathering cannot be healed until the poem's naïve hero Perceval starts asking questions about the Grail.

Chrétien's poem remained unfinished and the dish unexplained until about 1200, when a Burgundian poet named Robert de Boron expanded the story. This survives only in a prose adaptation known as the *Didot-Perceval*. Robert turns

---

[8] Cited in Roger Sherman Loomis, *The Grail: From Celtic Myth to Christian Symbol* (1963; new ed., Princeton, N.J.: Princeton University Press, 1991), 25.

[9] This section is taken from Sandra Miesel, "The Origins of the Holy Grail", *Catholic Twin Circle*, April 16, 1995, 4–5, which is in turn dependent upon *The Arthurian Encyclopedia*, ed. Norris J. Lacy et al. (New York: Peter Bedrick, 1986).

the dish into the cup of the Last Supper—serving as a ciborium rather than a chalice—and has the king wounded by the Holy Lance of Longinus that had pierced the side of Jesus.

Robert had previously written *Joseph d'Arimathie*, in which the Cup of the Last Supper feeds Joseph during years of captivity. Following adventures in the Near East, Joseph brings the Grail to England, where his relatives become the hereditary Grail-keepers and the ancestors of Perceval. Legend also made Joseph a missionary and first bishop of Britain, founder of the earliest British church at Glastonbury, where King Arthur was said to have been buried. His alleged grave and Guenevere's were discovered by the local monks in 1190. The eighteenth century saw a claim of Joseph's staff as the origin of the Glastonbury thorn tree that blooms at Christmastime, and Victorians added a fable about the Holy Well on site near the place where Joseph was supposed to have buried the Cup of the Last Supper.

The medieval parts of this material were gathered into the so-called Vulgate Cycle of Arthurian romances in prose (1215–1235). The portion entitled *Queste del Saint Grail*[10] shows Cistercian influence—it may have been written by a monk—and is the most explicitly Christian version of the Grail legends. The Vulgate Cycle was a major source for Malory, whose rendering is the "canonical" telling of the story for English speakers. In both the Vulgate and Malory, Sir Perceval/ Percivale is one of the three purest knights of the Round Table. Along with Sir Bors and the faultless Sir Galahad, he is privileged to take part in the Grail ritual and receive Holy Communion from the hands of Jesus himself. Finally, the Grail company sees the vessel taken back to heaven along

---

[10] Available in English as *The Quest of the Holy Grail*, trans. P. M. Matarasso (1969; New York: Penguin, 1979).

with the blood-dripping Holy Lance. Galahad dies soon after, Perceval dies a year after becoming a hermit, and Bors returns to Camelot to tell their tale. The Holy Grail is now permanently out of reach.

Arthurian stories, known as the "matter of Britain" spread from France all over Europe. A notable contribution to Grail lore was *Parzival* by the German poet Wolfram von Eschenbach (1210). He shows the Grail as a mysterious white stone left behind by the "neutral" angels of the War in Heaven. It generates whatever food and drink is desired, revives the dead, cures the sick, and keeps people who behold it young. A dove lays a Host upon it every Good Friday to feed the wounded king of the Grail Castle. Parzival finally heals him and replaces him as master of the Grail Knights.

Modern Myths of the Grail

Since the Middle Ages, Grail romances have been a favorite source of inspiration to writers, artists, musicians, and filmmakers.[11] Disentangling their sources has engaged scholars for generations. Magical food-producing vessels are found in the lore of many cultures, but Roger Sherman Loomis has been the foremost campaigner for a Celtic origin of the Holy Grail, for instance in *The Grail: From Celtic Myth to Christian Symbol.* He sees it derived from Irish tales about ever-filled cauldrons and drinking horns and journeys to the Happy Otherworld. The maiden Grail-bearer is based on the personified Sovereignty of Ireland who gives a cup only to the worthy. These motifs were transmitted to Wales, then to Brittany, with Breton storytellers spreading them around

[11] Sadly, they also inspired occultists and even Nazis. Heinrich Himmler organized SS members into a secret order of pseudo-Grail knights in Wevelsburg, Westphalia, to practice esoteric Aryan mysteries. D. Sklar, *The Nazis and the Occult* (1977; New York: Dorset, 1989), 99–101.

northern France, where the medieval romances first appear. Loomis assumes that the material had been much altered by misunderstandings and oral process: there was no one "original" Grail myth.

A newer and much more controversial theory of the Grail's origins is proposed by C. Scott Littleton and Linda A. Malcor in *From Scythia to Camelot*. They trace the motifs back to the ancient Scythian peoples of the Crimea, whose symbolic Cup of Sovereignty fell from heaven and whose modern descendants in the former Soviet Union still tell stories about a supernatural cup/cauldron that judges the merit of heroes—including an Arthur-like figure.[12] These myths were supposedly brought into Europe by two waves of Scythian-derived barbarian invaders in Roman times: the Sarmatians, who were sent to Roman Britain, and the Alans, who settled in Brittany and Provence. The old stories were perhaps mingled with historical incidents such as the looting of precious vessels (traditionally plunder from the Jewish Temple) taken during the sack of Rome in 410, which Littleton and Malcor see as the origin of the Grail procession.[13]

Another school of interpretation was made famous by Jessie L. Weston's *From Ritual to Romance*.[14] Under the influence of Sir James Frazer's *Golden Bough*, Weston imagined that the Grail was derived from fertility rites and vegetation folklore as well as from esoteric teachings of Oriental mystery religions, gnostics, Templars, and Cathars. These theories have long been discredited among academics but are still favored by occultists. Weston also popularized the notion of the Four

[12] C. Scott Littleton and Linda A. Malcor, *From Scythia to Camelot* (New York: Garland, 1994). The heroes were called the Narts, and the ever-filled vessel was the Nartamongae, "revealer of the Narts" (13).

[13] Ibid., 236–40.

[14] Jessie L. Weston, *From Ritual to Romance* (1920; Garden City, N.Y.: Doubleday, 1957).

Grail Hallows (Cup, Lance, Sword, Stone/Dish) being perpetuated in the suits of Tarot cards (Cups, Wands, Swords, Pentangles) and ultimately of the familiar card suits (Hearts, Diamonds, Spades, Clubs). Weston's system is not universal; Brown equates Cups, Swords, Scepters, Pentacles with Hearts, Spades, Clubs, and Diamonds (391). But Weston's non-Christian explanations are still favored by modern occultists, including Margaret Starbird, who calls the Tarot a Cathar catechism.[15]

Loomis firmly dismisses esoteric theories, including "Miss Weston's fascinating theory of a lost mystery cult conveyed by Eastern merchants from the Mediterranean to Britain, and of secret initiation rites enacted in remote ages—a theory also discredited by the absence of any reference to such a cult in the mass of medieval testimony of heresy".[16] He also discounts a Provençal (and presumably Cathar) source for *Parzival* as "preposterous".[17] Loomis does think that the Knights Templar inspired *Parzival*'s Grail Knights, the *Templeisen*,[18] but that does not mean they are to be taken as actual Templars. The Grail legends were "surely not the esoteric doctrines of heretical cults" and not intended as anti-papal propaganda.[19]

The Church and the Grail

Although the Church has never expressed an opinion about Grail romances and always remained ambivalent about knighthood, the Christian connection with the Holy Eucharist is

[15] Margaret Starbird, *The Woman with the Alabaster Jar: Mary Magdalen and the Holy Grail* (Rochester, Vt.: Bear, 1993), 104.
[16] Loomis, *Grail*, 63.
[17] Ibid., 197.
[18] Ibid., 214.
[19] Ibid., 276.

what fixed the Grail in the medieval mind.[20] The old myth motifs would never have gained such popularity without the Christianization that brought them in line with medieval devotional practices and iconography.

Medieval artists illustrated Grail romances with the costumes, props, and settings of their own day, just as they did with scenes from the Bible or classical antiquity. In manuscript illuminations, the banquets for Arthur's knights or the Grail Knights look as contemporary as medieval depictions of the Last Supper, except that a ciborium-like Grail floats above the table carried by angels. The mystical eucharistic vessel was expected to resemble ones actually used in the liturgy. Grail "accessories" such as the Holy Lance and the Sword of David recall relics, votive offerings of weapons, or royal regalia preserved in churches.

The furnishing of medieval altars could be dazzling. Altar vessels, reliquaries, monstrances, and so forth, for major churches were marvels of goldsmiths' work. Some of the best were containers from antiquity or the Islamic world fitted with bases and handles for liturgical use. Some magnificent examples carved from crystal or semiprecious minerals can still be seen in the treasury of San Marcos in Venice.

In addition to its use at the Last Supper, the Grail was supposed to have been used to catch the blood of the crucified Christ. This aspect may have been influenced by the

---

[20] Richard F. O'Gorman, "Grail", in *Arthurian Encyclopedia*, 260. The cathedral of Valencia, Spain, claims to have the actual vessel of the Last Supper, El Santo Grial, donated in 1437. This New Testament-period red hardstone cup, set as a chalice sometime during the Middle Ages, was supposedly brought to Rome from Jerusalem, sent to Spain, and long hidden from the Moors. Its legend has nothing to do with Grail romances. See Anton Legner, *Reliquien in Kunst und Kult: Zwischen Antike und Aufklärung* (Darmstadt: Wissenschaftenliche Buchgesellschaft, 1995), 87.

"chalice at the cross" art motif that emerged at the end of the first millennium and became increasingly popular as the Middle Ages wore on. Artists showed a chalice at the base of the Cross or carried up to Christ's wounds by angels. The most developed form has an allegorical woman representing *Ecclesia* (the Church) standing beside the Cross or beside Jesus alone to receive the Precious Blood in her chalice while holding a spear-like staff. Surely this resonated with the image of the female Grail-bearer.

Grail romances also tapped into medieval eucharistic devotion, such as the elevation of the consecrated Species during Mass, Corpus Christi processions, exposition, and *exempla* and miracle stories about the Blessed Sacrament. The elevation is a twelfth-century development, in an era when Communion was infrequent, probably catering to people's wish to see the Host. (Annual reception had to be commanded at the Fourth Council of the Lateran in 1215 because most of the faithful seldom communicated.) Devout contemplation of the elevated or otherwise exposed Host was believed to convey not only grace but also well-being and protection, just as seeing the Grail would. The feast of Corpus Christi, which originated in the thirteenth century, gave additional opportunities for solemn reverence toward the Body of Christ.

Preaching and teaching about the Eucharist was an important part of spiritual formation from the twelfth century onward. Thomas Aquinas' formula of transubstantiation equipped priests to expound the Real Presence to their flocks and counter objections from heretics. *Exempla* were invented preachers' parables. Historian Miri Rubin distinguished three general classes of these stories, which she credits with raising "eucharistic sensibility"; (1) visions or other sensory proofs of Christ's Real Presence as a reward for faith or to resolve honest doubt; (2) unusual behavior of men, animals, or nature when the Eucharist is near; (3) revelation of the Real Presence to the sacrilegious and their punishment.[21]

Exempla corresponded to miracles recorded as actual events. For example, in the Mass of St. Gregory, the pope saw the Man of Sorrows in his chalice at the Consecration. A hungry donkey refused food but adored the Blessed Sacrament held by St. Anthony of Padua. A Host levitated out of a stolen ciborium at Paris and was safely retrieved. Seeing a living Child in the Host and living on the Blessed Sacrament alone were miracles enjoyed much more often by women than by men (forty-five out of fifty-five reports).[22] But these two categories correspond to the experiences of Grail Knights.

Consider the climax of *The Quest of the Holy Grail*. As in eucharistic miracle accounts, the Grail distinguishes fit from unfit recipients. The worthy knights who have finished the quest hear Mass said by Bishop Josephus, son of Joseph of Arimathea, who had survived for years on miraculous Hosts from the Grail. At the moment of Consecration "there descended from above a figure like unto a child, whose countenance glowed and blazed as bright as fire; and he entered the bread, which quite distinctly took on human form before the eyes of those assembled there." Later, Josephus vanishes, and the company "saw the figure of a man appear from out of the Holy Vessel, unclothed, and bleeding from his hands and feet and side". Jesus gives each knight Communion as the usual wafer, but it tastes wondrously sweet. Afterward, he identifies the vessel as the platter for the paschal lamb at the Last Supper, called the Holy Grail "because it has made itself agreeable to all my people". Jesus blesses them all and vanishes. Then Galahad smears Christ's blood from the Holy

---

[21] Miri Rubin, *Corpus Christi: The Eucharist in Late Medieval Culture* (1991; New York: Cambridge University Press, 1992), 11–118.

[22] Ibid., 120.

Lance on the maimed Grail King to heal him.[23] Rubin summarizes the themes this way: "Moving from the child to the suffering man, Christ's crucifixion and death were represented as prerequisites for the grace which passed through the eucharist, to promise regeneration and salvation."[24]

Giving the Lady Her Due

Thus, despite its pagan roots in mythic food-producing and hero-honoring vessels, despite the (then) unorthodoxy of a woman carrying a eucharistic vessel, the Grail of medieval romance is firmly anchored in Catholic faith and devotion. There is nothing to support Dan Brown's claim that the stories were coded quests for the "lost sacred feminine".

Neither is the Holy Grail a hidden Cathar concept, as Starbird would have it. The flowering of Grail romances and eucharistic piety in the twelfth and thirteenth centuries coincided with heresies that denied the Eucharist. As Rubin notes, "Elsewhere, new types of dualist dissent, such as catharism in the south of France, had a rigorous antisacramental critique, inasmuch as matter could never be conceived of as containing spirit and definitely not as being capable of transformation into God."[25] Having no belief in the Eucharist, Cathars could not have imagined the Grail containing it, as all the romances describe.

Whether the Grail is imagined as a platter, chalice, ciborium, or stone, it carries the entire eucharistic Christ—"Body and Blood, Soul and Divinity" in Catholic teaching—and not his offspring or bloodline. Therefore, the only person with a proper claim to being the living Grail is the

[23] *Quest*, 275–77. This is a pun: *gré* means "agreeable" in medieval French.
[24] Rubin, *Corpus Christi*, 139.
[25] Ibid., 320.

great Mother of God, Mary Most Holy. The rose, which *The Da Vinci Code* appropriates for the Magdalene, is more properly the Virgin's traditional symbol, while the Magdalene's is the ointment pot. Our Lady was the guiding Star of the Sea more than a thousand years before the term "compass rose" existed.

Mother Mary has long been honored for her womb that bore and breasts that nursed the Savior. Even some of the titles in the Litany of the Blessed Virgin point out her woman-as-container role: Ark of the Covenant, House of Gold, Vessel of Honor, Singular Vessel of Devotion. Her pregnant and lactating state, in which she gave her blood and milk to become the Body and Blood of Jesus, were lovingly depicted in medieval art.[26] These are iconographic themes that deserve revival, to demonstrate that femininity can be celebrated within orthodox Christianity. What, after all, is more womanly than motherhood?

But the modern mind resents motherhood as the proper fulfillment of female sexuality. The absence of sexual experience disqualifies Mary for admiration—and the traditional Jesus as well. The manic enthusiasm for Mary Magdalene as wife or at least sexual partner of Christ requires the dethronement of the Blessed Mother as Queen of Heaven. This is a long-standing feminist strategy.

Consider these relatively restrained remarks of Marina Warner, feminist and former Catholic schoolgirl. "Mary establishes the child as the destiny of woman, but escapes the sexual intercourse necessary for all other women to fulfill this destiny. Thus the very purpose of women established by the myth with one hand is slighted by the other."[27] Warner, a

---

[26] Sandra Miesel, "Mothering God", *Crisis*, December 2001, 28–33.
[27] Marina Warner, *Alone of All Her Sex: The Myth and the Cult of the Virgin Mary* (1976; New York: Random House-Vintage, 1983), 336.

supporter of contraception and abortion, thinks that the Church's condemnation of these practices chains women to limitless unwanted pregnancies. The Virgin's sinless Motherhood degrades all other females. "The twin ideal the Virgin represents is of course unobtainable. Therefore the effect the myth has on the mind of a Catholic girl cannot but be disturbing, and if it does not provoke revolt (as it often does) it deepens the need for religion's consolation, . . . against the perpetual frost of being carnal and female. By setting up an impossible ideal the cult of the Virgin does drive the adherent into a position of acknowledged and hopeless yearning and inferiority." [28]

What Dan Brown and his sources, influences, and fellow travelers display is a radical refusal to engage the Catholic Church and her cultural artifacts on their own terms. The occultists, feminists, and gnostics who inspired Brown wish only to redefine and mutilate Catholicism unto its destruction.

[28] Ibid., 337.

Chapter 6

The Real Templars

> Above all things, whomsoever would be a knight of Christ,
> choosing such holy orders, you in your profession of faith
> must unite pure diligence and firm perseverance, which
> is so worthy and so holy, and is known to be so noble,
> that if it is preserved untainted for ever, you will deserve
> to keep company with the martyrs who gave their souls
> for Jesus Christ.
>
> —Prologue to the Primitive Rule, in *The Rule of the
> Templars*

Who were the Knights Templar, and how did they become
such darlings in occult circles? Why, one can hardly spin an
esoteric theory without involving the Templars in some capacity. They were fantasy favorites long before Dan Brown discovered them in the pages of *Holy Blood, Holy Grail* and *The
Templar Revelation.*

Brown relies on those sources to claim that secret purposes were at work in the founding and growth of the Templars. He makes the Templars masters of sacred geometry,
great builders, and the inventors of Gothic architecture yet
heterodox in their beliefs and symbols. He blames the power-
hungry papacy for their destruction. Despite Dan Brown's
repeated protestations of total accuracy, all of these notions

are false. To rebut them, let us look at the rise and fall of the Templars in history.

Protectors of Pilgrims

The Knights Templar—properly the Order of the Poor Knights of Christ and the Temple of Solomon—were founded in 1118 when nine French crusader knights led by Hugh de Payns took vows to protect pilgrims in the Holy Land. The King of Jerusalem gave them quarters in his palace on Temple Mount and the Canons of the Holy Sepulchre provided stables in the same area. But Templar fortunes did not flourish until Hugh de Payns, who was related to the counts of Champagne, returned to France. There he won approval for his new Order from a local Church council at Troyes in 1128. St. Bernard of Clairvaux, who had attended the council and who had a kinsman among the nine founders, wrote their rule patterned on that of his own Cistercians. St. Bernard—himself born into the knightly class—embraced the *novae militia Christi* (the new knights of Christ) hoping that these warrior-monks would counterbalance the brutality and pride of worldly knights. The appreciative Templars put on the white mantle of the Cistercians. The pope added a red cross to the mantle's left breast in 1147.

This symbol was a flared, equal-armed cross, called a "cross formy". Brown nudges the reader to see the Templar sign as special—"symbolic of balance and harmony" and gender balance (145), unlike the supposedly violent Latin cross.[1] But the crosses used by the other medieval military orders, the Knights Hospitallers and Teutonic Knights, as well as the honorary papal order called the Knights of the Holy Sepulchre,

---

[1] Brown implies that the Templars used a pagan symbol, even though the pope selected it for them.

also have arms of equal length. There is nothing unusual about a cross formy, which is a standard charge in heraldry.

The Templars' unique vocation earned them enthusiastic support throughout Europe. A papal bull of approval in 1139 made them independent of local bishops. This did not mean, as Brown puts it, that the Knights were "a law unto themselves" (159). They remained answerable to the papacy, as every religious congregation of pontifical right still is. The privilege was hardly unique, having first been granted to the monastic Order of Cluny in the ninth century. The Knights Hospitaller of St. John of Jerusalem (the present Knights of Malta) had been enjoying the same independence since 1113, before the Templars were founded and before the Hospitallers themselves acquired a military function.

The rapid expansion of the Templars was not the least bit unusual. Some new religious orders capture popular imagination and attract a flood of donations. This happened with the Hospitallers and with the Cistercians. The latter grew from one monastery to 351 in the lifetime of St. Bernard. (In our own day Mother Teresa's Missionaries of Charity and Opus Dei have seen explosive growth.) There is no need to invoke secret manipulations by puppet masters at an elusive community known as the Priory of Sion to explain the quick success of the Knights and the Cistercians.[2] But historical examples are not good enough for Brown. He sees something sinister in the Templars' speedy attraction of recruits and donations. He speculates on the source of their fortune: some valuable secret concerning Christ excavated from the site of the Jewish Temple. Perhaps the Knights blackmailed the Vatican or their silence was bought (159).

---

[2] This idea is especially silly with respect to the Cistercians, who emerged from a series of contingencies that the most devious plotter could not have controlled. Cf. Jean-François Leroux-Dhuys, *Cistercian Abbeys: History and Architecture* (Cologne: Konneman, 1998), 23–36.

Brown is borrowing a notion from *Holy Blood, Holy Grail* that the Knights were founded as a cover story to hide digging under the old Holy of Holies—wrongly imagined as a subterranean vault. The treasure is later said to have been in the Holy of Holies instead of under it (434). The Templars supposedly burrowed through solid rock in total secrecy. That is an incredibly clumsy way of doing something for which ample opportunities and easier means had existed during the previous thousand years. It assumes that the Romans did not know how to loot the site of Herod's Temple when they destroyed Jerusalem in A.D. 70 and that no one, from Romans to Arabs, noticed anything during their later building campaigns on Temple Mount. Why exactly would the "true" Christians have hidden the original Gospel source, copies of pre-Constantinian Scriptures, writings by Jesus himself, and Mary Magdalene's diary in that particular place, beneath the Temple ruins, and not in some hiding place under their own control? Moreover, if these documents were first-century originals, they would have been written on delicate papyrus in the form of scrolls, not pages. How likely would they be to survive a millennium of storage and several more moves across Europe during the past 900 years?

Brown also exaggerates Templar wealth. Historian Peter Partner states, "It is unlikely that the Temple in Paris held some vast treasure beyond the dreams of avarice." [3] Partner is rightly skeptical that the Paris Temple possessed 150,000 gold pieces—four times the average annual expenditures of a wealthy English earl. The Templars' internal expenses absorbed their reserves, and their ready cash was let out as loans. Although valuable, their landed properties were "far less than that of the Hospitallers, and only a half or two thirds that of

---

[3] Peter Partner, *The Murdered Magicians: The Templars and Their Myth* (1981; n.p.: Crucible-Aquarian: 1987), 66.

the Cistercians".[4] Their European holdings were supposed
to fund the military orders' activities in the East. It is also
worth noting that the Hospitallers were approximately as well
endowed in the South of France as the Templars—there was
no special affinity for Templars in Cathar country.[5] Neither
did the Templars have a special fondness for the South of
France, inasmuch as the greatest concentration of their houses
was in the east-central part of the country on both sides of
the River Seine.[6]

Romantic Image vs. Real Knights

Neither Brown nor his principal sources *Holy Blood, Holy
Grail* and *The Templar Revelation* explain how the Templars
were organized. Trading on the romantic image of knighthood, they let readers picture legions of elite white-robed
crusaders. Only a small number of the Templars were actually full-fledged knights. The rest served as sergeants (clad in
brown or black), squires, chaplains, servants, mercenaries, or
lay associates. The knights were largely drawn from the minor
nobility with people of lesser status filling the other ranks.
The head of the Order was called the Grand Master. Professed knights constituted only a small part of the Order.
Possibly no more than three hundred were ever stationed in
the Holy Land, but these commanded several thousand
brethren as support personnel.

The Templars' mission was to defend pilgrims and protect
the Crusader States. Admired for their gritty courage, they

[4] G. Mollat, *The Popes at Avignon, 1305–1378*, trans. Janet Love (1963; New
York: Harper and Row, 1965), 213.

[5] Michael Costen, *The Cathars and the Albigensian Crusade* (Manchester, U.K.:
Manchester University Press, 1997), 89.

[6] *Grosser Historischer Weltaltas*, 3 vols. (Munich: Bayerischen Schulbuch-
Verlag, 1979), 2:29.

fought well but not always wisely. Poor judgment by their Grand Master contributed to the Christian forces' crushing defeat by Saladin at the Horns of Hattin in 1187. Crusader fortunes slipped downward from that point until their last stronghold fell in 1291. The surviving Templars retreated to Cyprus and to Europe.

While their brethren had been fighting Muslims in the Holy Land, European Templars had developed into international bankers. Evading the Church's laws against usury, cash donations and the earnings from their properties were lent out at interest, ostensibly to generate profits for future crusading ventures. Templars accepted deposits, transferred funds between their far-flung houses, served as financial advisors, and were bankers for the kings of France.

Aside from the accounting skills these activities required, the Templars seldom developed their minds. They produced a few poets, but most members—including their last Grand Master—were illiterate. The spiritual texts, including the Bible, read aloud during their meals had to be in vernacular languages because only their chaplains knew Latin. Their houses held scarcely any books except liturgical ones. These are not the masters of mystic wisdom and "sacred geometry" depicted by Brown and his sources.[7]

In the words of art historian Paul Frankl, "It need hardly be said that no amount of knowledge of metaphysics can help one build a rib-vault."[8] The rib vault was the specific innovation that sparked the evolution of Gothic architecture out of the older Romanesque style. It appeared in building the cathedral of Durham, England, in 1093, six years before

---

[7] Partner, *Murdered Magicians*, 15, and Alan Forey, *The Military Orders: From the Twelfth to the Early Fourteenth Century* (Toronto: University of Toronto Press, 1992), 191.

[8] Paul Frankl, *Gothic Architecture*, rev. Paul Crossley (1962; New Haven: Yale University Press, 2000), 265.

the First Crusade began and a generation before the founding of the Templars. The Knights did not invent Gothic architecture or use it exclusively. They built solely for their own
needs and had nothing to do with the cathedrals of their day
or with the craftsmen who constructed them. Gold was the
mortar in medieval structures, but it was not Templar gold.
Brown's claim that the Templars were "master stonemasons"
(434) picks up notions from *The Templar Revelation*, which
makes huge claims for Templar involvement in Gothic building without any evidence or citations from professional historians of architecture.[9] Chartres' chapter of canons built that
cathedral, not the Templars.[10]

Even as patrons, the Templars lacked taste. Their structures were numerous but "mostly humble and utilitarian".[11]
According to the judgment of art historian Kenneth John
Conant, "Templars' works tend to be monotonous, and not
one of them ever rated high as an architectural masterpiece. . . . Their establishments were like contemporary con-
ventual structures, with little or nothing specifically Templar,
except, occasionally, the church."[12] They seldom built for-
tresses in Europe, with the Templar compound at Paris being
a notable exception. There was no standard design for a Templar church.[13] But Brown, speaking through his fictional historian Teabing, reads a secret message in the shape of their

[9] Lynn Picknett and Clive Prince, *The Templar Revelation: Secret Guardians of the True Identity of Christ* (1997; New York: Simon and Schuster, 1998), 110–16.

[10] A good popular survey is Jean Favier, *The World of Chartres* (1990; New York: Harry N. Abrams, 1998).

[11] Partner, *Murdered Magicians*, 12.

[12] Kenneth John Conant, *Carolingian and Romanesque Architecture 800–1200*, 2nd rev. ed. (1959; New York: Penguin, 1979), 334.

[13] Partner, *Murdered Magicians*, 12–13. One of Brown's other sources says the same thing, acknowledging only three round Templar churches in England. Charles G. Addison, *The History of the Knights Templar* (1842; Kempton, Ill.: Adventures Unlimited, 1997), 306.

churches, in this case the London Temple. Their architecture is alleged to be "pagan to the core" because the building is round, honoring the sun instead of God. The style was meant as an affront to the Vatican (339).

Brown picked up the supposed heterodoxy of round churches from *The Templar Revelation*, which cites no Church document as evidence.[14] Yet round churches have never been forbidden nor cruciform ones imposed by ecclesiastical authorities. Not all the great churches of the Middle Ages were shaped like a Latin cross. Teabing's allusion to the Pantheon (later repeated by Langdon) refers to a temple of all the gods in Rome that was rededicated as a Christian church in 609 in honor of St. Mary and the Martyrs.[15] There are also round churches in Rome built by Christians, S. Costanza (ca. 350) and S. Stefano Rotundo (ca. 475). The shape has been revived in recent decades, see for example the Catholic Cathedral of Liverpool, designed in the 1950s, and St. Louis Priory in St. Louis, Missouri, completed in 1962. Are we to imagine that all the architects who designed these and other round churches were crypto-sun worshippers? If there is an intrinsic connection between roundness and paganism, the ancient Greeks and Romans never heard of it, inasmuch as their temples were almost always rectangular.

The true inspiration for distinctive Templar churches was the Anastasis Rotunda, a high-domed circular structure that Constantine ordered built over the Tomb of Christ in Jerusalem, adjacent to the Church of the Holy Sepulchre (in use by 350).[16] Muslims adapted its double-walled design, building a circular core within an outer octagonal shell for their famous Dome of the Rock on Temple Mount (ca. 690). This

[14] Picknett and Prince, *Templar Revelation*, 110.
[15] Richard Krautheimer, *Early Christian and Byzantine Architecture*, 4th rev. ed. (1965; New York: Penguin, 1986), 66–67, 91–92.
[16] Ibid., 60–63, 74–75.

shrine was reclaimed as a church during the Crusader occupation and named the Temple of the Lord.[17] Medieval depictions of the original Temple of Solomon were often modeled on the re-christened Dome. It gave the Templars their name and appears on the reverse of their seal.[18] The image stuck: a domed, polygonal Temple appears in *Raphael's Espousals of the Virgin*, painted in 1504.

Few Templar churches were circular. St. Sepulchre's in Cambridge, England (1130), is a rare surviving example. The church within their huge Holy Land fortress Chateau Pélerin (ca. 1220) is imperfectly round but echoes the contours of the Anastasis Rotunda. The twelfth-century Paris and London Temples had circular naves with oblong choir sections added later. Teabing's claim of perfect circularity misrepresents the building's actual appearance. And Brown appears so unfamiliar with churches that he cannot tell one end from another. Brown's hero Langdon thinks the "boxy annex" of the oblong portion is the nave of the church (343). The oblong part is in fact the choir, not the nave.[19] (How did he overlook the opportunity to read an oblong part conjoined with a circular part as a pagan symbol of coition?) But not all round churches were built by Templars, and not all centrally planned Templar churches were round. Some were polygonal, recalling the Dome of the Rock.[20]

Brown's depiction of the London Temple is defective, although detailed descriptions exist in one of his sources,[21]

[17] Conant, *Carolingian and Romanesque Architecture*, 333.

[18] Partner, *Murdered Magicians*, opposite 106. "Tempel von Jerusalem", in *Lexikon der Christlichen Ikonographie*, ed. Englebert Kirschbaum et al., 8 vols. (1972; Freiburg: Herder, 1994), 4:225–39.

[19] The parts are correctly identified in Michael Baigent, Richard Leigh, and Henry Lincoln, *Holy Blood, Holy Grail* (1982; New York: Dell, 1983), plate 14.

[20] Conant, *Carolingian and Romanesque Architecture*, 333–36.

[21] Addison, *History of the Knights Templar*, 289–341.

not to mention ample data and photographs available on the Internet. Brown's characters are by turns too knowledgeable and too ignorant, as well as oblivious to what is in front of their eyes. For instance, the building's random patches of dark and light stonework caused by post World War II repairs are not noticed. The central arcade of columns somehow becomes a room-encircling stone bench. The characters count ten tomb effigies of stone knights before they notice that one tomb lacks an effigy. Teabing the expert historian wrongly assumes that the sculptures depict Templars when he should have known that they are figures of Templar admirers, including the famous Sir William Marshal and two of his sons.

The reason for belaboring these points is that fantasies about the Knights' intellectual and artistic achievements loom large in *Holy Blood, Holy Grail* and *The Templar Revelation*. Brown had the chance to learn the facts from Peter Partner's book *The Murdered Magicians*, which he lists in his bibliography, but he chose to ignore them. Brown's bibliography contains no standard reference works on medieval architecture—a poor basis for his pretensions to scholarship. But then, Brown distorts the fate of the Templars even worse than their buildings. What follows is their true story.

The Demise of the Templars

Driven from the Holy Land in 1291, the Knights had picked a bad time to become obsolete. Their reputation had already turned sour in Europe because of their pride and avarice. They refused to merge with the Knights Hospitaller and claimed that further crusading was impractical. These developments unfortunately coincided with a wave of panic about magical attacks at the papal and French courts where astrological "ceremonial magic" had been a trendy hobby among courtiers. Adding rumors of heresy and political conspiracy to the mix would doom the Templars.[22]

In 1305, a renegade Templar denounced the Order to King Philip IV of France. Despite having driven Pope Boniface VIII to his death, Philip was superstitiously pious. He sent agents to infiltrate the Knights. It may not have been difficult to convince him of scandalous doings because there were treasure and lands to be seized. (Philip had already mastered the art of canceling debts by destroying one's bankers in earlier moves against Italians and Jews.)

On Friday the thirteenth of October, 1307, French royal officials arrested every Templar in the kingdom, about two thousand persons. At most these included 150 professed Knights, the others being of lower rank. Philip had secured permission for his raid from the national Inquisitor General, who happened to be his own confessor. Only belatedly did he notify Pope Clement V, a fellow Frenchman, who was shocked by the affair.

The Templars were held in royal prisons, and although the French Inquisitor waved his hands over the process, royal torturers subjected the Knights to hideous torments unrestrained by the legal limits that restricted Inquisitional proceedings. At least thirty-six Templars died of maltreatment; more than twenty committed suicide. Enough confessed to stage a trial on charges of denying Christ, defiling the crucifix, sodomy, obscene practices, and idolatry. Although the confessions varied wildly and the accused later tried to retract them, the fate of the Templars was sealed.

After complex maneuvers involving royal ministers and the French Estates General, plus regional and papal Church commissions, Philip coerced the weak, sickly pope into con-

---

[22] Partner, *Murdered Magicians*, 54–58. The dynamics of the situation foreshadow the great witch-hunt that began in the fifteenth century.

demning the Order. In 1310, fifty-four Templars went to the stake together at Paris, proclaiming their innocence.²³ Nine more were burned at Senlis. An unknown number may have been executed later on Cyprus. The Grand Master Jacques de Molay and the superior of Normandy Geoffroi de Charnay were burned at Paris in 1314, two years after Pope Clement had suppressed their Order, in accordance with the French king's demand. Legend says that out of the flames de Molay called for the pope, king, and king's minister to appear before the judgment seat of God. In any event, all were dead within a year.²⁴

Knights who confessed were merely humiliated and released. Some joined other military orders, but most were pensioned off or simply disappeared. Portuguese Templars reconstituted themselves as the Knights of Christ. Philip held on to Templar properties in France until the Knights Hospitaller ransomed them for 200,000 pounds. The Hospitallers also had great difficulty taking possession of former Templar lands in the British Isles. The theory—unknown to professional historians—that some Templars secretly survived in Scotland is unnecessary for explaining the emergence of Freemasonry there almost three centuries later. In memory, the Templars became sad historical examples of either unjust persecution (Dante) or internal corruption (Bl. Raymund Lull).

²³ Desmond Seward, *The Monks of War: The Military Religious Orders* (1972; New York: Penguin, 1995), 218. Seward puts the total number executed at Paris at 120 as does Norman Cohn, *The Pursuit of the Millennium: Revolutionary Millenarians and Mystical Anarchists of the Middle Ages* (1957; London: Grenada-Paladin, 1978), 75–78. Cohn is particularly scathing about the Templar case. Stephen Howarth, *The Knights Templar* (1982; New York: Dorset, 1991), 299, adds additional burnings at Reims and Rouen.

²⁴ Mollat, *Popes at Avignon*, 232–42; Partner, *Murdered Magicians*, 59–83. Charnay was no relation to the family that once owned the Shroud of Turin: Partner, *Murdered Magicians*, 194, n. 79.

Brown's errors on Templar history range from simple carelessness to deliberate falsification. He even gets their original home wrong. The first Templars were not housed in a "meager residence" under the old Temple called Solomon's stables. They lived in a wing of the royal palace on Temple Mount, next to the Al-Aqsa Mosque (which still exists).

Who Was Responsible for Destroying the Templars?

Far more serious is Brown's twisted description of the Templar's fall. Although acknowledging a role for Philip of France, Brown puts the blame on Pope Clement V, stating that he planned a "sting operation" to destroy the Templars and take their treasure, therefore "taking control of the secrets held over the Vatican". Brown compares this alleged operation to a CIA maneuver and says Clement has sealed orders opened all across Europe on Friday, October 13, 1307 (159). Brown further claims that "Clement's Machiavellian operation came off with clockwork precision." The pope supposedly alleged that the sins of the Templars were revealed to him in a dream. The date of their arrest date is the reason that Friday the thirteenth is still considered unlucky (160).

But even *Holy Blood, Holy Grail* and *The Templar Revelation*—not to mention more legitimate histories—identify the king, not the pope, as the chief villain. French royal officials arrested the Templars, not papal soldiers. There were no simultaneous arrests across Europe. (Subsequent papal requests for action in other countries were not uniformly obeyed.) The prisoners were held in French prisons and tormented by royal torturers, not "an angry Pope". Thirteen had been an unlucky number since the days of ancient Babylon, intensified for Christians by the thirteen guests at the Last Supper. Good Friday made that day of the week ominous, and a Friday on the thirteenth was unluckier yet.

Brown makes much of the idolatry charges against the Templars, which, of course, did not spring from any papal vision. But the idol they were accused of worshipping was not the head of a horned fertility god "represented as that of a ram or a goat, a common symbol of procreation and fertility". Brown also tries to draw the cornucopia into his discussion of horn symbols by reading it as a pagan survival (317). But the use of a Roman sign of plenty (originally the horn of a she-goat who nursed the god Zeus) hardly points to secret paganism on the American Thanksgiving table. Symbols have multiple layers of meaning. Besides advertising fertility, picturing horns on a man's head can also be a way of calling him a cuckold, the dupe of a faithless wife. Furthermore, Brown claims that Satan's horns reflect the Church's policy of making the ancient horned pagan fertility god into an evil symbol (316). Brown has apparently not heard that the Middle Ages also interpreted the goat as a symbol of Christ[25] or that demons wore horns in ancient Mesopotamia millennia before Christianity.

But there was no consistency in the Templars' confessions about Baphomet. "Many Templars denied the idol, but those that did not tended to let their imaginations run riot in describing it: it was like a skull, like a reliquary, like a cat, like two or three cats, like a painting on a beam or wall, like a head of a man with a long beard."[26] It is possible that the Templars had special ceremonies honoring the severed head of their patron John the Baptist or even the Holy Mandylion depicting the face of Jesus. One confession claimed that the idol multiplied riches and promoted the growth of trees and flowers, which is the excuse for seeing a fertility connection.[27]

[25] T. H. White, trans., *The Bestiary: A Book of Beasts* (1954; New York: Putnam-Capricorn, 1960), 40–41.

[26] Partner, *Murdered Magicians*, 77–78.

[27] Ibid.

(Why would an order of celibates—who may have occasionally committed sodomy—worry about fostering reproduction?) No idols of any design were ever found in Templar sites. One silver reliquary in the form of a woman's head was found in the Paris Temple, but that was a common devotional object.[28] For instance, hundreds of head-reliquaries of St. Ursula's 11,000 virgin companions still exist. Brown and his sources are repeating speculations from nineteenth-century esoteric histories, especially an often-reproduced engraving of a goat-horned Baphomet by the mystic adept "Eliphas Levi".[29] Moreover, the nonexistent horns of the Templars' nonexistent idol did not add horns to the Christian image of Satan. Those had been part of the usual picture since the Council of Toledo described Satan that way in 447.[30]

Transforming the word "Baphomet" into "Sophia/Sofia" using the ancient Atbash code is something Brown picked up from *The Templar Revelation*.[31] The mysterious-sounding name "Baphomet" was actually an Old French name for "Mahomet", an obsolete version of "Muhammad".[32] For the Templars' accusers to imagine a statue of the prophet Muhammad as an idol for Christian heretics is a shocking slur on Islam. Muslims' antipathy to religious images was not understood in the medieval West.

Neither were the Templars connected with the dualist Cathar heretics of Southern France, a favorite theory among occultists. No charges of uniquely Cathar practices were made

---

[28] Cohn, *Pursuit of the Millennium*, 87.

[29] Partner, *Murdered Magicians*, plate opposite 107, 139–42.

[30] Jeffrey Burton Russell, *Lucifer: The Devil in the Middle Ages* (Ithaca, N.Y.: Cornell University Press, 1984), 69, n. 13.

[31] Picknett and Prince, *Templar Revelation*, 109–10, which gets the information from heterodox scholar Hugh Schonfield, author of *The Passover Plot: New Light on the History of Jesus* (New York: Bantam, 1967).

[32] Partner, *Murdered Magicians*, 109, 138. A Provençal poet, possibly a Templar, called Muhammad "Bafometz" in the late thirteenth century (35).

during their trials. Partner says: "Convincing or specific evidence that the Templars were Cathars cannot have existed, or the prosecution would have used it."[33] Once again Brown has chosen to ignore Partner, whom he claims among his sources.

Possibly Brown's silliest mistake about the Templars is charging that Pope Clement V not only burned hundreds of Templars but had their ashes "tossed unceremoniously into the Tiber River" (338). That the statement is put in the mouth of his "Royal Historian" character, Teabing, only adds to its irony. The largest burnings of Templars took place in Paris, with smaller holocausts in three other French cities and possibly Cyprus. There is no record of Knights burned at Rome. In any event, the pope could not have dumped any remains in the Tiber inasmuch as he resided at Avignon in Southern France and not in Rome. French-born Clement V, former archbishop of Bordeaux, never set foot in Rome, even for his coronation as pope. His reign (1305–1314) opened the era known as the Babylonian Captivity of the papacy, which lasted until 1378. During that time, popes were scarcely more than private chaplains to the kings of France, although not all were as weak-willed as Clement V.

The books Brown lists in his official web site[34] bibliography—including even *Holy Blood, Holy Grail* and *The Templar Revelation*—correctly blame the king of France for the destruction of the Templars. Yet Brown deliberately chooses to contradict his own sources and makes the papacy responsible for that tragedy. Whatever the cost to truth, the Church must be shown to be murderous, deceitful, and treacherous. Any stick will do for beating Catholics, even an invented one.

---

[33] Partner, *Murdered Magicians*, 84.
[34] www.danbrown.com.

Chapter 7

The Templar Myth

> It is sad that this dedicated group of men, who strove to
> unite the contrary virtues of monk and warrior, and who
> gave their lives willingly for their faith, should be mostly
> remembered as a source of fantasy and fairy tale.

—Stephen Howarth, *The Knights Templar*

Though the Order of the Temple perished, its memory lived
on. A new occult model of the Templars blazed up from
their ashes. According to esoteric historians, dissolution was
a mere temporary setback for the Knights. They supposedly
lived on as a secret organization in Scotland and won the
Battle of Bannockburn for Robert the Bruce in 1324, although
standard military histories know nothing of this.[1] Moreover,
the Templars discovered the New World a century before
Columbus and still found time to found Freemasonry, all to
spread that mystic wisdom they had inherited from Atlantis,
Egypt, the Phoenicians, the Essenes, the gnostics, the Assassins, the Cathars, and so forth, occultism without end.

A particularly inane version of these fancies can be found
in David Hatcher Childress' introduction to a 1997 reprint

[1] Hans Delbrück, *History of the Art of War*, trans. William J. Renfroe, Jr., 4
vols. (1982; Lincoln, Neb.: University of Nebraska Press, 1990), 3:438–42.
Mounted Templars did not ride to the rescue. The battle was won by infantry,
not by cavalry.

edition of *The History of the Knights Templars*, by Charles G. Addison. There is nothing in *The Da Vinci Code* to suggest that Brown actually read Addison's decorous Victorian pages, despite his listing that book as a source. But Brown's approach mirrors that of Childress, who claims that: "Clearly the Knights Templar saw themselves as inheritors of ancient knowledge that went back to Atlantis. They struggled for hundreds of years against the Vatican and the reign of terror known as the Inquisition. To the Templars, the true church, one that taught mysticism, reincarnation, and good works, was being suppressed by a dark power that called itself the one true faith." [2]

How a Catholic religious order, begun with high praise from St. Bernard, should gather such a lot of mystic moss has been elegantly explored by historian Peter Partner in *The Murdered Magicians*. The following summary of the Templar myth is heavily dependant on this book, which is considered a seminal study of the topic. (Brown also claims Partner as a source but reverses his judgments—when he does not simply ignore them.)

The Makings of a Myth

The Templar myth started with an offhand remark by a Renaissance expert on magic. When German scholar Henry Cornelius Agrippa of Nettesheim wrote *De occulta philosophia* (1531), he happened to mention "the detestable heresy of

---

[2] David Hatcher Childress, introduction to Charles G. Addison, *The History of the Knights Templar* (1842; Kempton, Ill.: Adventures Unlimited, 1997), 18. Childress is the author of *Lost Cities of Atlantis*. He also believes that the Templars discovered America long before Columbus and other preposterous ideas that originated with French writer Louis Charpentier (cf. Peter Partner, *The Murdered Magicians: The Templars and Their Myth* [1981; n.p.: Crucible-Aquarian: 1987], 175).

the Templars" as an example of evil magic alongside witches, dualist heretics, pagan sex rites, and gnostic abominations. The idea was picked up in France and embellished with lurid details about ancient gnostic orgies and infant sacrifice. From this unpromising spark, a durable fire would kindle.

But several developments had to occur before the Templars could light up the occultist world. Freemasons had to emerge as well as taste for various types of "illumined" mysticism. "Speculative" Freemasonry, as distinct from the "operative" craft of working stone, coalesced in Scotland in the 1590s when lodges of actual stoneworkers began to enroll outsiders who were interested in the symbolic possibilities of architectural knowledge. David Stevenson's *Origins of Freemasonry* traces the gradual process whereby guild practices and habits of secrecy evolved into a secret society.[3]

Freemasonry was nourished by intellectual enthusiasms first unleashed during the Italian Renaissance: Neoplatonist philosophy, Hermetian wisdom derived from Hellenistic Egypt, Christianized Cabala, alchemy considered as spiritual transformation, and Rosicrucianism that sought the renewal of all arts and the mastery of nature.[4] "The occult striving", says Stevenson, "was in essence an attempt to penetrate beyond the world of experience to the reality which underlay it and as such paralleled or overlapped with the artistic use of symbols and emblems."[5]

Although it may seem counterintuitive, the turn toward human reason so dear to the Renaissance and subsequent eras flowed beside an opposite current attracted to mysticism. Then as now, some intelligent people dipped from both

[3] David Stevenson, *The Origins of Freemasonry: Scotland's Century 1590–1710* (1988; New York: Cambridge University Press, 1990), 190–213.

[4] Ibid., 77–125, relates them to Freemasonry, but the best author to consult on these mysticisms is Frances Yates.

[5] Ibid., 78–79.

streams. Sir Isaac Newton worked at alchemy as well as mathematics and physics; contemporary computer programmers may practice wicca. This double stream was especially prominent in the eighteenth century, for the Age of Reason was also an Age of "Illuminism" that longed to be "enlightened" by secret wisdom. French historian A. Viatte observes: "Rather than obey the dictates of the real, and adjust himself to his reduced limits, late eighteenth century man took refuge among phantoms; satisfying his nostalgia with the marvels offered by imposters and necromancers." [6] Partner himself says, "The Age of Reason was an age of runaway superstition." [7] Not coincidentally, the same century saw Freemasonry attain its modern form—and the Lodge brought back the Temple. Freemasonry had already traveled from Scotland to England in the seventeenth century and created an aura of profundity around itself. Even members of Britain's Royal Society, the earliest organization of scientists, became Freemasons and absorbed Rosicrucian ideas.

The failure of Scotland's rebellion against English rule in 1715 sent Scottish refugees to France. Some of these leading "Jacobites" were Freemasons and spread their Craft among the French nobility. In 1736, one of these men, the Chevalier Ramsay, preached that Freemasons were heirs of Masonic crusaders who had learned biblical, Egyptian, and Greek wisdom during their service in the Holy Land. Building the Temple was a metaphor for self-development. Ramsay's talk played to French taste for chivalric pageants and honors. (Although early Freemasonry enrolled many Catholics, including Ramsay himself, Pope Clement XII strongly condemned the Craft in 1738 for deism and religious indifferentism. This

---

[6] Quoted in Partner, *Murdered Magicians*, 115.
[7] Ibid., 110.

prohibition has been repeated by subsequent popes, and Catholics are still forbidden to join Masonic organizations.)

The advanced "Scottish Rite" (sometimes called Red Lodge) degrees were developed to satisfy the taste for pageantry. In its final form, the twenty-nine degrees of this rite repeatedly refer to Solomon's Temple and include a Knight Rose Croix ("of the Rosy Cross", for that Rosicrucian touch). The parallel York Rite, which originated in the later eighteenth century, has the Knight Templar as its highest degree.

Oddly enough, Ramsay had not connected his Masonic crusaders with the Knights Templar. That step was taken in Germany—three times. In summary, the new myth of the Templars claimed that their Grand Masters had acquired Essene wisdom passed to them by the Canons of the Holy Sepulchre (a real group that actually had been associated with the Templars). The execution of the last Templar Master, Jacques de Molay, had opened a new era in world history. Surviving Templars had fled to Scotland and bided their time until they contrived the founding of Freemasonry. Members of the higher Scottish Rite degrees were implicitly swearing to avenge de Molay on the French monarchy, most notoriously in the thirtieth Knight Kadosch degree, where images of a king, pope, and traitor—"the three abominables"—are beheaded.

After the middle of the eighteenth century, two strains of German Templarism were dominant. The Templars of the Strict Observance were supposedly directed by "Unknown Superiors", one of whom was (mistakenly) thought to be Bonnie Prince Charlie. The other organization was the Canons of the Temple, whose initiations reeked of the occult. The two groups alternately cooperated and fought as German nobles patronized and joined them.

The revived Templars and the Canons were brought together in 1782 for the Convent of Wilhelmsbad, a Masonic conference that exposed the foolishness of both enterprises. The meeting is famous among occultists and conspiracy theorists because it also encompassed a French mystical brotherhood known as the Elus Coëns ("Illuminated Priests") and the notorious Bavarian Illuminati. The latter were plotting a radical restructuring of German society but had not gotten beyond the planning stage when the Bavarian government closed them down in 1785. "An enormous amount of rubbish has been written about the Illuminati", says Partner,[8] for they are invoked even today as the Secret Masters of the New World Order.

But the Illuminati connection fatally damaged the reputation of the revived Templars. They were described as heirs of the ancient gnostics, practitioners of sorcery and Satanism. The Italian charlatan Caligostro told the Roman Inquisition that the Strict Observance Templars were out to destroy Altar and Throne in vengeance for de Molay. Others claimed that the Jesuits were behind all the plotting.

The Occult Connection

In any event, the outbreak of the French Revolution in 1789 made tales of subversive plots grimly relevant. The beheading of King Louis XVI was revenge for the burning of de Molay. All the accusations came together in the hands of ex-Jesuit Abbé Augustin de Barruel to produce an all-encompassing theory of conspiracy in his three-volume work *Mémoires pour servir à l'histoire du Jacobinism* (1797–1798), which is still in print in an English edition as *Memoirs concerning the History of Jacobinism*. Partner calls Barruel "a passionate controversialist who combined the skills of a medieval inquisitor

[8] Ibid., 125.

with the mentality of an eighteenth century occultist".[9] To Barruel everything is connected, from the Templars' origins in dualist heresies (Manichees, gnostics, Cathars) to their continuation in Jacobin Freemasons who were responsible for the French Revolution. Every subversive or revolutionary movement—no matter how independent—has Templar inspiration and is part of a continuous historical plot. He oversold the linkage between revolution and secret societies so thoroughly that real revolutionaries obligingly founded "Illuminist" secret societies to carry out their designs.

Barruel has been a basic text of political paranoia down to the present.[10] Through him, "the idea of political Masonic conspiracy became a commonplace, and the Templars became stamped in the popular imagination as a suspect group who smelled slightly of the pit."[11] A sign of their dangerous aura was Napoleon's first request after looting the Vatican archives: he wanted to see the records of the Templars' trial.

But the diligent hand that drew all the Templar threads together was not French but German. Josef von Hammer-Purgstall's *Mystery of Baphomet Revealed* (1818) turned the Templars into duplicitous idolaters. Hammer, who had real credentials as an Orientalist, traded heavily on the appearance of erudition without a supporting framework of logic. His thinking is even wilder and woollier than Barruel's. Hammer made the Templars a medieval version of an ancient gnostic cult called the Ophites, who had been described by patristic writer Origen. The Templars' mysterious Baphomet was an androgynous idol also known as Achamoth or Sophia, which they worshipped with ritual orgies. The Knights' role as

---

[9] Ibid., 131.

[10] Ted Flynn, *Hope of the Wicked: The Master Plan to Rule the World* (Sterling, Va.: MaxKol, 2000), is a recent specimen of the genre, although it does not mention Barruel.

[11] Partner, *Murdered Magicians*, 133.

defenders of Christendom was a mere pose, and Freemasons are their heirs.

Hammer also tied the Templars to the Holy Grail because the Knights of the Grail in the medieval German romance *Parzival* are white-clad *Templeisen*. He made the Grail itself a symbol of gnostic illumination without Christian meaning. Moreover, the Grail story reflects the secret survival of pre-Christian paganism, traceable in ancient monuments all over Europe. Later fantasies about a universal Mother-Goddess and witchcraft as pagan worship, key concepts in the rise of modern neo-paganism, derive from Hammer. As Partner says, "No one can pick up a popular work on the Templars or the Grail without meeting his theories." [12]

The Da Vinci Code and its sources *Holy Blood, Holy Grail* and *The Templar Revelation* trade heavily on this supposed continuity between paganism, gnosticism, and the Templars, as well as on the supposed gnostic connotations of the Holy Grail. For instance, Brown spends a chapter demonstrating how "Baphomet" can be transformed into the word "Sophia" ("wisdom"), which is also his heroine's name (318–21).

These modern writers also carry on a nineteenth-century tradition that took Hammer's theories and turned them upside down so that worshipping Baphomet became a good thing rather than a bad thing. The Romantic era's taste for the perverse and conspiratorial led some people to regard the Templars as enlightened heroes, allies of the Cathars and opponents of the clerical order. All the heretics of the Middle Ages—even Muslim heretics called the Druze—were imagined to have actively collaborated against the monstrous impositions of Rome. Such opinions are precursors of Brown's hostile remarks about the Church.

---

[12] Ibid., 144.

Moreover, Frenchmen who fancied themselves as "Neo-Templars" produced a forged gnostic Gospel of St. John called the *Levitikon*, in which Jesus is a mortal initiate of the Egyptian mysteries of Osiris and whose ideas of hidden wisdom were transmitted by the Templars and their Masonic successors. *The Templar Revelation* presents Jesus—a mystic adept trained in Egypt—and Mary Magdalene as unloving partners in Egyptian sex rites. Fortunately, Brown did not borrow this notion. Perhaps he saw some limits to the credulity of the public. In 1831, an esoteric "French Catholic Church" was founded on *Levitikon* teachings. Failing to attract popular support, it lasted about a dozen years.

By the middle of the nineteenth century, the myth of the mystic Templars was so well established that the sometime Catholic deacon and sometime socialist Alphonse-Louis Constant attempted to integrate them into a total theory of esoteric knowledge. Writing as "Eliphas Lévi", Constant repeated the Egyptian connections of Christ transmitted to the Templars via the "Johannite" gnostic teachings of the apostle St. John. (Real biblical scholars, of course, see St. John as a foe of gnosticism.)

According to Constant, the Templars turned their esoteric inheritance into a form of pantheism centered on the adoration of Baphomet as a symbol of wisdom. Constant's own engraving of the androgynous idol shows a black-winged female body with the head and cloven hooves of a he-goat, bearing a pentacle on its brow.[13] This image is often reproduced as a picture of Satan, but Constant identified his so-called "Baphomet of Mendes" with a goat-god worshipped in that district of ancient Egypt. (Min, the principal Egyptian god of fertility, was not represented as a goat, although the Greeks equated him with their horned nature-

---

[13] In ibid., plate opposite 107.

god, Pan.) Constant also read Egyptian symbolism into the Greater Trumps or Major Arcana of Tarot cards besides linking the whole system to a Hebrew form of mysticism called Kabbalah.[14] Constant thus reinforced an esoteric reading of the Tarot that continues to the present day.

Built on a House of Cards

Although now often associated with magic and fortune-telling, Tarot cards had in fact been devised for an innocent game in Italy not long before 1450. Playing cards themselves had reached Europe from the Islamic world in the latter fourteenth century. They arrived with the suit-signs Cups, Coins, Swords, and Batons instead of our familiar Hearts, Diamonds, Spades, and Clubs. Although initially lacking the mystical significance they eventually acquired in Tarot packs, the original suit-signs have been retained on ordinary playing cards in Italy and the Hispanic world. The curious symbols of the Major Arcana, the twenty-two pictorial trumps added to a then-standard deck of fifty-six cards, were probably inspired by allegorical images called *trionfi* that appeared on floats in Italian festive processions. Occult interpretations of the Tarot emerged in eighteenth-century France and are now articles of unshakable faith in esoteric circles.[15]

The Da Vinci Code borrows directly from Margaret Starbird's *Woman with the Alabaster Jar* to claim that the Tarot trumps are a "flash-card catechism for the medieval heresy

[14] Robert Wang, *The Qabalistic Tarot: A Textbook of Mystical Philosophy* (York Beach, Maine: Samuel Weisner, 1983), is a random example of such syncretic mysticism but oddly fails to mention Constant.

[15] Ronald Decker, Thierry Depaulis, and Michael Dummett, *A Wicked Pack of Cards: The Origins of the Occult Tarot* (New York: St. Martin's Press, 1996), tells the true history of the Tarot.

of the Grail".[16] Brown repeats Starbird's phrase "flash-card catechism" and esoteric theories (390–91) and calls the Tarot a secret code for heresy (92). Brown forgets that the whole seventy-eight card deck, not just the twenty-two cards of the Major Arcana, is used to play Tarot as a game or as a means of telling fortunes. The latter practice is, of course, forbidden to Catholics. According to Starbird, the complex symbols of the Major Arcana recount the glorious doctrine of the Holy Blood descended from Jesus and Mary Magdalene and tell the sad tale of the Templars. Her silly books are, like Brown's novel, heavily influenced by *Holy Blood, Holy Grail.*

Departing radically from traditional Tarot lore, which only deals in universal qualities, Starbird's card interpretations are historically specific. These include the Papess as the alternate "Church of Love" opposed to the Catholic Church. The Papess card may have referred to heretics, although they were not Cathars but a Milanese sect known as the Guglielmites, who set up a female pope and cardinals.[17] Among her other identifications are the Empress as Mary Magdalene; the Emperor as Philip the Fair, who executed Templars, and the Pope as Clement V, who abolished them; the Lovers as the holy bloodline; the Hanged Man as a "Tortured Templar"; the Devil as the Inquisition, and so forth. Her reading requires a particular early Tarot deck to have been painted in France in 1392 under Cathar influence—fifty years before Tarot actually originated. But it has been recognized for well over a century that the cards in question are really Italian,

[16] Margaret Starbird, *The Woman with the Alabaster Jar: Mary Magdalen and the Holy Grail* (Rochester, Vt.: Bear, 1993). Starbird recycles her theories in *The Tarot Trumps and the Holy Grail: Great Secrets of the Middle Ages* (Boulder, Colo.: WovenWord, 2000).

[17] Stephen Wessley, "The Thirteenth-Century Guglielmites: Salvation through Women", in *Medieval Women*, ed. Derek Baker (Oxford: Basil Blackwell, 1978), 289–303.

painted around 1480.[18] Her card identifications are as far-fetched as her attempt to read heretical references into the *Noli me tangere* painted by Bl. Fra Angelico.[19] Starbird cannot distinguish between a red "X" and a four-petalled red flower. She also makes the saintly friar a follower of Hermetian occultism.

Starbird also sees evidence for the "Grail heresy" in medieval watermarks and vine leaf decorations, an absurd notion that would make almost every papermaker and manuscript illuminator of the Late Middle Ages a secret Cathar. And if crypto-heretics were so numerous—not to mention powerful—why were they not in control of society?

The "Templar" Temptation Lives On

The swoops of logic and twisted facts found in Starbird are much like those made by occultists and perfervid folklorists in the late nineteenth century. The now-discredited scholarship of figures such as Jessie Weston and Sir James Frazer sought remnants of pagan fertility cults behind Europe's Christian façade. The Templars as mystic adepts and proto-Grail Knights fit their program perfectly.

Occultists, too, absorbed the Templar myth in the 1890s when secret societies and high magic were chic. The name of Aleister Crowley's infamous Ordo Templi Orientalis (Order of the Eastern Temple) is a nod to the Knights and their association with Solomon's Temple. Crowley, who liked to style himself the Great Beast in reference to the Antichrist, presided over gnostic sex rites beginning in the years before World War I. The "sacred marriage" ritual enacted by the grandparents of *The Da Vinci Code*'s heroine, (140–43) which

---

[18] Decker, Depaulis, and Dummett, *Wicked Pack of Cards*, 28.
[19] Starbird, *Woman with the Alabaster Jar*, 122–25.

Brown himself cross-references to Stanley Kubrick's film *Eyes Wide Shut* (1999), may have Crowleyite roots.

The mystic Templars live on, seven centuries after the real ones were killed and disbanded. They live on in novels serious and popular, such as *Monsieur* by Lawrence Durrell, *Baphomet's Meteor* by Pierre Barbet, the *Illuminatus!* trilogy by Robert Anton Wilson et al., *Foucault's Pendulum* by Umberto Eco, and the Templar series of historical fantasies by Katherine Kurtz. The Templars are also the focus of countless Internet web sites.

Peter Partner calls the Templar myth "an eccentric but harmless theosophical dream, sometimes exploited by charlatans to the detriment of the credulous, but not used to encompass evil ends".[20] This is a curiously mild judgment, given the lunacies he chronicles in his original (1981) edition of *The Murdered Magicians*, published a year before *Holy Blood, Holy Grail*. Partner did not realize how powerful the new wave of Templar mythology that had already begun to emerge in France and England would prove. He could not have foreseen *The Da Vinci Code*'s phenomenal sales or its dire impact on its readers' religious beliefs.

---

[20] Partner, *Murdered Magicians*, 176.

Chapter 8

The Priory of Sion Hoax

> The underlying power of the Priory of Sion is at least partly due to the suggestion that its members are, and have always been, guardians of some great secret—one that, if made public, would shake the foundations of both Church and State.
>
> —Lynn Picknett and Clive Prince, *The Templar Revelation*

Whatever its popularity and influence, the Templar myth at its most mystical failed to satisfy some tastes. Deeper levels of mystification were devised by inventing the Priory of Sion, a secret society reputed to be the hidden power behind major events in Western history.

Ancient Society or Modern Fabrication?

First publicized by French writer Gérard de Sède in the 1970s, the Priory was revealed to English speakers by the 1982 best seller *Holy Blood, Holy Grail*, co-authored by Michael Baigent, Richard Leigh, and Henry Lincoln. So fundamental is this book to *The Da Vinci Code* that Dan Brown borrowed two of the authors' names for his character Leigh Teabing (whose surname is an anagram of Baigent). Both Baigent and Lincoln are Masonic historians, while Leigh is a fiction writer.

They fully accept the Templar myth connecting the Knights to Freemasonry and believe that Jesus married Mary Magdalene, leaving descendants who survive to this day under the Priory's protection.

Brown borrows the *Holy Blood, Holy Grail* theses with both hands. His fictional Priory likewise guards the "Grail Secret" of the Holy Blood—with documents to prove it—as well as the precious bones of the Magdalene. Coyly, the Priory of Sion's initials P.S. also stand for "Princess Sophie", the nickname of his heroine Sophie Neveu, born into the sacred bloodline. Brown's Priory continues the practice claimed in *Holy Blood, Holy Grail* by enrolling the best and brightest of the day. Sophie's personal attractions are presented as typical of the breed. Her brilliant, multi-talented grandfather Jacques Saunière is both a curator at the Louvre and Grand Master of the Priory. And as clinching proof of excellence, Priory members drive expensive cars to a gathering for worship of the divine feminine (140).

But so high-minded is Brown's Priory that it will not lift a finger to flick its ancient enemy the Catholic Church into what it sees as well-deserved oblivion. Rather than using its secret documents to blackmail the Church or unmask the "falsity" of her claims, the Priory will wait for imminent liberalization in Rome and let belief in the divine feminine re-emerge spontaneously. This is why the millennium passed without the overturning of altars.

This forbearance is a departure from the arguments of *Holy Blood, Holy Grail*, which outlined the ambition of the Priory's then-Grand Master Pierre Plantard to restore the French monarchy with himself as king. Four years later *Holy Blood, Holy Grail*'s 1986 sequel, *The Messianic Legacy*,[1] modified these plans

[1] Michael Baigent, Richard Leigh, and Henry Lincoln, *The Messianic Legacy* (New York: Dell, 1986).

to encompass a new (and counterintuitive!) European order based on popular enthusiasm for elite rule.

Because Plantard died in 2000 with "earth-shaking secrets" still unrevealed, Brown dropped the political angle but kept the Priory's pretensions as the ultimate secret society, more powerful than the Jesuits, the Holy Office, Opus Dei, the Mafia, the Freemasons, the Bilderbergers, and the Trilateral Commission. He does simplify the Priory's list of rivals, making its great enemy Opus Dei instead of the Knights of Malta, which *The Messianic Legacy* views as the Vatican's intelligence service. (The Knights' medical apostolate is dismissed in that book as mere cover for spying.)

Brown does cling to the following historically ludicrous claims made by *Holy Blood, Holy Grail*: Jesus was married to Mary Magdalene and intended his Church to be led by her, not St. Peter. They were the parents of at least one child. After the crucifixion—which is not followed by a resurrection—the Magdalene fled to southern Gaul with Joseph of Arimathea. There they found safe refuge among the local Jewish community. Some fifth-century descendant injected the Holy Blood into the Merovingian dynasty that took power in what is now France after Rome's fall. (The Merovingians were already themselves derived from the Hebrew tribe of Benjamin, transplanted to Greece, then Germany.) Although the last Merovingian king was deposed in 751, the lineage persisted in secret and linked up with various noble families, including the House of Lorraine, which produced the famous crusader Godfrey of Bouillon, Defender of the Holy Sepulchre.

Godfrey's election as civil ruler of the crusaders' Kingdom of Jerusalem in 1099 was supposedly arranged by the mysterious Abbey of Notre Dame du Mont de Sion, which *Holy Blood, Holy Grail* claims was also behind the founding of the Cistercians and the Knights Templar. The Abbey—afterward the Priory of Sion—supposedly did this in order to have the Knights excavate under the ruins of the ruined Jewish Temple to retrieve damaging documents relating to the Magdalene and perhaps the bones of Jesus or the Ark of the Covenant as well.

The Priory and the Templars, so the story goes, shared the same Grand Master until 1188 when the Priory severed ties following a curious incident involving a felled tree at Gisors in France. Thereafter, the roll call of Grand Masters includes high nobility, the alchemist Nicholas Flamel, painters Botticelli and Leonardo da Vinci, scientist-mathematician Sir Isaac Newton, writer Victor Hugo, composer Claude Debussy, and filmmaker-artist Jean Cocteau. (St. Joan of Arc and Nostradamus are also supposed to have been members.) A number of the Grand Masters are female. Women take the code name Jeanne and men Jean for St. John, apparently meaning St. John the Baptist, who is seen by some occultists as the founder of an alternative "Johannite" Christianity.

Although their nationalities range across Western Europe, the Grand Masters' supposedly steady purpose has been to restore the Merovingian bloodline to the throne of France. To this end they manipulated the sixteenth-century French Wars of Religion and fomented political conspiracies, all the while tending the flame of mystic wisdom and the Grail secret. Even St. Vincent de Paul was in on the game, which at times used the seminary of St. Suplice as its center. (St. Suplice appears in *The Da Vinci Code* as a possible hiding place for the Grail. Brown calls the seminary unorthodox [88].) Priory members were also in the thick of late nineteenth-century French occultism. The viciously anti-Semitic *Protocols of the Elders of Sion* were claimed to be based on a real document about the uniquely powerful Priory.

By the mid-twentieth century, the story goes on, the Priory was manipulating the Church, first in the person of member

Pope John XXIII, who took his unusual name as a tribute to the Grand Master of his day (Cocteau), who used the title "Jean XXIII". Pope John's apostolic letter *Inde a primis* on the Precious Blood is allegedly about the holy bloodline and implicitly denies the efficacy of Christ's death and Resurrection. But in order to cover all bases, the Priory also enrolled—or made a dupe of—Archbishop Marcel Lefèbvre and other French traditionalists. (Two of the accused clerics have denied any connection.)

Merovingian pretender and Grand Master Pierre Plantard, a hero of the French Resistance who helped General de Gaulle win power, brought the Priory partly out of the shadows by registering it with the French police in 1956. The ostensible purpose of this Prieuré de Sion was advocacy for low-cost housing, but it later claimed to have thousands of well-connected members in the worlds of finance, government, and intelligence services—not to mention those illustrious Grand Masters.

Dubious Dossiers and Unbelievable Beginnings

This list is only a thin summary of the sweeping claims that *Holy Blood, Holy Grail* and *The Messianic Legacy* make for the Priory of Sion. Their arguments depend heavily on the *Les Dossiers Secrets*, a batch of supposed Priory documents discovered in the French national library, the Bibliothèque Nationale, and first publicized by Gérard de Sède. (Copies of the *Dossiers* are glimpsed in the possession of Dan Brown's character Teabing [326].) Many of these references are simply typescripts with covers.

But *The Messianic Legacy* recounts much hugger-mugger about missing documentation and forged signatures until Baigent and Company begin to doubt Plantard's candor. Well, they should have, because the *Dossiers* give every appearance of having been "salted" into the library with pseudonymous by-lines and falsified publication dates. The process somewhat resembles recent cases of people inserting spurious information about works of art into existing library catalogues to create a false pedigree for their merchandise.

Dan Brown's other major source of esoteric ideas, *The Templar Revelation*, dismisses the *Dossiers* as fabrications. They were meant to mystify in order to preserve an even more startling secret: that St. John the Baptist rather than Jesus was the true Messiah of authentic—gnostic—Christianity.[2] Picknett and Prince regard the authors of *Holy Blood, Holy Grail* as "selective" in their evidence and seem to consider them naïve. They recognize the difficulty of proving medieval lines of descent and dismiss the Merovingian restoration claim as a front for the Priory's unconventional religious goals. Picknett writing alone is even more dismissive of the Priory and the Rennes-le-Château story.[3]

Unraveling the Priory hoax means starting back at the beginning with the alleged Jewish character of the Franks. Although Jews were widely distributed throughout the classical world, even before the Roman conquest of the Middle East, they had no relation whatsoever to the Germanic barbarians who came to call themselves "Franks" (meaning "fierce" or "free"). The tribe of Benjamin never betook itself en masse to Greece, much less Germany. Wishful thinking to the contrary is on a par with medieval legends that make Franks and Britons descendants of refugees from the Trojan War.

The Franks first impinged on the Roman world in the third century as a confederacy of tribes living on the east

---

[2] Lynn Picknett and Clive Prince, *The Templar Revelation: Secret Guardians of the True Identity of Christ* (1997; New York: Simon and Schuster, 1998), 39–57.

[3] Lynn Picknett, *Mary Magdalene: Christianity's Hidden Goddess* (New York: Carroll and Graf, 2003), 108–13.

bank of the Rhine near Cologne.[4] Their presence can be traced through archaeology, ancient historians, and linguistics. There are no Hebraic elements in their native culture whatsoever. Their language is ancestral to modern Dutch and Flemish. Jews are not noted for being tall, blond, and blue-eyed, as the Franks were. The Merovingians were not particularly well-disposed toward Jews and barred them from certain offices.[5] The Merovingians clung to Frankish names and intermarried with other Germanic peoples almost exclusively. Out of 125 persons known in the dynasty's genealogy, only one prince, Samson (who died in childhood), bears an Old Testament name.[6]

Although initially hostile, some Franks came to serve the Empire under Constantine in the fourth century. Within a hundred years, the war leader of the Salian Franks, named Chlogio (Clodio), led his people over the Rhine to what is now Belgium, and the Franks commenced on a path of conquest that would bring them dominion over Gaul by the fifth century. A legend first recorded around 600 says that Merovech (Meroveus), ostensible son (or brother) of Chlogio, may have been fathered by a monstrous bull-man living in the sea. This is the point at which the devotees of the holy blood theory think it entered the Merovingian dynasty named after Merovech—the bull-man was somehow a symbol for a Jewish seducer carrying the genes of Jesus and Mary Magdalene, who happened to have wandered into barbarian

---

[4] Frankish history in this section is taken from a recent survey, Edward James, *The Franks* (Oxford: Basil Blackwell, 1988), and from a classic older treatment by J. M. Wallace-Hadrill, *The Long-Haired Kings* (1962; Toronto: University of Toronto Press, 1982).

[5] James, *Franks*, 179, 193.

[6] Reiss-Museum, *Die Franken: Wegbereiter Europas*, 2 vols. (Mainz: Phillip von Zabern, 1996), 1:390–92.

territory. They might as well imagine that the Merovingians were really extraterrestrials.

In any event, a golden bull's head was found in the tomb of Merovech's son along with a unique swarm of golden bees that wound up 1350 years later on the coronation cloak of Napoleon. Merovech's grandson Clovis, conqueror of Gaul, converted to Christianity (traditional date 496). Support of the Church insured that the Franks would be the only Germanic barbarians to form a lasting kingdom, which is how Roman Gaul came to be called France.

Holy Blood, Holy Grail makes fantastic claims for the Merovingians as carriers of a sacred lineage that gave them the mandate to reign.[7] This was hardly unique among barbarian royalty—the ruling clans of the Visigoths in Spain and the Ostrogoths in Italy made the same claim. Several Anglo-Saxon dynasties boasted descent from the god Woden.[8] The significance of this genetic mystique lay in its independence from the Church—a good feature, in the opinion of *Holy Blood, Holy Grail's* authors. Religious anointing did not become part of the Frankish coronation ceremony until 751 with the crowning of the first Carolingian, Pippin the Short.[9]

Ignoring the dynasty's penchant for violence and polygamy, the authors of *Holy Blood, Holy Grail* greatly exaggerate the Merovingians' level of culture and enlightenment, likening them to Byzantium, on one hand, and modern constitutional monarchy, on the other. The Merovingians were in fact living off the past capital of Roman Gaul that enabled them to mint gold coinage, and their subjects still included literate Gallo-Romans. King Chilperic did attempt to write

---

[7] Michael Baigent, Richard Leigh, and Henry Lincoln, *Holy Blood, Holy Grail* (1982; New York: Dell, 1983), 234–37.

[8] Marc Bloch, *The Royal Touch: Monarchy and Miracles in France and England*, trans. J. E. Anderson (1961; New York: Dorset, 1989), 31.

[9] Ibid., 37.

Latin poetry—of mediocre quality—and tried to maintain Roman customs. But the Merovingian era was artistically undistinguished, and their manuscripts are written in the worst calligraphy ever seen in the West.

Aside from a miraculous cure attributed to the sainted King Guntram, the Merovingians did not possess mystic healing powers. "Touching" subjects to heal them starts only with the Capetian King Robert II the Pious (d. 1031) but continues for seven hundred years down to Louis XV. As for secret proponents of esoteric "Johannite" Christianity, the favorite patrons of the dynasty were Ss. Martin, Denis, Vincent, and Médard. St. John the Baptist is notably absent.

Margaret Starbird insists that the *fleur de lis* is a "heraldic emblem of the Merovingian bloodline".[10] But the Merovingians did not use that emblem; it, too, is a Capetian innovation, first employed by Robert II before the science of heraldry even existed.[11] Nevertheless it appears on the Priory of Sion's seal[12] and a bank vault key in *The Da Vinci Code* (110, 139), as well as on the self-acquired heraldic arms of modern Priory Grand Master and Merovingian pretender to the French throne Pierre Plantard as the ancient symbol of France.[13]

To summarize: the Merovingians were not as described in *Holy Blood, Holy Grail*. (Neither did they found Paris, as

---

[10] Margaret Starbird, *The Tarot Trumps and the Holy Grail: Great Secrets of the Middle Ages* (Boulder, Colo.: WovenWord, 2000), 43. Starbird conducts a ridiculous quest for Merovingian/Cathar symbols in the watermarks of medieval paper.

[11] William M. Hinkle, *The Fleurs de Lis and the Kings of France 1285–1488* (Edwardsville, Ill.: Southern Illinois University Press, 1991), 4–5. Late medieval poems make the arms of Clovis before his conversion show three "seatoads" or frogs that are turned into *fleurs de lis*. See 37–39, 67.

[12] Biagent, Leigh, and Lincoln, *Holy Blood*, 396.

[13] Paul Smith, "The 1989 Plantard Comeback". Accessed at http://priory-of-sion.com/psp/id60.html.

Brown's heroine Sophie says [257]—a mistake no educated
Parisian would make, inasmuch as Paris was originally a
Gallic village called Lutetia Parisiorum expanded into a city
by the Romans.)[14] Quite aside from the fact demonstrated
earlier that there was no holy blood to be transmitted because
Jesus was not married to Mary Magdalene, there was no
place for it to enter the Merovingian lineage or be continued after that dynasty's fall in 751. The Priory's arguments
are based on a claim that a late Merovingian king named
Dagobert II survived a murder attempt and went on to
father a son, Sigisbert IV, who continued the line in secret,
passing it down to Godfrey of Bouillon and modern Priory
of Sion founder Pierre Plantard. But Dagobert's marriage
was fabricated by the Priory.[15] Historians know that
Dagobert died violently without issue in 675. Because he
seems to have been murdered, he was considered a mar-
tyred saint. His nephew Childerich III, last of the Merovingians, was deposed and clapped in a monastery in 751 to
make room for the Carolingians.

The Real Priory of Sion

There really was, however, a medieval Church of St. Mary
in Sion, built by crusaders in 1099 over the ruins of an earlier Byzantine one called Hagia Sion.[16] The canons—priests

[14] For the true history of Paris, see *The Columbia Encyclopedia*, ed. Barbara
A. Chernov and George A. Vallasi, 5th ed. (New York: Columbia University
Press, 1993). Brown regularly fails the "desk encyclopedia test" by muffing
easily found facts.

[15] Robert Richardson, "The Priory of Sion Hoax", *Gnosis*, no. 51 (Spring
1999), 49–55. Accessed at http://www.alpheus.org/html/articles/esoteric_
history/richardson1.html.

[16] Jack Finegan, *The Archeology of the New Testament: The Life of Jesus and the
Beginning of the Early Church*, rev. ed. (Princeton, N.J.: Princeton University
Press, 1992), 239–40.

living under a rule—who served this imposing church on Mt. Sion were the original Prieuré du Notre Dame de Sion that *Holy Blood, Holy Grail* and other esoteric histories claim was the mysticism-mongering power behind the Knights Templar. No objective evidence supports this contention. This priory had no relationship with the Templars—unlike the Knights' friends the Augustinian Canons of the Holy Sepulchre, who also wore a white mantle and were originally located beside their quarters on Temple Mount. (Eighteenth-century neo-Templarism had imagined these canons as the vector for transmitting ancient Jewish Essene wisdom to the Knights, another baseless fantasy.)[17] The crusader Church of St. Mary was razed in 1219 by the Sultan of Damascus. One surviving pillar can still be seen near the Cenacle and the modern Church of the Dormition.[18] The canons withdrew to Sicily and were last heard of in 1617, when they joined the Jesuits.[19]

That real story is, of course, too simple for the occult mind. The Priory of Sion is supposed to have branched out into Europe before the loss of the Holy Land and separated from the Templars in 1188, an act that coincided with "the cutting of the elm" at Gisors. The giant tree was actually felled by order of an exasperated Philip II of France, whose parley there with Henry II of England was going badly.[20]

The now-independent Priory purportedly maintained an underground existence under lay Grand Masters. Never mind that only the military orders—not priories—called their superiors Grand Masters. That is the least of the problems with

---

[17] Peter Partner, *The Murdered Magicians: The Templars and Their Myth* (1981; n.p.: Crucible-Aquarian, 1987), 9, 111, 120.

[18] Finegan, *Archeology of the New Testament*, 239–40.

[19] Richardson, "Priory of Sion Hoax".

[20] W. L. Warren, *Henry II* (1973; Berkeley, Calif.: University of California Press, 1977), 620.

the resounding roll of nobles and cultural leaders who are claimed to have headed the Priory. How exactly did the far-flung organization coordinate activities across France, England, and Italy with pre-modern means of communication? How did they maintain such strict secrecy that academic historians of occult movements such as the magisterial Frances Yates failed to hear of them? Why did they leave no record before the twentieth century? Is this another case of the cliched claim: "The secret society was said to exist, but it was also said to be too secret to be proved to exist"?[21]

Plantard and the Priory Hoax

Such questions are moot because the mystic Priory of Sion is in fact a modern hoax conjured up by a Frenchman named Pierre Plantard and his associates. The following arguments are taken from researchers Robert Richardson and Paul Smith, who provide a wealth of credible detail attacking Plantard. Smith corrects Richardson on a few points. Understanding the context of Plantard's invention requires a detour back to nineteenth-century France and the esoteric enthusiasms mentioned previously in chapter 7, "The Templar Myth".

Following the fall of the Second French Empire in 1870, Freemasons took over the restored Republic and struggled bitterly with pro-monarchist, conservative, anti-Semitic, principally Catholic forces for the next three generations. Anti-government forces split into factions, some of which sought to combat Freemasonry with their own esoteric pseudo-Masonic groups, a "Grand Occident" to oppose the "Grand Orient" organization of the traditional Masons. (Fear of a supposed Judeo-Masonic plot ran strong among reactionary

[21] Ibid., 174.

Catholics and, indeed, still does today in certain French-influenced circles.)

In the 1880s, a noted Catholic and Hermetian mystic named Joseph Alexandre Saint-Yves d'Alveydre became enthralled with the Templar myth. He saw the Templars as the secret rulers of medieval Europe and wanted to replicate those conditions in his own time. From his obsessions "he produced the theory of theocratic 'synarchy' or joint rule, which aimed at an oligarchy of a chosen band of initiates who exercised their rule through bodies which represented the various orders of society."[22] The doctrines of Saint-Yves d'Alveydre percolated through esoteric groups for decades, and synarchy even influenced the Masons themselves.

During the politically explosive 1930s, a young man named Pierre Plantard, product of a strict Catholic home and sometime organizer of Catholic youth, took up Grand Occident ideas. In 1937 he attempted to form an anti-Semitic and anti-Masonic group for national renewal called the French Union. After the partition of France between German conquerors and their puppet government at Vichy, Plantard tried to found an association called French National Renewal, but the Nazis would not authorize it. Without permission he established a nationalist esoteric order known as Alpha Galates (meaning "First Gauls") in 1942. No Jew or Freemason could join. Plantard would be sentenced to four months in prison for unauthorized association, but he would later portray this as punishment for helping Jews just as he would try to explain away anti-Semitic pro-Nazi pronouncements in Alpha Galates' periodical as cunningly coded Resistance messages.[23]

---

[22] Partner, *Murdered Magicians*, 172.
[23] Richardson, "Priory of Sion Hoax", and Paul Smith, "Pierre Plantard and the Priory of Sion Chronology". Accessed at: http://priory-of-sion.com/psp/id22.html.

Plantard also served six months in jail for fraud and embezzlement in 1953. Three years later, while working as a draftsman in the town of Annemasse on the eastern French border, he and three friends founded a duly registered club called the Priory of Sion. The name came from a local hill and originally had nothing to do with Mt. Sion in Jerusalem.[24] This version of the Priory dissolved a year later. But Plantard was positioning himself for recognition as an expert in esoterica who also took a hand in world affairs. He claimed (without proof) to have helped General Charles de Gaulle gain power in 1958 and caused pseudo-historical writings to be deposited in the French national library.

Plantard's chance for fame came in 1962 with the publication of two popular works of pseudo-history, Gérard de Sède's *Les Templiers sont parmi nous* (The Templars are among us) and Robert Charroux's *Treasures of the World*. Thereafter Plantard would revive the Priory of Sion and weave a web of obfuscation around it. Richardson claims that much was plagiarized from a late nineteenth-century esoteric society called the Order of the Rose-Croix of the Temple of the Grail, including association with famous occultists, the mystic Templars, "the survival of supposedly lost monarchy; association with prominent cultural figures; sensationalistic announcements of the discovery of the tomb of Jesus; the supposition of a higher esoteric order with supreme knowledge; the Cathars, and other themes."[25]

Among the other themes was the "mystery" of Rennes-le Château in the old Cathar country of Southern France. There a priest named Bérenger Saunière was supposed to have found a Templar treasure that made him fabulously rich: mysterious

[24] Paul Smith, "The Real Historical Origin of the Priory of Sion". Accessed at: http://priory-of-sion.com/psp/id43.html.

[25] Richardson, "Priory of Sion Hoax".

coded parchments from inside a hollow pillar in his church and a tomb hinted to be Christ's or perhaps the Magdalene's. Although Abbé Saunière lends his name to the Louvre curator murdered in *The Da Vinci Code*, he was in fact a simoniac priest whose wealth came from selling overbooked Masses until he was suspended by his bishop in 1911. The parchments were fake, the pillar was not hollow, and the tomb was not painted by Nicholas Poussin in his two works entitled *Et in Arcadia Ego*. The so-called mystery was invented by a local restaurant owner in the 1950s to attract tourists.[26] ("Et in Arcadia Ego" is the motto on Pierre Plantard's self-acquired coat of arms.)[27]

Spurious documents, interviews, and admiring books multiplied. Lists of famous Grand Masters were produced. Goddess worship, however, was not part of the agenda, unlike Brown's version of the Priory. In 1975, Plantard began calling himself "Plantard de St. Clair" to pretend a connection with a noble Scottish family involved with Freemasonry who had built the strange Chapel of Rosslyn near Edinburgh. (This is why *The Da Vinci Code* claims the blood of Christ survived most directly in the Plantard and St. Clair families [260, 442]. According to the story the Priory spun, however, the Hapsburgs carry it, too.) Plantard appeared on BBC television as a Templar expert in 1979. He came to the attention of Michael Baigent and his partners, resulting in the publication of *Holy Blood, Holy Grail* (1982) and *The Messianic Legacy* (1986).

These authors believed Plantard's pretensions that the Priory was a marvelously astute society numbering thousands of important people while guarding a secret that would topple

---

[26] Paul Smith "Rennes-le-Château Debunked", accessed at: http://www. anzwers.org/free/rlcdebunked/; Smith, "Priory of Sion Parchments and Steven Mizrach", accessed at: http://anzwers.org/free/parchments; and Paul Smith, "Et In Arcadia Ego", accessed at: http://smithppo.tripod.com/psp/id17.html.

[27] Paul Smith, "The 1989 Plantard Comeback". Accessed at http://priory-of-sion.com/psp/id60.html.

the Catholic Church. They were, however, puzzled by forged signatures that called into question the authenticity of Saunière's parchments and noted that his aims had abruptly changed from a restoration of himself as holy-blooded Merovingian pretender to more diffuse political plans. Plantard had in fact resigned from the Priory in 1984 and was in the process of revamping his myth.

Plantard regained the Grand Mastership in 1989—or so he said. Old documents were repudiated and new ones cited. New lists of Grand Masters were created. The works of Baigent and team were dismissed as springing from their imaginations. The Priory no longer went back to Godfrey of Bouillon and the Knights Templar but only to 1681 and was linked with St. Vincent de Paul. Instead of a mysterious treasure, their focus was on a mysterious black rock containing "immense energy". By 1990 he was no longer claiming to be a Merovingian pretender.

Unfortunately the man that Plantard had claimed as his immediate predecessor in the revived Priory was a prominent financier who had committed suicide under the cloud of scandal. The death investigation brought a search of Plantard's house where Priory documents were found claiming him as the "true King of France". Plantard was compelled to swear under oath that the whole business was a fabrication. Warned to stay away from the Priory and out of trouble, Plantard died in obscurity in 2000. A few people still claim to speak for the Priory, trying to continue the myth. Smith's final verdict is simple and to the point: "The whole history of the Priory of Sion is one of deception and confidence trickery—it was a fake society that never existed." [28]

---

[28] Paul Smith, "Priory of Sion Debunked", accessed at: www. anzwers.org/ free.posdebunking/; and data from Paul Smith, "Pierre Plantard and the Priory of Sion Chronology", accessed at: http://priory-of-sion.com/psp/id22.html.

Although the false history of the Priory has been repeatedly exposed in France and on the BBC in 1996, not to mention tireless debunking by researcher Paul Smith since at least 1985, Dan Brown wants his readers to think it is real and that its preposterous claims are genuine. The commercial need to feed the public's taste for conspiracy clearly is trumping truth.

Chapter 9

The *Code* Puts on Artistic Errors

I know of no serious scholar who has proposed this notion.

—Joseph Forte, an art historian at Sarah Lawrence College, responding to speculation that Leonardo's artwork secretly depicts a marriage between Jesus and Mary Magdalene.

As its title suggests, *The Da Vinci Code* is filled with references to Leonardo da Vinci (1452–1519), among the most enigmatic and legendary artists in history. *Mona Lisa*—arguably the most famous painting in the world—mysteriously stares out from the novel's cover, and the novel contains a number of key plot devices involving the life and work of the famed Italian painter. Leonardo has fascinated people for centuries; even during his lifetime he was renowned for his eccentric nature and obvious genius. Some of the appeal of Brown's novel is undoubtedly due to its use of the Renaissance genius and its striking claims about the meaning and content of his paintings.

Interest in Leonardo and his paintings—notably the *Mona Lisa*, *The Last Supper*, and *The Virgin of the Rocks*—is evident in comments by readers and reviewers of *The Da Vinci Code*. Salon.com applauds the novel for providing an "art history lesson".[1] The ABC special "Jesus, Mary and Da Vinci"[2] featured reporter Elizabeth Vargas speaking to art historians regarding Brown's claims about Leonardo's paintings, searching to discover information that might validate the novelist's bold comments. Bookreporter.com states that Brown's "surprising revelations on Da Vinci's penchant for hiding codes in his paintings will lead the reader to search out renowned artistic icons as *The Mona Lisa*, *The Madonna of the Rocks* and *The Last Supper*. *The Last Supper* holds the most astonishing coded secrets of all and, after reading *The Da Vinci Code*, you will never see this famous painting in quite the same way again."[3]

The Art of Fact

Readers might not ever see the painting in quite the same way again, but will they be seeing it correctly? Does Brown provide valid insights into the work of Leonardo da Vinci? Do his claims stand up to the evidence, scholarly consensus, and historical fact? As we have noted previously, Brown insists that his novel is factual and historically accurate in all areas, including artwork and architecture. In addition, he has made it known in interviews that his wife, Blythe, to whom the novel is dedicated, is an art historian. In an interview on *The Today Show*, Brown and host Matt Lauer had the following exchange:

> LAUER: How much of this is based on reality in terms of things that actually occurred? I know you did a lot of research for the book.

---

[1] From www.danbrown.com.
[2] ABC television special, "Jesus, Mary and Da Vinci", November 3, 2003.
[3] From www.danbrown.com.

MR. BROWN: Absolutely all of it. Obviously, there are—
Robert Langdon is fictional, but all of the art, architecture,
secret rituals, secret societies, all of that is historical fact.

LAUER: So what'd you do? You traveled the world, you know,
running into museums and—and . . .

MR. BROWN: Essentially, yeah.

LAUER: . . . interviewing a lot of historians.

MR. BROWN: My—well, I'm very fortunate. I married an art
historian who, you know, with whom I travel, and we have
a great time.[4]

Like other interviewers, Lauer never really questions the novelist about his interpretations of Leonardo's artwork. Noting
that Brown claims his novel is based on fact, they seem willing to accept his remarks at face value. When interviewing
Brown for "Jesus, Mary and Da Vinci", ABC reporter Elizabeth Vargas treated Brown as though he were a historian
and a scholar, although he admits he is neither. Brown offered
up clichés ("Our history books have been written by the
winners") and errors (Leonardo Da Vinci lived in "an age
when science was synonymous with heresy") without elic-
iting so much as a blink from Vargas. He described Leonardo
as a man of reason living in a superstitious age, a genius fear-
ful of what the Catholic Church might do to him if he were
indiscreet about his scientific studies.

This is not just simplistic; it is wildly off the mark. Although
there was often tension between Church officials, secular leaders, and various artists, the Church often supported (implicitly

---

[4] Matt Lauer and Dan Brown, NBC's *The Today Show*, June 9, 2003. Tran-
script accessed at www.danbrown.com.

and explicitly) the scientific and technological advances of the Renaissance.[5] Ironically, Brown admits this general fact (although he is incorrect about the details) and contradicts himself when he states that Leonardo lived well off of "hundreds of lucrative Vatican commissions" (45). Although the Vatican often commissioned artwork (consider, for instance, Leonardo's contemporary Michelangelo and the Sistine Chapel), it commissioned only one piece of art from Leonardo—not "hundreds".[6] Regardless, the Church did not consider science to be "synonymous with heresy"[7] and was not seeking to persecute Leonardo for any supposed heterodoxy in his beliefs or artwork. On the contrary, as historian C. W. Previté-Orton writes in his lengthy history of the medieval era, the Renaissance was the culmination of centuries of progress and growth, much of it at the hand of the Church. "Taken as a whole," Previté-Orton writes, "the history of the Middle Ages after the ruin in the West of the ancient civilization is one of progress, progress in society, government, order and organization, laws, the development of human faculties, of rational thought, of knowledge and

[5] For a popular introduction to this topic, see "Christ and Science" in Vincent Carroll and David Shiflett's *Christianity on Trial* (San Francisco: Encounter Books, 2002), 54–85.

[6] See Bruce Boucher, "Does 'The Da Vinci Code' Crack Leonardo?" *New York Times*, August 3, 2003. Accessed at www.nytimes.com. Boucher is the curator of European decorative arts and sculpture at the Art Institute of Chicago.

[7] Brown explores this same theme in *Angels and Demons* (New York: Pocket Star Books, 2000). Near the opening, Langdon declares that "the unification of science and religion is not what the church wanted." Another character, a scientist, responds: "Of course not.... The union would have nullified the church's claim as the *sole* vessel through which man could understand God. So the church tried Galileo as a heretic, found him guilty, and put him under permanent house arrest" (33). Compare to Teabing's remark in *The Da Vinci Code* that Constantine's actions at the Council of Nicaea meant that "followers of Christ were able to redeem themselves only via the established sacred channel—the Roman Catholic Church" (233).

experience, of art and culture." [8] Unfortunately, Brown's novel adheres to the common myth that the Middle Ages were dark, superstitious times filled with little more than violence, oppression, and squalor.

The Life of Leonardo

In a *New York Times* article titled "Does *The Da Vinci Code* Crack Leonardo?" art historian Bruce Boucher noted that Leonardo's enigmatic personality and life provide plenty of fodder for sensationalistic explanations of his work. "Controversial in life," Boucher writes, "Leonardo still provokes a bewildering range of admirers and detractors. No other artist is burdened with such baggage, but then, the ambiguity and gaps in our knowledge render him a blank sheet onto which almost anything can be projected." [9]

Brown takes up this projection in earnest. Early in *The Da Vinci Code*, the novel's main (male) character, Professor Robert Langdon, makes these statements about Leonardo (45):

1. He was a "flamboyant homosexual".
2. He is "an awkward subject for historians", especially Christian historians.
3. He was also a "worshipper of Nature's divine order".
4. He produced an "enormous" amount of "breathtaking Christian art".
5. He had a reputation for "spiritual hypocrisy".
6. He accepted "hundreds of lucrative Vatican commissions".
7. He painted in order to fund a "lavish lifestyle".

---

[8] C. W. Previté-Orton, *The Shorter Cambridge Medieval History*, vol. 2: *The Twelfth Century to the Renaissance* (Cambridge, U.K.: Cambridge University Press, 1952), 1119–20.

[9] Boucher, "Does 'The Da Vinci Code' Crack Leonardo?"

As Boucher points out in his article, most of these statements are dubious at best or completely incorrect. Both major issues and minor details indicate that Brown's knowledge of Leonardo's life and work is suspect. For example, Boucher notes that Leonardo was not called "Da Vinci"—as he is referred to in *The Da Vinci Code*. That phrase referred to where Leonardo was from (a small Tuscan village).

There are far more significant errors, including the remark about Leonardo's "flamboyant" homosexuality. There was an alleged incident of homosexuality in Leonardo's youth. In 1476, he and three other young men were charged with sodomy involving a seventeen-year-old male prostitute. The charges were dropped after two hearings for lack of evidence.[10] Little else is known of the incident, and there are no other records of similar activity. "This episode is the only hint of sexual activity by Leonardo, and those who have been the most painstaking students of his life assume it never happened."[11] If Leonardo was homosexual—and there is little evidence that he was—he was definitely not "flamboyant". In fact, he was known for being very private and revealing little about himself to the public.

The use of the word "awkward" implies that historians are embarrassed by Leonardo or afraid of his supposedly outrageous beliefs. On the contrary, many historians are naturally drawn to complex, mysterious historical figures. Such figures understandably fascinate students of history and ordinary readers, which explains why so many books have been written about the man who painted the *Mona Lisa*. For example, a search on amazon.com for books about "Leonardo Da Vinci" turns up nearly five thousand titles. And it is misleading to say that Christian historians are somehow

[10] Sherwin B. Nuland, *Leonardo da Vinci* (New York: Penguin, 2000), 28–29.
[11] Ibid., 29.

embarrassed or flummoxed by Leonardo. It is not as though there were no nominal Christians or even agnostics in the Middle Ages or the Renaissance or that every important Catholic personage was a saint.

Leonardo was infamous for his meager production of finished artwork. According to the *Encyclopedia of World Art*, "Leonardo's output of paintings was unusually small. A total of seventeen commonly accepted works has been preserved, and of this total, four are unfinished." [12] Many of Leonardo's notebooks have been preserved, filled with sketches and drawings of human anatomy, buildings, architectural ideas, plants, animals, weapons, and advanced technological concepts. His religious works are indeed breathtaking, but there are very few of them in existence, simply because he did not complete many paintings. There were not "hundreds" of commissions from the Vatican, or even dozens. The best estimate, according to existing records, is that Leonardo received a single, solitary commission from the Vatican; [13] during his relatively long life he spent little time in Rome.

Stating that Leonardo was a "worshipper of Nature's divine order" is reading far too much into the blank slate of Leonardo's life. Leonardo undoubtedly had a fascination, even love, for nature, evidenced by his numerous sketches of landscapes, plants, and animals. But this fascination seems to have been mostly devoid of a supernatural or religious element. "Leonardo was not a very religious man, but he was not antagonistic to religion or even to the Church (he did not share Michelangelo's passionate desire for ecclesiastical reform)", states art scholar D. M. Field, "And he was certainly no atheist. Like some scientists today, he felt that the very complexity and efficiency of nature argued some supreme

---

[12] *Encyclopedia of World Art*, vol. 9 (New York: McGraw-Hill, 1964), 210.
[13] Boucher, "Does 'The Da Vinci Code' Crack Leonardo?"

creative agency beyond it." [14] It is not at all evident that Leonardo had a reputation for "spiritual hypocrisy". That is hyperbole on the part of Brown, who is apparently portraying the artist as something of a hedonistic, neo-pagan playboy. Although Leonardo apparently did enjoy the finer things in life and liked living well (hardly a unique trait), the descriptive "lavish" is debatable.

Near the beginning of *The Da Vinci Code*, the French police officer Fache tells Langdon that the symbologist must be "aware that Leonardo da Vinci had a tendency towards the darker arts" (45). According to Alessandro Vezzosi, an expert on Leonardo and the founder and director of the Museo Ideale Leonardo Da Vinci, this is inaccurate. "Leonardo was severely critical of the pseudo-sciences and the occult: astrology, necromancy, chiromancy, and alchemy", he writes. "Yet, he acknowledged that the latter was respectable when it approached chemistry." [15] In his famed *Notebooks*, Leonardo strongly criticized alchemy, writing: "The false interpreters of nature declare that quicksilver is the common seed of every

[14] D. M. Field, *Leonardo Da Vinci* (n.p.: Regency House, 2002), 415. There is evidence that Leonardo ended his life in communion with the Church. Giorgio Vasari (1511–1574) was a biographer of many of the Renaissance artists, recording them in *The Lives of the Artists*. He described the final days of Leonardo in this way: "At length, having become old, he lay sick for many months, and seeing himself near death, he desired to occupy himself with the truths of the Catholic Faith and the holy Christian religion. Then, having confessed and shown his penitence with much lamentation, he devoutly took the Sacrament out of his bed, supported by his friends and servants, as he could not stand. The king arriving, for he would often pay him friendly visits, he sat up in bed from respect, and related the circumstances of his sickness, showing how greatly he had offended God and man in not having worked in his art as he ought" (Giorgio Vasari, *The Lives of the Artists*. Accessed at http://www.artist-biography.info/). Some scholars are dubious about various details of Vasari's work, but his book is the best contemporary account of Leonardo's life in existence.

[15] Alessandro Vezzosi, *Leonardo Da Vinci: The Mind of the Renaissance* (New York: Harry N. Abrams, 1997), 145.

metal, not remembering that nature varies the seed according to the variety of the things she desires to produce in the
world. And many have made a trade of delusions and false
miracles, deceiving the stupid multitude." [16]

Apparent in Leonardo's sketches and notes is a lifelong
interest in the physical sciences; also apparent is the notable
absence of interest in esoteric belief systems, goddess worship, the occult, or related matters. Leonardo's *Notebooks*,
which provide much of our information about his views on
a host of topics, focus on technical aspects of painting and
drawing (including perspective, light and shading, and color),
the "proportions and movements of the human figure", bot-
any, landscape painting, "precepts" for painting, sculpture,
metalwork, architecture, astronomy, and mechanics.

Yet Brown refers to the artist's "eerie eccentricities" and
how they supposedly "projected an admittedly demonic aura"
(45). Admitted by whom? Where? No answer or explanation is given.[17] Some of the alleged "eerie eccentricities" are
the exhumation of corpses for the study of anatomy (then
not an uncommon practice) and the famous journals written
in "illegible reverse handwriting". Although the journals were
difficult to translate, they must not be completely illegible,
otherwise it would not be evident that they were written in
reverse, nor would they have been translated, as they have
been. Langdon claims that Leonardo believed he could turn
lead into gold and could create a potion that would "postpone death" (45). No evidence exists for these remarks; all

---

[16] Leonardo da Vinci, *The Notebooks of Leonardo da Vinci*, pars. 1207–8.
Accessed online at the Online Books Page at http://onlinebooks.library.
upenn.edu/.

[17] Brown is likely relying on Lynn Picknett and Clive Prince's *The Templar
Revelation: Secret Guardians of the True Identity of Christ* (1997; New York: Simon
and Schuster, 1998), which claims that Leonardo was a master of occult and
esoteric practices (19–35).

indications are that Leonardo would have scoffed at such notions.

Langdon also remarks that Leonardo's "inventions included horrific, never-before-imagined weapons of war and torture" (45). Here, at last, the novel is closer to the mark, for Leonardo's ingenious ideas for new weapons and military equipment were well known in his day, and his ability in this realm was in regular demand from kings and princes. He was repulsed by war, but he believed it was a necessary evil—a standard position among Renaissance thinkers. "His drawings of battle and its tools number in the hundreds; they are powerfully evocative, beautiful, and sometimes quite theatrical."[18] In a famous letter sent in 1482 to Ludovico il Moro, the ruler of Milan, Leonardo provided a list of his skills in the realm of weaponry and military engineering, describing his mobile bridge designs, scaling ladders, mortars, sea vessels, and catapults.

There is, however, no mention of torture devices, and there is no evidence that Leonardo designed any such instruments. Oddly, the claim that Leonardo devised weapons of war and torture devices goes against the notion, developed in *The Da Vinci Code*, that Leonardo was a sensitive, nature-worshipping man with a strong attachment to the "sacred feminine". Langdon states that Leonardo was concerned "over the Church's elimination of the sacred feminine from modern religion" and was frustrated by the "Church's demonization of the goddess" (46). But is not the hallmark of those concerned with the goddess and the "sacred feminine" a rejection of warfare and torture and a desire for balance and peaceful harmony? Was Leonardo a hypocrite? Or merely confused?

The distorted nature of the novel's depiction of Leonardo culminates in the assertion that from 1510 to 1519 the artist

---

[18] Vezzosi, *Leonardo Da Vinci*, 66.

presided as Grand Master over the Priory of Sion, the secret society that protected the "truth" about Jesus and Mary Magdalene (113).[19] Langdon states that Saunière, the murdered curator of the Louvre, shared a "historical fraternal bond" with Leonardo and that both men were fascinated with "goddess iconology, paganism, feminine deities, and contempt for the Church" (113). This is a bold statement; it is also a seriously flawed one, as an examination of Brown's "evidence"—the artwork of Leonardo—will demonstrate.

Will the Real Leonardo Stand Up?

Langdon describes Leonardo as a "prankster" who found it amusing to gnaw "at the hand that fed him". He adds that many of Leonardo's "Christian paintings" contain hidden symbolism that is decidedly non-Christian—"tributes to his own beliefs and a subtle thumbing of his nose at the Church" (45–46). (Readers are also told that Langdon had once delivered a lecture at the National Gallery in London titled "The Secret Life of Leonardo: Pagan Symbolism in Christian Art" [46].) Not only are these remarks baseless, they do not even fit with *The Da Vinci Code*'s depiction of Leonardo.

For example, are we to believe that the Grand Master of a secret society possessing an incredible and damning secret was a "prankster" who placed hidden messages in his paintings like some sort of ingenious schoolboy? And if the great artist did leave those messages, for whom were they left? One answer, the Priory of Sion, makes no sense—would the members not already know about the alleged relationship between Jesus and Mary Magdalene? And if the Priory had agreed to keep quiet about that relationship, upon fear of persecution

[19] See chap. 8 above, "The Priory of Sion Hoax", for a refutation of these claims.

and death, why would the Grand Master so glibly endanger himself and the society he headed? The picture that emerges is of a sort of fifteenth-century rock artist who loved the thrill of danger and the excitement of pushing the social and lawful limits to see how much he could get away with, hardly a depiction that serious historians and scholars of Leonardo's life and work would accept.

Also, if Leonardo were a "flamboyant homosexual" who had no problem openly defying Church teaching and social law regarding sexual mores, why would he prove to be so secretive about spurning Church beliefs when it came to his beloved paintings, some of which he did not even turn over to those who had commissioned them (for example, the *Mona Lisa*)? Yet, on the other hand, the novel claims that Leonardo's painting *The Virgin of the Rocks* (ca. 1483–1485) was filled "with explosive and disturbing details" and was rejected by the Confraternity that had commissioned it. So did Leonardo openly thumb his nose at the Church? Was his "hidden symbolism" not so hidden? It seems to be a classic case of the proverbial cake: having it both ways in order to satisfy the author's literary and ideological needs.

The Virgin of the Rocks

The Da Vinci Code's claim to accuracy quickly goes awry with its description and interpretation of *The Virgin of the Rocks*, which Brown prefers to call by its other name, *The Madonna of the Rocks*. The masterpiece is described as a "bizarre scene" depicting "an awkwardly posed Virgin Mary" with the Christ Child, John the Baptist, and the angel Uriel (131). The painting, Langdon adds, "was notorious among art historians for its plethora of hidden pagan symbolism"—just "like the *Mona Lisa*" (134). While the painting is rather unusual in style and

The Virgin of the Rocks (Paris)   *The Virgin of the Rocks (London)*

composition, describing it as "bizarre" and "notorious" smacks of hyperbole.

The novel correctly notes that there are two versions of this painting—the earlier one is in the Louvre in Paris and the later one is housed at the National Gallery in London. But Brown twice describes the first painting as a "a five-foot-tall canvas" (131–33), whereas it is actually 198 × 123 centimeters, or about 6.5 feet tall (1.99 meters tall × 1.22 meters wide, according to the Louvre web site). It was originally painted on wood panel but was transferred to canvas (the second version of the painting, in London, is still on a wood panel). The novel describes Sophie, at the Louvre, pulling the painting from the wall and moving it with relative ease. Its backing "flexed" as she pulled it from the wall (132).

In reality, Sophie's action would be a remarkable feat, for the painting, at six and a half feet in height and in a wooden frame, is undoubtedly very heavy and awkward. Even if she would have been able to remove it from the wall, it is doubtful it would have flexed, since that possibility would make the painting vulnerable to cracking or other damage. Normally, such artistic license would not be of much concern, but Brown insists his details are accurate, claims that he attended art school in Spain, and points out that his wife is an art historian. And yet he is completely wrong about the dimensions of a painting, even though the information can be obtained in a few minutes at the library or on the Internet.

Langdon states that "the nuns" of the Confraternity of the Immaculate Conception gave Leonardo specific dimensions and themes (138). But there were no *nuns* in the Confraternity; it was an all-male group, consisting of either brothers or laymen or a combination of both. More importantly, Brown states that "the nuns" had asked for a painting that would include Mary, Jesus, John the Baptist, and the angel Uriel, and he fulfilled that request, but his first painting was filled "with explosive and disturbing details" (138). Actually, Leonardo did not follow the Confraternity's directives as to the subject matter of the painting. The original contract was to include a depiction of God the Father overhead, with two prophets on the side panels (*The Virgin of the Rocks* was the centerpiece). There has been much scholarly discussion about the exact nature of the contract and what exactly transpired between Leonardo and the Confraternity. What is clear is that Leonardo deviated substantially from the original plan for the subject matter. The painting is a depiction of a legend taken from the early events in Jesus' life. This legend, unknown prior to the fourteenth century, "described the meeting between the Holy Family and the future St. John the Baptist in the desert under the protection of the Angel

Uriel, after they had fled to escape King Herod's slaughter of the innocents."[20]

Brown's interpretation then takes an even stranger turn, as Jesus and John the Baptist are misidentified. He writes that the Virgin Mary sits with "her arm around an infant child, presumably Baby Jesus", while Uriel sits with a baby, "presumably baby John the Baptist" (138). Presumably? Brown has it backward, once again following the lead of *The Templar Revelation*. That book's interpretations of Leonardo's paintings are so overwrought that it is not surprising to learn that the authors, Lynn Picknett and Clive Prince (who are described as "writers, researchers, and lecturers on the paranormal, the occult, and historical and religious mysteries"), believe that the Shroud of Turin is a photograph of Leonardo da Vinci.[21] They state that the child closest to Mary must "logically" be Jesus and conclude that Leonardo's commitment to occult, heretical beliefs led him to depict John the Baptist blessing Jesus.

Yes, the composition is unique. But is it heretical? Art historians and scholars have always understood that the infant on the left, under the right arm of the Virgin Mary, is John the Baptist; the infant on the right, next to the angel Uriel, is Jesus. The angel supports the Christ Child, "emphasizing his divinity";[22] he also sits closest to the water, prefiguring the baptism he will receive as an adult from John the Baptist. His cousin kneels in adoration, while Mary acts as both a compositional and a theological mediator, the biological tie between the two children. Why does Brown transpose the identities of the two

---

[20] Field, *Leonardo Da Vinci*, 153.

[21] Picknett and Prince, *Templar Revelation*, 24–25, 33. See their book *The Turin Shroud: In Whose Image?* (New York, HarperCollins, 1994). The authors believe that Leonardo had mastered the alchemical secret of photography, with which he created the Shroud of Turin. This theory has not been taken seriously by those directly studying the Shroud.

[22] Field, *Leonardo Da Vinci*, 153.

infants? So he can write that instead of the "usual" depiction of Jesus blessing John, "it was baby *John* who was blessing Jesus . . . and Jesus was submitting to his authority!" (138). No reason for this supposed action is given in *The Da Vinci Code*, but *The Templar Revelation* offers the following: Leonardo was "obsessed" with John the Baptist and believed him to be superior to Jesus. Why? Because he believes the "Church of John" has existed since the time of Christ as a parallel Church, kept intact by groups such as the Priory of Sion.[23]

Speaking of the painting now in London's National Gallery, Brown writes that Leonardo "mollified the confraternity by painting them a second, 'watered-down' version of *Madonna of the Rocks* in which everyone was arranged in a more orthodox manner" (139). Clearly, if the original were "unorthodox" in part because it depicted John the Baptist blessing Jesus, we would expect the second, "orthodox" painting to have that blasphemous act changed. But the second painting is nearly identical to the first, including the poses and positions of the two babies. The similarities between the two paintings do not align with Brown's strange description of the first painting. Yet, in order to promote his theory that Leonardo was conveying hidden, dangerous anti-Christian messages about the "sacred feminine", Brown must grasp at straws—and apparently calculates that most readers will not examine reproductions of the two paintings for themselves.[24]

Describing the painting in the Louvre, Brown writes about Mary's hand, placed over the head of Jesus (whom Brown identifies as John), as "making a decidedly threatening gesture— her fingers looking like eagle's talons, gripping an invisible head"

---

[23] Picknett and Prince, *Templar Revelation*, 349.

[24] *The Da Vinci Code* repeatedly fails the "desk encyclopedia test", meaning it makes claims that a decent encyclopedia will expose as erroneous. However, Brown apparently (and correctly) guessed that most readers will not bother to examine the novel's statements in any detail—if at all.

256   *The Da Vinci Hoax*

(139). This description comes straight from *The Templar Revelation*, which quotes a biographer of Leonardo who describes Mary's hand as "reminiscent of an eagle's talons".[25] Brown also adopts Picknett and Prince's description of "the most obvious and frightening image": Uriel's hand making "a cutting gesture . . . as if slicing the neck of the invisible head gripped by Mary's claw-like hand" (139). Whose head? Why? What is the point? No explanation is given by Brown, but Picknett and Prince interpret it as a sign of John the Baptist's beheading and further proof that the child on the right is Jesus' cousin.[26]

Rocking the Conspiracy Boat

The authors of *The Templar Revelation* inform readers that "this kind of examination of Leonardo's work reveals a plethora of provocative and disturbing undercurrents."[27] Of course, "this kind of examination" is predicated on looking specifically for any possible "provocative and disturbing undercurrents", regardless if they exist or not. What sort of sinister and dark secrets might we discover in the Sistine Chapel, Monet's water lilies, Van Gogh's sunflowers, or Norman Rockwell's nostalgic depictions of American life if we *really* looked?

The sensational ideas found in *The Da Vinci Code* and *The Templar Revelation* will appeal to readers unsatisfied by more mundane explanations. They will also fit, to one degree or another, into a conspiracy theory so large that the makers of *X-Files* would be proud. This is not to say that the full story behind *The Virgin of the Rocks* is known or that Leonardo's intentions were entirely in keeping with the artistic criteria of his day. But finding heretical, anti-Church, pro-goddess messages

---

[25] Picknett and Prince, *Templar Revelation*, 30.
[26] Ibid.
[27] Ibid., 31.

at every turn is not convincing, nor does it square with the existing evidence.

The first version of *The Virgin of the Rocks* was painted in 1483 to 1486. It was intended for the Chapel of the Order of the Immaculate Conception of the Church of S. Francesco in Milan. It was commissioned by the Confraternità dell' Immaculata Concezione. Leonardo worked on the triptych (he painted the centerpiece) with Ambrogio de Predis (who painted the outer panels). The artists eventually brought a lawsuit against the Confraternity over the fee, and it took ten years before it was settled, in 1506, in favor of the artists.[28] Such conflicts between artists and patrons were not uncommon, Sherwin Nuland notes, but "were more common for Leonardo because of his reputation for abandoning projects to which sponsors had committed themselves, or at least delaying them for long periods of time".[29] Although the records are sketchy, it appears that Leonardo, in the midst of the protracted dispute, sold or gave away the original painting and then painted (or co-painted, as seems to be the case) the second version. The original painting, Field speculates, may have been "sent by the Duke of Milan to the German emperor-elect, Maximilian I, as part of the dowry of his niece, Bianca Maria Sforza, on her marriage to Maximilian in 1493."[30]

Even though Leonardo apparently did not follow the direction provided by the Confraternity, his version "is a classical rendition" of the theme of the legend of John the Baptist's meeting with the Christ Child in the desert.[31] Although "classic" in many ways, *The Virgin of the Rocks* was rather strange for its time, including the obscure event it depicts. But, again, contrary to what Brown implies, the two versions are almost

<hr />

[28] *Encyclopedia of World Art*, 213.
[29] Nuland, *Leonardo da Vinci*, 52.
[30] Field, *Leonardo Da Vinci*, 159.
[31] *Encyclopedia of World Art*, 214.

identical, especially compositionally. The only significant differences are the addition of a cross (for iconographic reasons) in the arms of John the Baptist in the second painting, the addition of halos, and the lowering of Uriel's hand.

Leonardo's sketches for the painting show that he originally began with a more traditional pose for the Virgin Mary (bent forward, with hands clasped in front of her) and moved to the more unique pose seen in the painting. Mary's hand remains the same; far from being "claw-like", it is in a maternal position, protectively placed above her son. "The expressive blessing hand of the Virgin, emerging from the darkness, appears to float in space." [32] The Virgin's left hand bears a more than passing resemblance to the right hand of Christ in *The Last Supper*—both are masterful depictions of suspended movement, with Mary's hand providing a sense of tension and a carefully placed focal point. As Field explains, her outstretched arms make up the "most remarkable feature of the composition", with her left hand "hovering protectively over the infant Jesus" [33] and her right arm holding onto the infant John the Baptist.

Uriel's hand is not making a cutting or threatening motion; rather, it points to the infant John the Baptist. The compositional power of this gesture is evident in comparing the two versions—the second version lacks the movement and power of the first, in large part due to the withdrawn hand. Again, it is Jesus who is blessing John—and this is identical in both paintings. So how is the latter painting "watered-down"? After all, even *The Templar Revelation* admits that the cross, which clearly identifies the child on the left as John the Baptist, was probably added much later. Are we to believe that the Confraternity would accept the second version, but not the first, even when the second version contained the same offending features?

[32] Ibid.
[33] Field, *Leonardo Da Vinci*, 157.

The Mona Lisa

Although it appears on the cover of *The Da Vinci Code*, the *Mona Lisa* (ca. 1510) gets less attention in the novel than *The Virgin of the Rocks* and *The Last Supper*. Langdon remarks that the painting is "one the world's most documented inside jokes" (119). Then, with irritating condescension and disingenuousness, he remarks that the painting's "collage of double entendres and playful allusions" has been understood by art critics for the longest time—"and yet, incredibly, the public at large still considered her smile a great mystery" (119). However, few, if any, of those double entendres and playful allusions are explained by Langdon, who continually proves adept at offering theories without producing evidence for them.

The professor of symbology does offer that it is "quite possible" that the *Mona Lisa* is a portrait of Leonardo as a woman (120). He again notes that "Da Vinci" was a "prankster" and that a computerized comparison of the *Mona Lisa* and Leonardo's self-portraits "confirm some startling points of congruency in their faces" (120). Of course, points of congruency can be found in many faces, and computers make such morphing and comparison easy—and easily misleading. Not surprisingly, Brown connects this idea to the gnostic ideal of androgyny, writing that Leonardo's *Mona Lisa* is not male or female but "carries a subtle message of androgyny. It is a fusing of both" (120). What is that message? According to Langdon, who is depicted lecturing on the subject at a prison, it is that Mona Lisa's "name is an anagram of the divine union of male and female"—that is the reason for the smile (121). It is more likely, but less sensational, that "Mona Lisa" comes from *Mona*, or "M'lady"—a common title of respect in Florence in the sixteenth century—and "Lisa", possibly the wife of Francesco del Giocondo, a local merchant.

Granted, there are numerous theories about who Mona Lisa was or was not, what her relationship was to Leonardo, and what her smile means or does not mean. But most of the theories advanced by experts rely far more on historical data than on unsubstantiated appeals to secret societies, gnosticism, goddess worship, and a longing for an androgynous identity. Vezzosi writes that it is "absurd" [34] to think that the *Mona Lisa* depicts Leonardo as a woman. *The Encyclopedia of World Art* states, "Questions concerning the sitter's person-

[34] Vezzosi, *Leonardo Da Vinci*, 125.

ality are of doubtful value. The *Mona Lisa* represents the ideal female portrait, the type continued from Raphael to Corot." [35] It is a view that has been endorsed by many, but others are convinced that proof of an exact identity of the sitter does exist. *The Dictionary of Art* claims that the sitter was "M[ad]o[n]na Lisa", the wife of Francesco del Giocondo (hence the painting's alternate name, *La Gioconda*) was confirmed in 1991 "with the publications of the 1525 death inventory of Leonardo's assistant of thirty years, Gian Giaconno Caprotti, who seems to have been in possession of a number of his master's works, including this portrait." [36] Another intriguing possibility (and the subject of much recent literature) is that the painting is an idealized portrait of Leonardo's mother, Caterina. If so, it would account for any physical resemblance. "He was describing his mother," explains Sherwin Nuland, an advocate of this position, "and he was describing himself. How close to consciousness either description was, we can only guess. The author was creating biography and autobiography at the same time." [37]

The Last Supper

The waves of controversy that have gone out from *The Da Vinci Code* have been caused, in large part, by two key claims: Jesus and Mary Magdalene were married, and Mary Magdalene is depicted on the right of Jesus in Leonardo da Vinci's *Last Supper*. We will now examine the latter claim.

In an interview segment included in ABC's "Jesus, Mary and Da Vinci", Brown explained that he was first exposed to this "fact" by an unnamed instructor while attending an

[35] *Encyclopedia of World Art*, 216.
[36] Jane Turner, ed., *The Dictionary of Art*, vol. 19 (New York: Macmillan, 1996), 185.
[37] Nuland, *Leonardo da Vinci*, 83.

unidentified art school in Spain. Brown's instructor told the class that although there is not a chalice depicted in the painting, the Holy Grail can still be found, seated next to Jesus— the person of Mary Magdalene. Brown's story may be true, but there is little doubt where nearly all—if not all—of his "insights" into *The Last Supper* came from: *The Templar Revelation*, which is prominently mentioned in Brown's novel.[38] A comparison of the conversation between Langdon, Teabing, and Sophie (230–50) and the first chapter of *The Templar Revelation*, titled "The Secret Code of Leonardo da Vinci",[39] reveals that Brown's vaunted research largely involved reading Picknett and Prince's book.

In the midst of the lengthy lecture given by Teabing and Langdon to the befuddled Sophie, the supposed truth about *The Last Supper* is revealed. Looking at a reproduction of the painting, she is astonished to realize (at the prodding of the two scholars) that the person seated at Jesus' own right side is a woman. She sees what she believes is feminine hair and hands—"and the hint of a bosom. It was, without a doubt . . . female. 'That's a woman!'" (243). Teabing explains that this "glaring discrepancy" is missed because the viewer's mind has such a powerful preconception about the painting that the truth that it depicts is blocked out. In other words, only certain special people, with a sort of *gnosis*, can see "the truth" about the work. Following the lead and language of *The Templar Revelation*, Teabing points out that the two figures are mirror images of one another, having clothes with the same colors (red and blue) and sitting in very similar poses ("*Yin* and *yang*", he says) (244).

It is worth noting that *Holy Blood, Holy Grail*, upon which Brown relies so heavily for information in other parts of his

---

[38] Brown, *The Da Vinci Code*, 253.
[39] Picknett and Prince, *Templar Revelation*, 19–35.

novel, ignores this theory but proposes an equally strange one: Leonardo believed in the heretical notion that Jesus had a twin and so *The Last Supper* depicts "two virtually identical Christs".[40] This idea is repeated in *The Messianic Legacy*,[41] the sequel to *Holy Blood, Holy Grail*, which informs readers that "Jude Thomas, or Jude the Twin" may have been Jesus' twin brother and depicted as such in *The Last Supper*.[42] Jesus' twin brother, the authors state, "is conspicuous in certain of Leonardo da Vinci's works, especially 'The Last Supper'".[43] It appears that there are as many conspiracies as there are conspiracy theorists.

Both Brown's interpretation (based on the writings of Picknett and Prince) and the ideas found in *Holy Blood, Holy Grail* rely on unfounded speculation and anti-Christian ideology far more than they do on historical evidence, scholarly analysis, or simple logic. Much ink has been spilled about *The Last Supper* and its history, context, purpose, meaning, and artistic merit. The goal here will be to touch on some key issues and show how far outside the realm of scholarship are the ideas found in *The Da Vinci Code*. We will specifically examine these key claims:

1. The "missing" chalice indicates that Leonardo is sending a hidden message about the true Holy Grail.
2. The figure to the right of Christ is Mary Magdalene, not the apostle John. This is evident due to the feminine appearance of the figure, as well as a V shape ("the Grail, the chalice, and the female womb") and an M shape (Magdalene) in the composition (244–45).

[40] Michael Baigent, Richard Leigh, and Henry Lincoln, *Holy Blood, Holy Grail* (1982; New York: Dell, 1983), 423–44.

[41] Michael Baigent, Richard Leigh, and Henry Lincoln, *Messianic Legacy* (New York: Dell, 1986).

[42] Ibid., 96–97.

[43] Ibid., 97.

3. Peter is depicted making a threatening, cutting gesture across the neck of Mary Magdalene (248). Meanwhile, the hand wielding a dagger is "disembodied" and belongs to no one.

The Missing Chalice

At the urging of Teabing, Sophie looks at *The Last Supper* and sees that there is "no chalice in the painting. No Holy Grail" (236). Brown, working from a central claim of *The Templar Revelation*[44] has Teabing inform Sophie that there is no chalice because the Holy Grail is not a thing, but a person—Mary Magdalene.

The absence of a large chalice with bold letters declaring it is the Holy Grail is important only if we assume that that is what the scene *should* include—an assumption the reader is pushed toward by Teabing's remarks. But *why* should we assume that Leonardo would depict Jesus' cup as being different from that used by the apostles? In fact, an examination of the painting reveals that each of the figures, including Jesus, has a cup and a piece of bread before him; Jesus' cup is next to his left hand, his right hand raised over the bread. But Brown and *The Templar Revelation* seem to imply that, since Jesus is not holding a cup or bread, the painting has nothing to do with the Eucharist—and, hence, nothing to do with the Holy Grail. However, it has been commonly understood (and explained in detail by numerous scholars) that *The Last Supper* is a depiction of John 13:21–30. That passage focuses upon Judas' betrayal of Jesus; John's explanation of the Eucharist, which is highly theological, is found in John 6. Noted art historian and critic E. H. Gombrich explains,

[44] See Picknett and Prince, *Templar Revelation*, 19–28.

One thing we can be sure about: Leonardo, like any other artist in his situation, had two sources on which to rely, the traditions of his art and the text of the Gospels, which, naturally, also form part of this tradition. It is remarkable that of the four accounts in the Gospel, tradition had long favoured the one in *St John*, despite the fact that St John does not mention the institution of the Eucharist which we generally associate with the Last Supper. The reason for this preference on the part of the painters may perhaps be found in the vivid episode that describes the action and the postures of the participants which, as you will see, also inspired Leonardo.[45]

Leonardo was masterful at portraying inner emotions and psychological states, and his masterpiece is a brilliant and multi-layered portrayal of the reactions of the apostles following Jesus' prediction of betrayal. But rather than show the moment when Jesus directly confronts Judas (see Jn 13:26–27), Leonardo depicts the very moment following Jesus' statement, "Truly, truly, I say to you, one of you will betray me" (Jn 13:21). "But the traditional gesture of Christ offering the bread to Judas, a gesture of denunciation and accusation, has been omitted by Leonardo; and the meaning and resonance of Christ's words are grasped only in the reactions of the apostles, which spread like a chain from one end of the table to the other." [46]

Acclaimed art critic Leo Steinberg analyzes the painting with incredible precision and thoroughness in his book *Leonardo's Incessant Last Supper*.[47] He makes the compelling argu-

---

[45] E. H. Gombrich, "Papers Given on the Occasion of the Dedication of The Last Supper (after Leonardo)", Magdalen College, Oxford, March 10, 1993. Accessed online at http://davinci.ntu.ac.uk/gombrich/oxford.htm.

[46] Anna Maria Brizzio, Maria Vittoria Brugnoli, and André Chastel, *Leonardo the Artist* (New York: McGraw-Hill, 1980), 49.

[47] Leo Steinberg, *Leonardo's Incessant Last Supper* (New York: Zone Books, 2001).

ment (substantiated with a wealth of evidence, quotes, and citations), that the painting has suffered from the "impoverishment of its content down to pure psychodrama", which is the "legacy [of] the Age of the Enlightenment".[48] Steinberg insists that *The Last Supper* depicts both the Consecration of the Eucharist *and* the betrayal by Judas, since those two key aspects of the event are concurrent and intertwined. "The conjunction of the two themes of the Supper", he writes, "is embedded in Scripture and liturgy."[49] This can be seen in the description given by Paul, who writes, "For I received from the Lord what I also delivered to you, *that the Lord Jesus on the night when he was betrayed took bread*, and when he had given thanks, he broke it, and said, 'This is my body, which is for you. Do this in remembrance of me'" (1 Cor 11:23–24; emphasis added). As *The Dictionary of Art* notes, "The theme of the institution of the Eucharist signaled by Christ's gestures towards the wine and bread, would also have been readily understood" by Leonardo's contemporaries.[50]

The Apostle John vs. Mary Magdalene?

When interviewed for ABC's "Jesus, Mary and Da Vinci", Brown repeated the character Teabing's belief that people see what they are told to see: "Our preconceived notions of this scene are so powerful that our mind blocks out the incongruity and overrides our eyes" (243). The person to Jesus' right, Brown declared, is "clearly a woman", echoing his novel: "It was, without a doubt . . . female" (243). It is ironic that Brown insists that we see what we are told to see—and then tells them what to see. Does that apply only to those

[48] Ibid., 31.
[49] Ibid., 35.
[50] Turner, *Dictionary of Art*, 19:189.

who disagree with his claims, or are his remarks held to the same dismissive standard?

The identity of the three apostles to Jesus' right has never been in doubt. In *The Last Supper*, Steinberg writes, St. Andrew (from left to right) "is followed by Peter, Judas, and John, the three whose identity in the mural was never doubted."[51] These three have distinctive qualities: Peter's intense movement forward and wielding of the knife (prefiguring his use of a sword in the Garden), Judas recoiling and grasping the bag of money (he was the treasurer for the group—see Jn 13:29), and John's youthful appearance and contemplative pose. There is also physical evidence. A par-

---

[51] Steinberg, *Leonardo's Incessant Last Supper*, 76.

ish church of Ponte Capriasca near Lake Lugano contains a mid-sixteenth-century fresco copy of *The Last Supper*. On that fresco are the names of the twelve apostles, left to right. The grouping of John, Judas, and Peter is purposeful. "The group [of three] at Christ's right, John, Judas, and Peter", Steinberg points out, "clusters the three who are destined for roles in the Passion." [52] Judas betrays Jesus, Peter denies Jesus, and John—"the disciple whom Jesus loved" (Jn 13:23; 19:26; 20:2; 21:7, 20)—was the only apostle to stand at Jesus' Cross (Jn 19:26–27). Steinberg states that there are also "significant pairs" in the painting, including Peter and John, and Jesus and John. Peter and John are often companions (see Lk 22:8), and personify "the active and contemplative life" and are "shown putting their heads together".[53] Hearing the prophecy of impending betrayal, Peter lunges forward, his hot temper and desire to defend his Master evident. John is the quiet, reflective contemplative who internalizes the distressing news, his hands folded in a prayerful manner appropriate to the coming death of Jesus. These two true apostles frame Judas, the traitor, who personifies greed and disloyalty. Although Jesus and John are depicted as being apart from each other, their mirrored images indicate that they are "soulmates . . . matched in outline, in (original) hue of garment and tilt of head." [54]

Viewing a reproduction of the painting, Sophie sees "flowing red hair, delicate folded hands, and the hint of a bosom" (243). The figure *is* undoubtedly effeminate, as Leonardo depicted the youthful John in the early fifteenth-century Florentine style. This approach can be seen in other paintings of the period, including Leonardo's own *Saint John the Baptist*

[52] Ibid., 80.
[53] Ibid., 78.
[54] Ibid.

(ca. 1413–1416), which depicts a young man who is quite effeminate in appearance and also has flowing hair and delicate hands. As for the "hint of bosom", it can only be found in the feverish imagination of those subscribing to Brown's theory—Leonardo's painting reveals no "hint" at all, unless viewers are willing to see what Brown suggests they see, despite lack of visual evidence.

There is no suggestion, in Leonardo's sketches or writings, that the figure is Mary Magdalene. There is, however, evidence that it is the apostle John. In a sketch for the painting, Leonardo depicts John "leaning over, face down; Christ resting one arm on John's back as he turns toward Judas." [55] Gombrich describes the sketch in detail:

> It is well known that the description of that text of the apostle St John "leaning on Jesus' bosom" is explained by the ancient habit of lying on couches during meals, though this had largely been forgotten and the apostles were usually represented sitting at table. But tradition still had St John leaning against Christ, and the only rapid sketch we have by Leonardo for this composition indicates that he originally meant to adopt this tradition as well as the action of Christ reaching across the table to give the sop to Judas, who was generally placed there in isolation from the others.[56]

Always searching for a new way to explore character and interrelationships in his paintings, Leonardo opted to show the apostle John as a mirror image of Christ (for the reasons

---

[55] Ibid., 275, fig. 188. "The motif of the arm on the back of the drowsing favorite occurs in Romanesque relief sculpture and persists throughout Fra Angelico, Bonifacio Bembo, and Perugino to Titian, as well as throughout Northern art from Strasbourg Cathedral to Lucas Cranach" (276; figures 190–94).

[56] Gombrich, "Papers".

noted by Steinberg) and to isolate Christ dramatically against the open window behind him.[57]

Teabing states that a "V" shape representing the Grail and the female womb is "at the focal point" of *The Last Supper* (244), but this does not hold up to an examination of the painting. The figure of Christ is clearly "the focal point of the painting"; the entire composition is based around his figure and his silhouetted head. Likewise, the "M" shape (244–25) is a brilliantly conceived compositional motif, with the three open windows providing a field of perspective and sense of depth.[58]

What Is Peter Trying to Do?

According to *The Da Vinci Code*, the painting of *The Last Supper* also conveys Peter's dislike for Mary Magdalene, shown by him "leaning menacingly" toward her and "slicing his blade-like hand across her neck" (248). This also fails the "see for yourself" test. If Peter's motion with his left hand really were threatening, why does the figure lean toward him with complete trust? Is that really the action of a woman being accosted by an angry rival? The motion, in fact, conveys trust and intimacy, which would be expected of the relationship between the two disciples Peter and John. It also

[57] Questions to consider in responding to Brown's theory include: If the apostle John, described in Scripture as the "beloved disciple", is not in the painting, where is he? And if the woman to the right of Jesus is a woman, why must we assume it is Mary Magdalene? Why could it not be Mary, the Mother of Jesus, her pose reflecting her quiet, withdrawn nature? Finally, why is it assumed that Mary Magdalene is young and beautiful, the perfect match for a thirty-something Jesus? Could she not just as easily have been middle-aged or even older? Or homely?

[58] On a symbolic level, might it not make more sense to see the windows as foreshadowings of the three crosses, with Christ's cross in the middle, and the crosses of the two thieves on either side?

indicates Peter's surprise, and one can imagine him asking John to repeat what Jesus had just said, so stunned was the head apostle at the prophecy of betrayal.[59]

Pointing to a hand holding a dagger, Langdon tells Sophie that it is "disembodied" and that a count of the arms will reveal that it belongs to "no one at all" (248). This also fails a "see for yourself" examination: on Christ's right, there are six apostles and twelve arms. The dagger is being held by Peter; it represents the sword he will use a few hours later in the garden to cut off the ear of a slave who is with the arresting party (Jn 18:10–11).[60] Leonardo mentions the knife-wielder in his *Notebooks*: "Another who has turned, holding a knife in his hand, upsets with his hand a glass on the table."[61] So what is the importance of Langdon's claim? *The Da Vinci Code* does not explain, but *The Templar Revelation* indicates that it is yet another threat to Mary Magdalene: "An anomalous hand points a dagger at a disciple's stomach one person away from" her.[62] It also states that almost no commentators say anything about it; however, almost every art book we consulted mentions that the hand is Peter's and that the dagger foreshadows his violent act in the garden.

---

[59] "Peter, who is the farthest away, having heard the words of the Lord, rises quickly, in keeping with his vehement character, behind Judas who, terrified and looking upwards, leans over the table tightly gripping the purse in his right hand but making, with his left, an involuntary convulsive movement as if to say 'What does this mean? What is to happen?' Peter in the meantime has grasped with his left hand the right shoulder of John who is leaning towards him, and—at the same time pointing to Christ—signals to the favourite disciple that he should ask who is the traitor" (Gombrich, "Papers").

[60] "Peter's right hand points the knife he will ply a few hours hence at the arrest. And the interlocked hands of the beloved disciple are prepositioned for their grieving at Calvary" (Steinberg, *Leonardo's Incessant Last Supper*, 89).

[61] Leonardo da Vinci, *Notebooks of Leonardo da Vinci*, par. 668.13.

[62] Picknett and Prince, *Templar Revelation*, 22.

Gothic Style and the Goddess

Dan Brown makes several assertions about architecture including the claim that the Knights Templar were "master masons", that they created the Gothic style, and that Gothic cathedrals encode secret messages about goddess worship. On the latter point, notes found in Teabing's study make a cathedral's entrance a vaginal symbol and its nave a tribute to the womb (325–26).

These notions are lifted directly from *The Templar Revelation*[63], which in its turn is influenced by Barbara G. Walker's *Women's Encyclopedia of Myths and Secrets*. The latter work, a matchless collection of anti-Christian misinformation, declares that "like a pagan temple, the Gothic cathedral represented the body of the Goddess who was also the universe, containing the essence of male godhood within herself."[64] Building on that background, Picknett and Prince argue that Gothic cathedrals cryptically continued the worship of the divine feminine. They were "goddess hymns carved in stone, and the 'Notre Dame' to which so many of them were dedicated was really the feminine principle itself—Sophia."[65] They speak of the labyrinth on the floor of Notre Dame de Chartres as a sign of female mysteries and conclude: "Clearly this place was not intended for the praise of the Virgin Mary."[66] Brown absorbed all their views.

---

[63] Ibid., 110–16. The same pages of the *Templar Revelation* also supplied Brown's ideas about the paganism of round Templar churches honoring the divine feminine.

[64] "Rose", in Barbara G. Walker, *The Woman's Encyclopedia of Myths and Secrets* (San Francisco: Harper and Row, 1983), 867. Walker does correctly make the rose a symbol of our Lady rather than Mary Magdalene as in *The Da Vinci Code*, but rose windows supposedly stand for femininity as opposed to the masculinity of the Cross (866).

[65] Picknett and Prince, *Templar Revelation*, 115.

[66] Ibid., 116.

The Templars as builders and proprietors of round churches have already been dealt with earlier in "The Real Templars". But it is worth mentioning that the sheer magnitude of medieval building precluded any one order, however wealthy, from financing it. Each cathedral cost the equivalent of hundreds of millions of dollars. France built eighty of them, England twenty-seven, not to mention hundreds of abbeys and major churches and tens of thousands of parish churches in just those two countries over the course of four hundred years—not to mention secular buildings. Funding for cathedral construction came from bishops and chapters of canons, royalty and nobility, guilds, townspeople, and pilgrims. Interruptions in cash flow were what lengthened cathedral construction to an average of three centuries, although Chartres was completed in a speedy sixty-six years.[67]

Why are the Templars credited with Gothic structures and not the Romanesque ones built during the first century of their existence as an order? Who was building the Gothic cathedrals put up after the dissolution of the Templars? If there was a persistent underground current of pagan sentiment, why do esoteric histories fail to detect it in buildings of the Dark Ages, such as Charlemagne's imperial chapel at Aachen, or early medieval ones, such as the Norman cathedrals of the eleventh and twelfth centuries? "Gothic" is the right word to conjure with because most people have a mental image of Gothic churches but not of Romanesque ones. Many people have at least heard of Gothic Chartres but not Romanesque Moissac, so there is no romance in arguing from the latter. Gothic emerged from the older Romanesque style in the twelfth century, although there was no sharp turnover. Fine Romanesque buildings continued to rise in the

---

[67] For the financial aspects, see Henry Kraus, *Gold Was the Mortar: The Economics of Cathedral Building* (London: Routledge and Kegan Paul, 1979).

south of France while Gothic ones were already under construction in the north. The architectural innovations that made Gothic possible—the rib vault, the pointed arch, and the flying buttress—had been employed by Romanesque builders. The first rib vault was used at Durham, England, in 1093, a decade before the founding of the Templars. It was based on practical experimentation, not secret knowledge dating back to the pyramid builders of Egypt and brought back from the Crusades.

Starting with renovations at the French Abbey of Saint-Denis begun in 1137, Gothic became a distinct style instead of a set of structural inventions when architects changed the way they looked at structures. Like its Romanesque predecessor, a Gothic cathedral had a rectangular nave, a choir, apse, and usually transepts, but it was designed to float and soar, a dynamic rather than a static beauty. Instead of barrel vaults, round arches, thick walls, and small windows that made a Romanesque church a fortress of faith, a Gothic one was a cage of stone sealed with large expanses of glorious colored glass. The new approach to construction redirected weight and thrust from load-bearing walls to the framework. A building no longer needed to be massive to hold together.

"Gothic emerged with its own aesthetic theory, based on light, mathematics, and music. The light admitted by the new stained glass windows was likened to the Divine essence permeating the world. The architect imitated God's work building the cosmos out of geometrical relationships that corresponded to musical harmonies. . . . The perfect mathematical ratios of its plan took form with the unpredictable regularity of Nature itself, in a sense 'grown' as much as 'constructed.' " [68] A Gothic cathedral is a triumph of geometry,

[68] Sandra Miesel, "Medieval Architecture: A Prayer in Light and Stone", *Catholic Twin Circle*, February 5, 1995, 10–11.

every measurement generated from a modular square so all the parts fit together harmoniously. Yes, the builders used—but did not necessarily understand—the Golden Mean/ Proportion called *phi* that Dan Brown discusses. The "sacred geometry" employed in their work ranged from simple number symbolism, such as three levels in a structure representing the Trinity, to complex mathematical operations that related words and numbers.

For a small sample of the intricacies involved, consider the thirty-seven glass openings in the western rose window at Chartres. According to architectural historian John James, "Thirty-seven is the thirteenth prime, and there are thirteen months in the lunar year. Multiply this by the Trinity and you get 111, which is itself the Trinity again, and is the sum of each line on one of those fascinating arrangements known as magic squares." The six-by-six magic square, called the square of the Sun, adds up to 111 in every direction, which is also the total of the letters coded as numbers for "Jesus Maria".[69] Assuming James' interpretations of the process are correct, these kinds of manipulations go back to antiquity, but the purpose to which they are harnessed is entirely Christian.

Using modular planning and the Golden Mean to achieve the Augustinian ideal of perfect proportions "led builders of great churches to conceive of architecture as applied geometry, geometry as applied theology, and the designer of a Gothic cathedral as an imitator of the divine Master".[70] As a literal representation of heaven, a cathedral was meant to reveal "the

[69] John James, *Chartres: The Masons Who Built a Legend* (1982; London: Routledge and Kegan Paul, 1985), 164–65. James demonstrates how the building was laid out from the original square and how messages were encoded, pp. 105, 117.

[70] Robert A. Scott, *The Gothic Enterprise: A Guide to Understanding the Medieval Cathedral* (Berkeley, Calif.: University of California Press, 2003), 125.

nuptial vision that divine reason had established throughout the cosmos".[71] The organic unity of Gothic buildings reflects the logical order of scholasticism and gives pride of place to light, God's own element.

So where among these noble aspirations investigated by generations of historians is there room for a Gothic cathedral to represent the body of "the goddess"? What part of a womb is a transept—or two transepts in some English cathedrals? What part are the chapels that radiate from the back of the apse? What does the bend in the axis of Chartres and other cathedrals mean, since it was deliberately introduced and not a construction flaw? If western rose windows are feminine, what of the ones adorning the south and north transepts? At Chartres, those three windows respectively show the Last Judgment (west), Christ of the Apocalypse (south), and the Glorification of the Virgin (north).

Brown claims that a Gothic cathedral's front (west) door depicts intimate female anatomy and invites the reader to find this "fact" titillating (325–26). (What do the two doors flanking the middle one depict?) Both Gothic and Romanesque buildings handle decoration the same way in the arched spaces above the triple entrances: concentric bands of carving framing a major subject. At Chartres, the subject of the central "Royal Portal" on the west front is Christ in Majesty surrounded by the symbols of the Four Evangelists within rows of the twenty-four elders of the Apocalypse and heads of cherubim. Where is the femaleness in that? The panels over transept doors use the same concentric composition. At Chartres, the central entrance on the north depicts the Glorification of the Virgin, and the south one, the Last Judgment. In both cases the paired doors are separated by a carved column. Cinquefoil roses do not appear over doorways

---

[71] Otto von Simson, quoted in ibid., 121.

here or elsewhere. Vine and oak leaves are more common motifs than roses in Gothic carvings. Medieval builders were not obsessed with pagan tributes to female genitalia.

Like other medieval cathedrals, Chartres has no overall decorative pattern. Besides paying special honor to Christ and the Virgin, its glass and sculptures present biblical stories and characters, saints, figures from antiquity, the labors of the months, and other scenes of work or daily life. Its incarnational vision reaches out to embrace the universe. There is no occult significance to the appearance of zodiac signs at Chartres; they were simply used as time markers for the months. They also appear in that capacity in most medieval laymen's prayer books.

The mysterious labyrinth drawn on the floor of Chartres and elsewhere is not a maze but a circuitous route to a central six-petalled rosette. John James takes it as a symbol of the Christian's pilgrim way through life but also as a tribute to architects, because Daedalus, the first architect in Greek mythology, also designed the first labyrinth.[72] Any feminine symbolism would relate Ariadne, the Cretan princess who showed the way through the original labyrinth, to the Virgin who leads Christians through life.[73]

The Templar Revelation makes much of a single window at Chartres commemorating Mary Magdalene, the first known example.[74] That is one tribute out of nearly 120 medieval lancet (tall) windows. Aside from the Blessed Virgin and St. Anne, only one other window depicts female saints, these being Catherine and Margaret together. And the "Mary" honored by Notre Dame de Chartres is not cryptically the Magdalene; specific features of the Virgin Mary's life, death,

[72] James, *Chartres*, 130.
[73] Ibid., 86–89.
[74] Picknett and Prince, *Templar Revelation*, 110.

assumption, and glorification are depicted in its stone and glass.

Although not a model for ornate Westminster Abbey, austere Chartres is the best-loved and best preserved of the first Gothic cathedrals. It is a monument of Christian faith, a "living work that bears witness to the world",[75] a temple of the Living God and not a pagan goddess. "Here the transient and the eternal embrace in stone."[76]

[75] Favier, *The World of Chartres* (1990; New York: Harry N. Abrams, 1998), 8. Facts and figures on Chartres are all taken from this book, a beautiful tribute to the building.

[76] Sandra Miesel, "The Glory of Chartres", *Catholic Heritage*, January–February 1993, 14.

Chapter 10

More Errors and Final Thoughts

> Personal friends are taking *The Da Vinci Code* as Gospel
> truth. . . . What bothers me is that these people who call
> themselves Catholic will believe some fiction story by a
> person they don't know because he states his book is well
> researched, yet they won't take up any single article about
> their faith written by a Catholic.
>
> — e-mail from reader

As the past several chapters demonstrate, there is no lack of
evidence for stating frankly that *The Da Vinci Code* is filled
with errors big and small. In this final chapter, we will look
at some of the novel's claims that did not fit naturally into
previous chapters. We will then conclude with some final
thoughts about *The Da Vinci Code* and what its success tells
us about popular culture.

Witch Numbers Can You Trust? [1]

About a quarter of the way into the novel (124–25), readers
are treated to a page-long diatribe about the Catholic Inquisition, the murder of witches, and the supposed hatred of

[1] Most of the material in this section has been taken from Sandra Miesel's
article "Who Burned the Witches?", *Crisis*, October 2001, 20–26.

women found within conservative religious bodies—especially the Catholic Church. It begins with Langdon reflecting on the "deceitful and violent" history of the Catholic Church, which is said to include the re-education and murder of pagans and worshippers of the "sacred feminine". The following claims are made:

1. The witch-hunters' manual *Malleus Maleficarum* (*Hammer of the Witches*, or *The Witch's Hammer*), published in 1486, is "arguably" the most "blood-soaked" work in human history. It proclaimed the dangers posed by "freethinking women" and provided instructions to clergy about the torture and destruction of those women. These women included "all female scholars", gypsies, mystics, lovers of nature, gatherer of herbs, priestesses, and any female "suspiciously attuned" to nature (125).[2]

2. Midwives were killed because they used natural medicine in easing the pain caused by childbirth. This pain was not meant to be alleviated, the novel states, since it was the proper punishment for Eve eating from "the Apple of Knowledge". This belief about Eve produced the doctrine of Original Sin (125).

3. Over a three-hundred-year period, the Catholic Church was responsible for burning a total of five million women at the stake (125).

4. All of this propaganda and intimidation has led to the banishment of women from "the temples of the world". Thus,

[2] In this section, the novel places two phrases within quotes—"the dangers of freethinking women" and "suspiciously attuned to the natural world"—without any indication where they are taken from. The context indicates that Brown is suggesting they are found in *Malleus Maleficarum*, but they do not appear in that document.

women are not allowed to be Catholic priests, Orthodox Jewish rabbis, or Islamic clerics (125).

5. This also means that the sacred act of *hieros gamos*, described as a sexual union in which a man and woman become sexually whole, has been turned into something shameful. Women were suspected of working with the devil in bringing about sexual temptation; they were his "favorite" accomplices (125).

6. The Church slyly defamed women further by linking the term "left-hand side", which has a "feminine association", with irrational, sinister behavior, while "right" became linked with goodness, righteousness, and dexterity. And so radical thinking is now considered "left wing" and associated with the "left brain" (125).

Plenty of Smoke, but How Much Fire?

Malleus Maleficarum, authored by the Dominican inquisitors Jacob Sprenger and Heinrich Kraemer, was indeed a vicious, misogynist work. It depicted women as the sexual playmates of Satan, declaring, "All witchcraft comes from carnal lust, which is in women insatiable." Sprenger and Kraemer proclaimed that not believing in the reality of witches was heresy. Witches regularly did physical as well as spiritual harm to others, they wrote, and allegiance to the devil defined witchcraft. Sprenger and Kraemer exhorted secular authorities to fight witches by any means necessary.

By itself, the *Malleus* started no new witch-panics, but it was used freely by later witchcraft writers, Protestant and Catholic alike. The Spanish inquisitors were nearly alone in scoffing at its lack of sophistication. Christians cannot deny that people were executed and that works such as the *Malleus Maleficarum* played a part in those abhorrent acts. But modern-day writers, such as Brown, are in no position to disparage early modern Europe, especially since the twentieth century witnessed the murder of tens of millions in the name of atheism, anti-Semitism, and anti-Christianity. It is hard to deny that those witch-hunts have much in common with our own political purges, imagined conspiracies, and rumors of ritualized child abuse, each often involving irrational fears, hatreds, and stereotypes.

As with all historical matters, context and careful scholarly research are crucial. Unfortunately, there are a number of stubborn modern myths about the witch-hunts of 1400–1800. Five million women killed, the number given in *The Da Vinci Code*,[3] is a bit more accurate than the number of nine million still used in some feminist circles, but not by much. The nine million number was actually created out of the blue by American feminist Matilda Joslyn Gage (1826–1898) in 1893.[4] Radical feminists have made much of this mass "gynecide", as antipornography activist Andrea Dworkin has called it. The feminists see witches as the natural enemy of patriarchy; for them, as for pagans, playing the politics of victimization strengthens solidarity. Fifty years ago, one of the neo-pagan movement's founders, Gerald Brosseau Gardner (1884–1964), coined the term "the Burning Times" to describe this time of persecution. Although Gardner's historical expertise has since been seriously questioned,[5]

---

[3] It is not clear where Brown came up with "five million". One of his sources, *The Templar Revelation*, states that "hundreds of thousands" of women were killed during three centuries of witch trials: Lynn Picknett and Clive Prince, *The Templar Revelation: Secret Guardians of the True Identity of Christ* (1997; New York: Simon and Schuster, 1998), 158.

[4] See Philip G. Davis, *Goddess Unmasked: The Rise of Neopagan Feminism Spirituality* (Dallas, Tex.: Spence, 1998), 289.

[5] Ibid., "Gardner and the Goddess", 327–43.

neo-pagan proponents Margot Adler and Starhawk (née Miriam Simos) are still preaching Gardner's teachings as though they were established facts.

Gage's estimate of nine million women burned is more than two hundred times the best current estimate of 30,000 to 50,000 killed during the four hundred years from 1400 to 1800—certainly a significant number, but not comparable to the Holocaust or Stalin's purges.[6] Many of those deaths did not involve burning. Witches were hanged, strangled, and beheaded as well. In addition, witch-hunting was not woman-hunting: at least 20 percent of all suspected witches were male. Midwives were not especially targeted; nor were witches liquidated as obstacles to professionalized medicine and mechanistic science.

The 30,000 to 50,000 casualties of the European witch-hunts were not distributed uniformly through time or space, even within particular jurisdictions. Three-quarters of Europe saw not a single trial. Witch persecution spread outward from its first center in alpine Italy in the early fifteenth century, guttering out in Poland, where witchcraft laws were finally

---

[6] The Gendercide Watch web site states: "[Jenny Gibbons] points out that estimates made prior to the mid-1970s, when detailed research into trial records began, 'were almost 100% pure speculation.' [Jenny Gibbons, "Recent Developments in the Study of The Great European Witch Hunt", *Pomegranate* (Lammas, 1998). Accessed at www.cog.org/witch_hunt.html]. 'On the wilder shores of the feminist and witch-cult movements', writes Robin Briggs, 'a potent myth has become established, to the effect that nine million women were burned as witches in Europe; gendercide rather than genocide. This is an overestimate by a factor of up to 200, for the most reasonable modern estimates suggest perhaps 100,000 trials between 1450 and 1750, with something between 40,000 and 50,000 executions, of which 20 to 25 per cent were men'. Briggs adds that 'these figures are chilling enough, but they have to be set in the context of what was probably the harshest period of capital punishments in European history.' " Accessed at www.gendercide.org.

repealed in 1788. The center had generally stopped trying witches before the peripheries even started.[7] Dr. Brian A. Pavlac, associate professor of history at King's College, has pinpointed a number of the modern myths about the witch-hunts. In addition to the nine million figure, false ideas include the belief that the witch-hunts reflect a culture of brute barbarism, that the Church was exclusively to blame, that the witch-hunts were all the same in focus and nature, and that modern-day practitioners of wiccan and "magick" are direct descendants of those executed during the witch-hunts of 1400–1800.[8] Pavlac notes,

> Historians have been unable to establish a concrete connection between any popular folk magic or witch traditions from before 1800 and modern organized witch movements. Most seem to have been inspired by the writings of Aleister Crowley (1875–1947) and Gerald Brosseau Gardner (1884–1964), who created for themselves new versions of witch rituals and organizations based on a loose interpretation of modern

[7] The regional tolls demonstrated the patchwork pattern of witch-hunting. The town of Baden, Germany, for example, burned 200 witches from 1627 to 1630, more than all the convicted witches who perished in Sweden. The tiny town of Ellwangen, Germany, burned 393 witches from 1611 to 1618, more than Spain and Portugal combined ever executed. The Catholic prince-bishop of Würzburg, Germany, burned 600 witches from 1628 to 1631, more witches than ever died in Protestant Sweden, Norway, Finland, and Iceland combined. The Swiss canton of Vaud executed about 1,800 witches from 1611 to 1660, compared with Scotland's toll of between 1,300 and 1,500 and England's toll of 500. The claim of some Catholic apologists that Elizabeth I executed 800 witches a year is false. In Southwest Germany alone, 3,229 people were executed for witchcraft between 1562 and 1684—more than were executed for any reason by the Spanish, Portuguese, and Roman Inquisitions between 1500 and 1800. All three of these inquisitions burned fewer than a dozen witches in total.

[8] See Brian A. Pavlac, "Ten Common Errors and Myths about the Witch Hunts, Corrected and Commented", *Prof. Pavlac's Women's History Resource Site* (October 31, 2001). Accessed at www.kings.edu/womens_history/witch/werror.html on February 29, 2004.

superstition and historical legacies. Many different people founded branches of witches in the 1960s and 1970s. While some of these diverse witch circles use historical research to establish some of their ideas, most seem to rely on imagination, fantasy and a robust eclecticism.[9]

Original Sin and the Ordination of Women

The book of Genesis never identifies the fruit of the "tree of the knowledge of good and evil" (Gen 2:17) as an apple. The popular notion that the fruit was an apple is a result of the Latin translation in the Vulgate. The Latin word for evil is *malus* and the word for "apple" is *malum*; "apple tree" is *malus*. The word *malum* appeared in the Vulgate translation of Genesis in the phrase "the tree of knowledge of good and evil", and readers began associating the apple with the fruit eaten by Eve. Both Adam and Eve suffered punishment for their disobedience: Eve would suffer pain in giving birth (Gen 3:16), and Adam would have to toil and sweat in order to provide food and sustenance for his family (Gen 3:17).

The doctrine of Original Sin is not, as Brown insinuates, based on Eve's actions alone (125). Both Adam and Eve shared responsibility for their disobedience and for the rupture of the communion they had shared with God. Original Sin is not personal sin but refers to the result of that broken communion: "Adam and Eve transmitted to their descendants human nature wounded by their own first sin and hence deprived of original holiness and justice; this deprivation is called 'original sin.' As a result of original sin, human nature is weakened in its powers; subject to ignorance, suffering,

---

[9] Ibid.

and the domination of death; and inclined to sin".[10] This belief has a long and complicated history, but it is based in part on statements made by Paul in his epistles to the Romans and the Corinthians: "Therefore as sin came into the world through one man and death through sin, and so death spread to all men, because all men sinned" (Rom 5:12) and "For as by a man came death, by a man has come also the resurrection of the dead. For as in Adam all die, so also in Christ shall all be made alive" (1 Cor 15:21–22).

Insisting, as *The Da Vinci Code* does (125), that women are not ordained or allowed to be Catholic priests, Orthodox Jewish rabbis, or Islamic clerics because of propaganda and intimidation is disingenuous and conveniently simplistic. The Catholic Church has a number of theological reasons for not allowing women to be ordained priests. Although a treatment of this topic is beyond the scope of this book, a couple of points should be made. First, although his circle of disciples included women such as Mary Magdalene and his own Mother, Jesus specifically selected twelve men to be his apostles. This was not due to cultural norms or societal pressures; rather, it was according to his divine plan. Pope John Paul II writes, "In calling only men as his Apostles, Christ acted in a completely free and sovereign manner. In doing so, he exercised the same freedom with which, in all his behavior, he emphasized the dignity and the vocation of women, without conforming to the prevailing customs and to the traditions sanctioned by the legislation of the time." [11]

Catholic doctrine holds that the male and female sexes are uniquely different and that these differences and what they represent have significant meaning. As Manfred Hauke has

---

[10] *Catechism of the Catholic Church* (CCC), 2nd ed. (Washington, D.C.: United States Catholic Conference—Libreria Editrice Vaticana, 1997), nos. 417–18.

[11] John Paul II, Apostolic Letter *Mulieris Dignitatem* (August 15, 1988), 26.

demonstrated in detail in *Women in the Priesthood?* the order of creation itself shows that male and female are equal and complementary but also distinctly different. Male and female are powerful symbols, with man symbolizing God in his transcendence and female symbolizing creation. But while men are not God, women specially and powerfully symbolize creation, since "symbol and reality are in agreement." [12] The Son of God, Hauke states, "became man as *male* in order to illustrate the representation of the heavenly Father vis-à-vis man and the 'official' representation of mankind before God".[13] This hardly removes the feminine element from the "symbolic structures of creation", however, since the Son of God not only assumed "his human nature from a woman and indeed, only from a woman".[14] Thus, the relationship between Christ and Mary is a central one; upon it rests a correct understanding of the nuptial relationship between Christ the Bridegroom and his Bride, the Church (see Eph 5). On the same principles, the greatest human person and the pinnacle of creation is a woman, the Blessed Virgin Mary, who represents the perfecting of the human race by the grace of Christ.

The issue ultimately comes full circle and returns to two different anthropological perspectives. Feminists seek an androgynous wholeness and seek to eliminate differences between male and female; Christians believe that the unique differences between male and female have been purposely created by God and speak volumes about man's relationship to him. This has been summarized well by Joyce Little in *The Church and the Culture War*:

---

[12] Manfred Hauke, *Women in the Priesthood? Systematic Analysis in the Light of the Order of Creation and Redemption* (San Francisco: Ignatius Press, 1988), 189.

[13] Ibid., 472.

[14] Ibid.

Catholicism has traditionally understood human sexuality to be of enormous importance, particularly with regard to the differentiation of the human race into male and female. The significance which the Church attaches to this differentiation can be seen most strikingly in the importance which the Church gives to sexual morality. But at a much deeper level, the vision of the Church regarding human sexuality is grounded ... first, in the revelation given in Genesis that our imaging of God is realized precisely in our creation as male and female (Gen 1:26–27), and second, in the revelation given in Ephesians 5 of the Christ/Church relationship, which is the covenantal and marital union of Christ the bridegroom with his bride, the Church. Indeed, the sacramental character of human marriage is rooted in the fact that human marriage images not only the Trinity but also the union of Christ and the Church.[15]

Sacred Sex and the Right-Wing Conspiracy

Brown apparently takes his cues about *hieros gamos*—the so-called "sacred marriage" involving ritualistic intercourse—from the works of Margaret Starbird, who refers to that ceremony on numerous occasions. She states in *The Goddess in the Gospels* that the gematria, or number codes, of the New Testament reveal that the *hieros gamos* was an "original teaching" of Jesus but that it was later obscured by the Church.[16] This conclusion is reached by a convoluted series of tenuous connections made between the number 666, yin and yang, the Song of Solomon, "lunar and Earth principles", and Jesus' parable of the mustard seed.

---

[15] Joyce Little, *The Church and the Culture War: Secular Anarchy or Sacred Order* (San Francisco: Ignatius Press, 1995), 127.

[16] Margaret Starbird, *Goddess in the Gospels: Reclaiming the Sacred Feminine* (Rochester, Vt.: Bear, 1998), 157–58.

Although Christianity (as well as Judaism and Islam) has nothing to do with ritualized sex, it does teach that husband and wife do achieve a state of wholeness in the marriage bed: "For this reason a man shall leave his father and mother, and shall be joined to his wife; and the two shall become one." This is first quoted in Genesis 2:24, repeated by Jesus in Matthew 19:5, and then quoted by Paul in the passage in Ephesians 5 relating human marriage to the marriage of Christ to the Church (Eph 5:31). Although the Church has consistently warned about the dangers of sexual sin and though some Christians throughout history have had less than positive attitudes toward sex, the Church has never taught that sex is shameful or bad.[17]

The claim that the Church has defamed women by destroying the meaning of the word "left" is patently ridiculous. It is true that the word "left" in French is *gauche*, and in Latin it is *sinister*. It is also true that the left side is often linked to femininity, unconsciousness, intuition, repression, and introversion, while the right side is linked to masculinity, consciousness, logic, action, and extroversion. However, these connections cross cultural and religious boundaries and are found in a number of cultures in many different epochs of history.[18]

But what did the Church have to do with that? Apparently very little, if anything. The word "right" comes from the pre-Christian, Germanic term *riht*, which describes a sense

---

[17] For a detailed theological reflection on sexuality and marriage, see John Paul II's *The Theology of the Body: Human Love in the Divine Plan* (Boston: Pauline Books and Media, 1997).

[18] These connections were often based, in ancient cultures, on observation of the skies, sunrise and sunset, and lunar cycles. Since the sun rose in the east, the right side was the connection to light and awareness. This is found in Hinduism as well as in ancient Egyptian beliefs. See J. E. Cirlot, *A Dictionary of Symbols*, 2nd ed. (New York: Barnes and Noble, 1995), 300–303.

of justice or balance that tribal elders attempted to achieve when determining the size of the *Bot*—that is, the proper order within the universe that would ensure peace and harmony. The word "left" became associated with radical thinking in pre-revolutionary France. This occurred in 1789, when the parliamentary body the French National Assembly was created to remove control from the king and turn power over to the citizenry. In the chamber where the National Assembly met, members of the Third Estate—the revolutionaries—sat on the left side, and members of the First Estate—the nobles—sat on the right. Therefore, the left side of the room was more liberal politically, and the right side was more conservative. The word "wing" is a military term, with the term "left wing" (dating back to the early 1700s) referring to the geographically left side of an army. It was picked up and applied to the French National Assembly, resulting in the "left wing" and "right wing" terminology still in use (for better or for worse) in political and cultural discourse today.

Kabbalah and the Shekinah

Not only does *The Da Vinci Code* display an appalling lack of knowledge of Christian practice and belief, it does little better when it comes to Judaism and Jewish beliefs. A good example is found in Langdon's explanation of the origin of the tetragrammaton—YHWH (pronounced as Yahweh)—the sacred name of God, which observant Jews believe should not be uttered. Langdon claims that YHWH comes from the name *Jehovah*, which he insists is an androgynous "union between the masculine *Jah* and the pre-Hebraic name for Eve, *Havah*" (309). A quick trip to the encyclopedia (or theological dictionary, if you prefer) shows that Langdon is wildly off the mark. The name "Jehovah" did not even exist until the thirteenth century at the earliest (and was not common until the sixteenth century) and is an English word. It was created by artificially combining the consonants of YHWH (or JHVH) and the vowels of *Adonai* (which means "Lord"), the name substituted for YHWH in the Old Testament by Jews.[19] The Hebrew—not "pre-Hebraic"—word for Eve is *hawwâ*, (pronounced "havah"), which means "mother of all living". There is absolutely nothing androgynous about any of this, but that dubious assertion is in keeping with the neo-gnostic flavor of the novel.

Langdon also claims that "the early Jewish tradition" involved acts of ritualistic sex in the Temple. These alleged acts were based on the "early" Jewish belief that the Holy of Holies was home to "not only God, but also His powerful female equal, Shekinah" (309). Men seeking to achieve spiritual wholeness, the novel states, would visit the Temple in order to have sex with a *hierodules*, or priestess, with whom they experienced the divine through sexual union. This is a remarkable claim in light of the fact that two of the most unique features of ancient Judaism were its monotheistic

---

[19] See David Noel Freedman, ed., *Eerdmans Dictionary of the Bible* (Grand Rapids, Mich.: W. B. Eerdmans, 2000), 682. *The Jewish Encyclopedia* says this about *Jehovah*: "A mispronunciation (introduced by Christian theologians, but almost entirely disregarded by the Jews) of the Hebrew 'Yhwh', the (ineffable) name of God (the Tetragrammaton or 'Shem ha-Meforash'). This pronunciation is grammatically impossible; 'Jehovah' is generally held to have been the invention of Pope Leo X's confessor, Peter Galatin ('De Arcanis Catholicæ Veritatis,' 1518, folio xliii.), who was followed in the use of this hybrid form by Fagius (= Büchlein, 1504–1549). Drusius (= Van der Driesche, 1550–1616) was the first to ascribe to Peter Galatin the use of 'Jehovah', and this view has been taken since his days (comp. Hastings, 'Dict. Bible', ii. 199, *s.v.* 'God'; Gesenius-Buhl, 'Handwörterb.' 1899, p. 311; see Drusius on the tetragrammaton in his 'Critici Sacri', i. 2, col. 344). But it seems that even before Galatin the name 'Jehovah' had been in common use (see Drusius, *l.c.* notes to col. 351). It is found in Raymond Martin's 'Pugio Fidei.' written in 1270 (Paris, 1651, iii., pt. ii., ch. 3, p. 448; comp. T. Prat in 'Dictionnaire de la Bible', *s.v.*)." Accessed at www.jewishencyclopedia.com.

character and its avoidance of the sort of ritualistic sex that was common in the ancient Near East.

The *hierodules*, who were essentially female cultic slaves, were part of the pagan cults surrounding the Hebrews in ancient Palestine. However, they were not part of the activities at Solomon's Temple, for the "house of Yahweh" (see Ps 27:4) was to be undefiled by immorality, fornication, or corruption.[20] The desire for purity is apparent throughout the Old Testament: "You shall not bring the hire of a harlot, or the wages of a dog, into the house of the LORD your God in payment for any vow; for both of these are an abomination to the LORD your God" (Deut 23:18). The Jews believed that any sort of wrong practice or immorality performed in the Temple would result in God removing his presence from it.

The word *Shekinah* does not appear in the Bible, although the concept can be found in several places. The Shekinah is "the in-dwelling presence of God, from the root *shakah*, 'to dwell' ".[21] In Rabbinic literature, the Shekinah refers both to the abiding of God in a specific place and as "a divine name irrespective of spatial location".[22] Brown's claims about the Shekinah appear to be based on a poor understanding of the Kabbalah. Kabbalah (which means "tradition") is a mystical and theosophical system of Jewish philosophy/theology that arose in the eleventh and twelfth centuries. It is a gnostic-like form of Judaism, emphasizing secret knowledge and doctrines, fused with mysticism and esotericism.

The Kabbalah teaches that there are two parts to the Deity: "God as He is in Himself and God in manifestation. God as

[20] For a detailed study of the Temple and Jewish worship, see Roland de Vaux, *Ancient Israel: Religious Institutions*, vol. 2 (New York: McGraw-Hill, 1961).

[21] Louis Jacobs, *The Jewish Religion: A Companion* (Oxford: Oxford University Press, 1995), 459.

[22] Ibid.

He is in Himself is known as En Sof, the Limitless, the Infinite, the ineffable Ground of Being."[23] The En Sof is manifested through a process of emanation in ten Sefirot, "the powers and potencies in the Godhead". As *The Jewish Companion* explains, one startling aspect of Kabbalistic doctrine "is the division of the Sefirot into male and female".[24] The female principle of the Sefirot is called the Shekinah. "In the Kabbalistic scheme, the sex act between husband and wife becomes a mirror of the divine processes on high."[25] However, Kabbalists stress that the use of male and female terms in referring to the Sefirot should never be understood as a reference to a goddess or a pagan notion of Godhead or to some sort of sexual activity "on high".[26] Needless to say, this understanding of God is not part of traditional, orthodox Judaism, and it remains highly controversial among Jews. Once again *The Da Vinci Code* misrepresents chronology ("early Jewish tradition") and belief ("His powerful female equal, Shekinah") in an apparent attempt to mislead readers and blur the lines between different belief systems.

Concluding Thoughts

Imagine a novel based on the premise that the Holocaust had never happened but was the invention of a powerful group of Jewish leaders who have used that "myth" to garner themselves power and fortune. Or consider a theoretical novel claiming that Muhammad was not a prophet at all but a drug-addled homosexual who married multiple wives in order to hide his deviant behavior and who killed non-Muslims in fits of rage against heterosexuals. Needless to say, such novels

[23] Ibid., 295.
[24] Ibid., 296.
[25] Ibid.
[26] Ibid.

would be immediately and rightly condemned by a majority of critics and readers. Yet *The Da Vinci Code*, a novel claiming that Christianity is fraudulent, that the Catholic Church is a violent, misogynist institution run by murderers and liars, and that androgyny is the answer to life's problems has met, not with condemnation, but with incredible success and even significant critical acclaim.

Just as important, the novel's dubious and often ridiculous claims about historical events and persons are taken seriously by many readers and members of the media. Brown has drawn upon the old stereotype of the Catholic Church as a blood-soaked, evil institution, an image that has sold well in the United States for decades, even centuries. As Philip Jenkins notes in *The New Anti-Catholicism*, "Most contemporary attacks on Catholicism or the Catholic Church draw heavily on history, or at least on a kind of mythic history that has become deeply imbedded in popular thought."[27] And so *The Da Vinci Code* is filled with talk of murder, intrigue, hatred of women, sexual repression, mass murder, religious oppression, and intolerance. "Today, likewise," Jenkins explains, "hypercritical examinations of Catholic misdeeds are intended to support contemporary political positions, commonly in debates over morality and sexuality."[28]

---

[27] Philip Jenkins, *The New Anti-Catholicism: The Last Acceptable Prejudice* (New York: Oxford University Press, 2003), 178.

[28] Ibid. Jenkins, who is non-Catholic, also writes, "Binding together the various historical accusations against the Catholic Church is what might be termed a whole alternative history, or historical mythology. Though modern anti-Catholics rarely share the religious orientation of their nineteenth-century predecessors, they agree with the older critique that the Catholic Church betrayed the truths symbolized by Jesus and his earliest followers, replacing them with oppressive practices borrowed from the Roman Empire. Though feminists have been particularly active in seeking to rewrite early Church history for their ideological ends, this strategy has also been exploited by many liberals anxious to discredit contemporary Catholicism" (ibid., 180–81).

Some readers, puzzled by the concern over *The Da Vinci Code*, insist that it is "just a book" or "only a novel".[29] However, what we read says much about who we are, both individually and as a culture. G. K. Chesterton once wrote, "Truth, of course, must of necessity be stranger than fiction, for we have made fiction to suit ourselves."[30] *The Da Vinci Code* is custom-made fiction for our time: pretentious, posturing, self-serving, arrogant, self-congratulatory, condescending, glib, illogical, superficial, and deviant. It has managed to tap into a deep reservoir of spiritual longing, restlessness, distrust, suspicion, and credulity. But how ironic is it that a novel that continually advocates distrust of authority is so easily trusted by millions of readers? How strange is it that a book so bent on criticizing religion in general and Christianity specifically so overtly *preaches* the gospel of the "sacred feminine"?

It is also strange that the novel is presented as a thriller but is rarely, if ever, thrilling. We estimate that over 20 percent of the book consists of lectures, almost all of them directed at the character Sophie, who first appears with "a haunting certainty to her gait" (50) and with a striking "boldness" (64) but is soon little more than an empty-headed and helpless student in the impromptu classrooms of Langdon and Teabing. Symbologist Robert Langdon is hardly any more believable than Sophie, a sort of emasculated pseudo-intellectual who is continually surprised that others know

---

[29] Recall that Rolf Hochhuth's 1963 play *Der Stellvertreter* (*The Representative*, or *The Deputy*) was responsible for radically influencing perceptions of Pope Pius XII (1939–1958), eventually resulting in a host of books (mostly published in the 1990s) questioning the Catholic Church's activities (or alleged lack of them) during the Holocaust.

[30] G. K. Chesterton, *Heretics*, in *The Collected Works of G. K. Chesterton*, vol. 1 (San Francisco: Ignatius Press, 1986), 66.

anything at all and is constantly offering up lectures that are as flawed as they are unbelievable.

The novel brings to mind Mark Twain's classic essay "Fenimore Cooper's Literary Offenses", in which the great wit dryly complains that Cooper violated eighteen of the nineteen rules—"some say twenty-two"—governing literary art in the domain of romantic fiction. Many of the same criticisms can be applied to Brown's novel: "A tale shall accomplish something and arrive somewhere"; "the talk shall sound like human talk, and be talk such as human beings would be likely to talk in the given circumstances"; "the author shall make the reader feel a deep interest in the personages of his tale and in their fate"; and "avoid slovenliness of form".[31] The effusive praise that many readers have for the book's "plot" is puzzling, for there really is not much of a plot, save a set-up and twist that is more in keeping with *Days of Our Lives* than it is with best-selling thrillers such as *The Bourne Identity* or *Eye of the Needle*. It is standard romance novel fare: boy meets girl; they get into a bind; they get out of the bind; and they kiss. Characters stand around and loiter endlessly, very little ever happens, and the ending is a bust. The "story" is simply a vehicle for a lengthy indictment against Christianity and the Catholic Church and an excuse, much like the *Left Behind* books, for endless lecturing and proselytizing. Brown appears to have little respect for his readers—and many of them do not seem to mind or to notice.

To revisit some of our opening thoughts, *The Da Vinci Code* is a perfect postmodern myth, pulp-fiction style. Occasionally clever and hip, it is never wise or insightful. Often cheesy, it is never artful. Seriously contrived, it is never

---

[31] Mark Twain, "Fenimore Cooper's Literary Offenses", in Joe Queenan, ed., *The Malcontents: The Best Bitter, Cynical, and Satirical Writing in the World* (Philadelphia: Running Press, 2002), 641–52.

believable or engaging. As Amy Welborn acidly notes, the characters are one-dimensional, and the novel "is neither learned nor challenging—except to the reader's patience. Moreover, it's not really suspenseful, and the writing is shockingly banal, even for genre fiction. It's a pretentious, bigoted, tendentious mess." [32]

So what is *The Da Vinci Code*? Is it just a fad? A one-hit wonder? A novelty novel? Will people remember it in ten years? Will it matter? Is it worth writing an entire book in response to it? We think it is necessary, especially considering the impact and influence the novel has had and continues to have. Our hope is that readers will not only consider the truth about specific topics and issues but will agree that Truth does exist and needs to be respected. "Truth, once it is rightly apprehended," wrote Ronald Knox, "has a compelling power over men's hearts; they must needs assert and defend what they know to be the truth, or they would lose their birthright as men." [33]

[32] Amy Welborn, "'Da Vinci' Code for Catholic Bashing", *Our Sunday Visitor*, June 8, 2003. Accessed at http://amywelborn.com/reviews/davinci.html.
[33] George J. Marlin, Richard P. Rabatin, and John L. Swan, *The Quotable Knox* (San Francisco: Ignatius Press, 1996), 205.

SELECTED BIBLIOGRAPHY

Adam, Karl. *The Christ of Faith.* Pantheon Books: New York, 1957.

Baigent, Michael, Richard Leigh, and Henry Lincoln. *Holy Blood, Holy Grail.* 1982; New York: Dell, 1983.

——. *The Messianic Legacy.* New York: Holt, 1986.

Bleeker, C. J., and S. G. F. Brandon, eds. *The Savior God: Comparative Studies in the Concept of Salvation Presented to Edwin Oliver James.* Manchester, U.K.: Manchester University Press, 1963.

Boucher, Bruce. "Does 'The Da Vinci Code' Crack Leonardo?" *New York Times,* August 3, 2003.

Brizzio, Anna Maria, Maria Vittoria Brugnoli, and André Chastel. *Leonardo the Artist.* New York: McGraw-Hill, 1980.

Brown, Dan. *Angels and Demons.* New York: Pocket Books, 2000.

Brown, Raymond. *An Introduction to the New Testament.* New York: Doubleday, 1996.

Brown, Raymond E., Joseph A. Fitzmyer, and Roland E. Murphy, eds. *New Jerome Biblical Commentary.* Englewood Cliffs, N.J.: Prentice Hall, 1990.

Carroll, Vincent, and David Shiflett. *Christianity on Trial.* San Francisco: Encounter Books, 2002.

Chadwick, Henry. *The Early Church.* 1967; Harmondsworth, U.K.: Penguin Books, 1973.

Clifton, Chas S. *Encyclopedia of Heresies and Heretics.* New York: Barnes and Noble, 1992.

Conway, Msgr. J. D. *Times of Decision: Story of the Councils.* Notre Dame, Ind.: Fides, 1962.

Costen, Michael. *The Cathars and the Albigensian Crusade.* Manchester, U.K.: Manchester University Press, 1997.

Cross, F. L. and E. A. Livingstone, eds. *The Oxford Dictionary of the Christian Church.* 3rd ed. New York: Oxford University Press, 1997.

Daly, Mary. *Beyond God the Father: Towards a Philosophy of Women's Liberation.* Boston: Beacon Press, 1973.

———. *Gyn-Ecology: The Metaethics of Radical Feminism.* Boston: Beacon Press, 1978.

Daniélou, Jean, S.J. *The Bible and the Liturgy.* Notre Dame, Ind.: University of Notre Dame Press, 1956.

———. *Myth and Mystery.* New York: Hawthorn Books, 1968.

Davis, Philip G. *Goddess Unmasked: The Rise of Neopagan Feminist Spirituality.* Dallas, Tex.: Spence, 1998.

Decker, Ronald, Thierry Depaulis, and Michael Dummett. *A Wicked Pack of Cards: The Origins of the Occult Tarot.* New York: St. Martin's Press, 1996.

Ebertshäuser, Caroline, et al. *Mary: Art, Culture, and Religion through the Ages.* Translated by Peter Heinegg. New York: Crossroad, 1998.

Ehrman, Bart D. *Lost Scriptures: Books that Did Not Make It into the New Testament.* New York: Oxford University Press, 2003.

———. *Lost Christianities: The Battles for Scripture and the Faith We Never Knew.* New York: Oxford University Press, 2003.

Favier, Jean. *The World of Chartres.* 1990; New York: Harry N. Abrams, 1998.

Field, D. M. *Leonardo Da Vinci.* N.p.: Regency House, 2002.

Forey, Alan. *The Military Orders: From the Twelfth to the Early Fourteenth Century.* Toronto: University of Toronto Press, 1992.

Freedman, David Noel, ed. *Eerdmans Dictionary of the Bible.* Grand Rapids, Mich.: W. B. Eerdmans, 2000.

Groothuis, Douglas. *Searching for the Real Jesus in an Age of Controversy.* Eugene, Ore.: Harvest House, 1996.

Hauke, Manfred. *God or Goddess? Feminist Theology: What Is It? Where Does It Lead?* San Francisco: Ignatius Press, 1995.

_____. *Women in the Priesthood? A Systematic Analysis in the Light of the Order of Creation and Redemption.* San Francisco: Ignatius Press, 1988.

Herrick, James A. *The Making of the New Spirituality: The Eclipse of the Western Religious Tradition.* Downers Grove, Ill.: InterVarsity Press, 2003.

Hitchcock, James. "Fantasy Faith". *Touchstone*, December 2003, 14–16.

Hughes, Philip. *The Church in Crisis: A History of the General Councils, 325–1870.* New York: Image, 1964.

Jacob, Margaret C. *Living the Enlightenment: Freemasonry and Politics in Eighteenth-Century Europe.* New York: Oxford University Press, 1991.

James, Edward. *The Franks.* Oxford: Basil Blackwell, 1988.

James, E. O. *The Ancient Gods: The History and Diffusion of Religion in the Ancient Near East and the Eastern Mediterranean.* New York: G. P. Putnam's Sons, 1960.

_____. *Christian Myth and Ritual: A Historical Study.* New York: Meridian Books, 1965.

_____. *The Cult of the Mother-Goddess.* New York: Barnes and Noble, 1994.

James, John. *Chartres: The Masons Who Built a Legend.* London: Routledge and Kegan Paul, 1982.

Jansen, Katherine Ludwig. *The Making of the Magdalen: Preaching and Popular Devotion in the Later Middle Ages.* Princeton, N.J.: Princeton University Press, 2000.

Jenkins, Philip. *Hidden Gospels: How the Search for Jesus Lost Its Way.* New York: Oxford University Press, 2001.

_____. *The New Anti-Catholicism: The Last Acceptable Prejudice.* New York: Oxford University Press, 2003.

Johnson, Luke Timothy. *Living Jesus: Learning the Heart of the Gospel*. San Francisco: HarperSanFrancisco, 1999.

——. *The Real Jesus: The Misguided Quest for the Historical Jesus and the Truth of the Traditional Gospels*. San Francisco: HarperSanFrancisco, 1996.

Johnson, Paul. *A History of Christianity*. New York: Atheneum, 1976.

Jonas, Hans. *The Gnostic Religion: The Message of the Alien God and the Beginnings of Christianity*. 1958; Boston: Beacon Press, 1963.

Jones, A. H. M. *Constantine and the Conversion of Europe*. Toronto: University of Toronto Press, 1978.

Kelly, J. N. D. *Early Christian Creeds*. 3rd ed. London: Longman, 1972.

——. *Early Christian Doctrines*. 5th rev. ed. San Francisco: Harper and Row, 1978.

King, Karen L. *What Is Gnosticism?* Cambridge, Mass.: Belknap Press of Harvard University Press, 2003.

Kreeft, Peter. *Fundamentals of the Faith*. San Francisco: Ignatius Press, 1988.

Kreeft, Peter, and Ronald K. Tacelli. *Handbook of Christian Apologetics*. Downers Grove, Ill.: InterVarsity Press, 1994.

Lacy, Norris, et al., eds. *The Arthurian Encyclopedia*. New York: Peter Bedrick, 1986.

Lebreton, Jules, S.J., and Jacques Zeiller. *The Emergence of the Church in the Roman World*. New York: Collier Books, 1962.

——. *Heresy and Orthodoxy*. New York: Collier Books, 1962.

Levack, Brian P. *The Witch-Hunt in Early Modern Europe*. 2nd ed. Essex: Pearson Education, 1995.

Loomis, Roger Sherman. *The Grail: From Celtic Myth to Christian Symbol*. 1963; new ed., Princeton, N.J.: Princeton University Press, 1991.

Malory, Thomas. *Le Morte d'Arthur*. Edited by Janet Cowen. 2 vols. New York: Penguin, 1969.

Metzger, Bruce M. *The Canon of the New Testament: Its Origin, Development, and Significance.* Oxford: Clarendon Press, 1987.

_____. *Historical and Literary Studies: Pagan, Jewish, and Christian.* Grand Rapids, Mich.: W. B. Eerdmans, 1968.

Miesel, Sandra. "Dismantling *The Da Vinci Code*". *Crisis*, September 2003, 18–23.

_____. "Medieval Architecture: A Prayer in Light and Stone". *Catholic Twin Circle*, February 5, 1995, 10–11.

_____. "Who Burned the Witches?" *Crisis*, October 2001, 20–26.

Molnar, Thomas. *The Pagan Temptation.* Grand Rapids, Mich.: W. B. Eerdmans, 1987.

Momigliano, Arnaldo, ed. *The Conflict between Paganism and Christianity in the Fourth Century.* Oxford: Clarendon Press, 1963.

Nash, Ronald H. *The Gospel and the Greeks: Did the New Testament Borrow from Pagan Thought?* 2nd ed. Phillipsburg, N.J.: P and R Press, 2003.

_____. "Was the New Testament Influenced by Pagan Religions?" *Christian Research Journal*, Winter 1994.

Neumann, Erich. *The Great Mother: An Analysis of the Archetype.* Translated by Ralph Manheim. Bollingen series, 47. 1955; Princeton, N.J.: Princeton University Press, 1972.

Newman, John Henry Cardinal. *The Arians of the Fourth Century.* 1833; repr., Eugene, Ore.: Wipf and Stock, 1996.

Nuland, Sherwin B. *Leonardo da Vinci.* New York: Penguin, 2000.

Olson, Carl E. "The Cardinal and the Code". *National Catholic Register*, February 22, 2004.

_____. "Jesus, Mary, and Da Vinci". *National Catholic Register*, November 16, 2003.

Olson, Carl E., and Sandra Miesel. "Fact: *The Da Vinci Code* Is Worse than Fiction". *The Catholic Answer*, forthcoming.

_____. "Cracking the Anti-Catholic Code, Part One". October 2003. Accessed at www.envoymagazine.com.

_____. "Cracking the Anti-Catholic Code, Part Two". January 2004. Accessed at www.envoymagazine.com.

Pagels, Elaine. *The Gnostic Gospels.* 1979; New York: Vintage Books, 1989.

_____. *Beyond Belief: The Secret Gospel of Thomas.* New York: Random House, 2003.

Partner, Peter. *The Murdered Magicians: The Templars and Their Myth.* 1981; New York: Oxford University Press, 1987.

Picknett, Lynn. *Mary Magdalene: Christianity's Hidden Goddess.* New York: Carrol and Graf, 2003.

Picknett, Lynn, and Clive Prince. *The Templar Revelation: Secret Guardians of the True Identity of Christ.* 1997; New York: Simon and Schuster, 1998.

Previté-Orton, C. W. *The Shorter Cambridge Medieval History.* Volume 2: *The Twelfth Century to the Renaissance.* Cambridge, U.K.: Cambridge University Press, 1952.

The Quest of the Holy Grail. Translated by P. M. Matarasso. New York: Penguin, 1969.

Rahner, Hugo, S.J. *Church and State in Early Christianity.* San Francisco: Ignatius Press, 1992.

_____. *Greek Myths and Christian Mystery.* London: Burns and Oates, 1957.

Raschke, Carl A. *The Interruption of Eternity: Modern Gnosticism and the Origins of the New Religious Consciousness.* Chicago: Nelson-Hall, 1980.

Read, Piers Paul. *The Templars.* Cambridge: Da Capo Press, 1999.

Robinson, James M., general editor. *The Nag Hammadi Library.* 3rd rev. ed. San Francisco: HarperSanFrancisco, 1988.

Rubin, Miri. *Corpus Christi: The Eucharist in Late Medieval Culture.* 1991; New York: Cambridge University Press, 1992.

Ruether, Rosemary Radford. *Sexism and God-Talk: Toward a Feminist Theology*. Boston: Beacon Press, 1983.

Russell, Jeffrey Burton. *Witchcraft in the Middle Ages*. London: Cornell University Press, 1972.

Scott, Robert A. *The Gothic Enterprise: A Guide to Understanding the Medieval Cathedral*. Berkeley, Calif.: University of California Press, 2003.

Seward, Desmond. *The Monks of War: The Military Religious Orders*. Rev. ed. New York: Penguin, 1995.

Starbird, Margaret. *Goddess in the Gospels: Reclaiming the Sacred Feminine*. Rochester, Vt.: Bear, 1998.

———. *Tarot Trumps and the Holy Grail: Great Secrets of the Middle Ages*. Boulder, Colo.: WovenWord, 2000.

———. *The Woman with the Alabaster Jar: Mary Magdalen and the Holy Grail*. Rochester, Vt.: Bear, 1993.

Steichen, Donna. *Ungodly Rage: The Hidden Face of Catholic Feminism*. San Francisco: Ignatius Press, 1991.

Steinberg, Leo. *Leonardo's Incessant Last Supper*. New York: Zone Books, 2001.

Stevenson, David. *The Origins of Freemasonry: Scotland's Century 1590–1710*. 1988; New York: Cambridge University Press, 1990.

Stoyanov, Yuri. *The Other God: Dualist Religions from Antiquity to the Cathar Heresy*. New Haven: Yale University Press, 2000.

Struder, Basil. *Trinity and Incarnation: The Faith of the Early Church*. Collegeville, Minn.: Liturgical Press, 1993.

Turner, Jane, ed., *The Dictionary of Art*. New York: Macmillan, 1996.

Ulansey, David. *The Origins of the Mithraic Mysteries*. New York: Oxford University Press, 1991.

Veith, Gene Edward, Jr. *Postmodern Times*. Wheaton, Ill.: Crossway Books, 1994.

———. *Reading between the Lines: A Christian Guide to Literature*. Wheaton, Ill.: Crossway Books, 1990.

Vezzosi, Alessandro. *Leonardo Da Vinci: The Mind of the Renaissance*. New York: Harry N. Abrams, 1997.

Walker, Barbara G. *The Woman's Encyclopedia of Myths and Secrets*. San Francisco: Harper and Row, 1983.

Wallace-Hadrill, J. M. *The Long-Haired Kings*. 1962; Toronto: Toronto University Press, 1982.

Warner, Marina. *Alone of All Her Sex: The Myth and the Cult of the Virgin Mary*. 1976; New York: Vintage-Random House, 1983.

Whitehead, Kenneth D. *One, Holy, Catholic, and Apostolic: The Early Church Was the Catholic Church*. San Francisco: Ignatius Press, 2000.

Wright, N. T. *Jesus and the Victory of God*. Minneapolis, Minn.: Fortress Press, 1996.

Yamauchi, Edwin M. *Pre-Christian Gnosticism: A Survey of the Proposed Evidences*. Grand Rapids, Mich.: W. B. Eerdmans, 1973.

_____. *The World of the First Christians*. Tring, U.K.: Lion, 1981.

Yates, Frances A. *The Rosicrucian Enlightenment*. 1972; Boulder, Colo.: Shambala, 1978.

ART CREDITS

Page	Source
252	*The Virgin of the Rocks*

252   *The Virgin of the Rocks*
(*The Virgin with the Infant Saint John adoring the Infant Christ accompanied by an Angel*)
Leonardo da Vinci
Transferred from wood to canvas
H 1.99m; W 1.22 m
Date of work: 1483–1486
Photo: Gerard Blot/Jean
Louvre, Paris
© Réunion des Musées Nationaux/ Art Resource, New York

252   *The Virgin of the Rocks*
(*The Virgin with the Infant Saint John adoring the Infant Christ accompanied by an Angel*)
Leonardo da Vinci
Oil on wood
189.5 cm × 120 cm
Date of work: about 1493–9 and 1506–8.
The National Gallery, London
© Alinari/Art Resource, New York

Page   Source

259   *Mona Lisa*
       Leonardo da Vinci
       Photo: R. G. Ojeda
       Louvre, Paris
       © Réunion des Musées Nationaux/ Art Resource,
       New York

262   *The Last Supper*
       Leonardo da Vinci
       S. Maria delle Grazie, Milan
       © Scala/Art Resource, New York

268   *Saint John the Baptist*
       Leonardo da Vinci
       Louvre, Paris
       © Réunion des Musées Nationaux/ Art Resource,
       New York

INDEX

In this index, the abbreviation DVC is used for Dan Brown's novel *The Da Vinci Code*.